Low Impact Building

Low Impact Building
Housing using Renewable Materials

Tom Woolley

A John Wiley & Sons, Ltd., Publication

This edition first published 2013
© 2013 John Wiley & Sons, Ltd

Blackwell Publishing was acquired by John Wiley & Sons in February 2007. Blackwell's
publishing program has been merged with Wiley's global Scientific, Technical and Medical
business to form Wiley-Blackwell.

Registered Office
John Wiley & Sons, Ltd, The Atrium, Southern Gate, Chichester, West Sussex,
PO19 8SQ, UK

Editorial Offices
9600 Garsington Road, Oxford, OX4 2DQ, UK
The Atrium, Southern Gate, Chichester, West Sussex, PO19 8SQ, UK
2121 State Avenue, Ames, Iowa 50014-8300, USA

For details of our global editorial offices, for customer services and for information about
how to apply for permission to reuse the copyright material in this book please see our
website at www.wiley.com/wiley-blackwell.

Library of Congress Cataloging-in-Publication Data

Woolley, Tom, author.
  Low impact housing : building with renewable materials / by Tom Woolley.
    pages   cm
  Includes bibliographical references and index.
  ISBN 978-1-4443-3660-3 (pbk. : alk. paper)   1. Ecological houses.
2. Building materials–Environmental aspects.   3. Green products.   4. Recycled products.
I. Title.
  TH4860.W67 2013
  690.028'6–dc23
                                                    2012031588

A catalogue record for this book is available from the British Library.

Wiley also publishes its books in a variety of electronic formats. Some content that appears
in print may not be available in electronic books.

Cover design by His and Hers Design.
Front cover: Tomorrow's Garden City, Letchworth © Morley von Sternberg
www.vonsternberg.com.
Back cover: Drumalla Park, Carnlough, courtesy of Brian Rankin, Oaklee Homes Group.

Set in 10/12.5pt Avenir by SPi Publisher Services, Pondicherry, India
Printed and bound in Malaysia by Vivar Printing Sdn Bhd

1   2013

For the pioneers of natural and renewable construction materials

Contents

Acknowledgements

There are many people who have assisted in the production of this book and I hope not too many have been overlooked. In particular it would not have been possible without the help of: Rachel Bevan, Leonie Erbsloh, Graeme North, Madeleine Metcalfe and Beth Edgar (Wiley-Blackwell); Gary Newman, Neil May, Alison Pooley, Ceri Loxton, Rob Elias, Jack Goulding (University of Central Lancashire); John Littlewood, Nigel Curry and the Technology Strategy Board Energy Efficient Bio-based Natural Fibre Insulation Project group.

Information and assistance was kindly provided by:

Alliance for Sustainable Building Products
Iris Anderson
Carol Atkinson
Russell Ayres
John Bedford
Matt Bridgestock
Luke Brooker
Peter Burros
James Byrne
Jim Carfrae
Peter Chalkley
Paul Chatterton
Michael Cramp
Robert Delius
Cathie Eberlin
Andrew Evans
Frances Geary
Jonathan Gibson
John Gilbert
Steve Goodhew
Tracy Gordon
Sahra Gott
Paul Green

Keeley Hale
Mike Haynes
Wai Lun Ho
Glen Howells
Nigel Ingram
Muzinee Kistenfeger
Simon Lawrence
Stephen Lawson
Niall Leahy
Bobby Leighton
Simon Linford
Donald Lockhart
Dave Mayle
Donal MacRandal
Kevin McCloud
Gerry McGuigan
Eamon McKay
Claire Morrall
Carl Mulkern
Daniel Mulligan
Niall Murtagh
Clinton Mysleyko
Natureplus
Tony Nuttall
Mark Patten

Robert Pearson
Gina Pelham
Brendan Power
Ian Pritchett
Paul Raftery
Brian Rankin
Jimm Reed
John Retchless
Frank Reynolds
Haf Roberts
Francois Samuel
Peter Seaborne
David Tibbs
Julie Watson
Darren Watts
Byron Way
Craig White
Jayne Wilder
John Williams
Keith Wood
Louisa Yallop
Myles Yallop
Marissa Yeoman
Gary Young

Figure credits

Introduction

Sustainability is not about energy, composting or insulation. Sustainability is nothing more than leaving the world a little richer than you found it.

(Watkins 2009)

This book is about changing the way we construct buildings and houses to reduce their carbon footprint and to minimise environmental damage. One of the ways this can be done is by reducing the energy and environmental impact of the materials and resources we use to construct buildings by using alternative products and systems. In particular, we need to recognise the potential for using *natural* and *renewable* construction materials as a way to reduce carbon emissions and also build in a more benign and healthy way. This book is an account of some attempts to introduce this into mainstream house construction in the UK, and the problems and obstacles that need to be overcome to gain wider acceptance of genuinely environmental construction methods.

Natural and renewable building and insulation materials can be made from biological sources such as hemp, flax, wood, straw, sheep's wool and so on. They can be combined with benign or low impact materials, such as lime and earth, into composites. Many building problems can be solved by using these materials, opening the possibility of significant benefits in terms of less pollution, less energy used, better and healthier buildings. Advocates of natural and renewable materials include those who just see a business opportunity in a new market for environmentally friendly products but others embrace Tony Watkins' holistic philosophy and see the use of natural materials as enriching a more holistic approach to living.

Many think of natural and renewable materials using hemp, earth, lime and so on as a fringe activity, only relevant to self-builders in the countryside using 'handmade' approaches (Olsen 2012). This was a frequent criticism of the book *Natural Building* (Woolley 2006). There have been, and continue to be, pioneers of low impact ways of building and 'handmade houses' such as in eco-villages like the Lammas project in Wales (Lammas 2012). With the support of Welsh Government planning policies, people who want to live in a sustainable and self-sufficient way, have been given permission to build houses in the countryside, where normally such development might not be allowed. They have used a variety of low impact building methods and in many cases are 'off-grid' so their energy consumption and environmental impact is very low. Despite this they have run into difficulties with the authorities, as their natural earth and timber structures do not comply with energy efficiency and building regulations (Dale and Saville 2012).

Regulations intended to force mainstream builders and developers to reduce energy wastage, are instead used against those whose aim in life is to do exactly that. Such are the contradictions of current policies as they fail to adopt a holistic approach. Instead, as will be argued in this book, policies have tended to support expensive technological solutions and the use of synthetic petrochemical based materials rather than low impact solutions.

On the other hand there has been some progress in recent years for alternative ecological materials and methods of building to become accepted in the mainstream as solutions for public sector bodies, housing associations and even major businesses. These clients and their architects have taken a decision to explore alternatives to petrochemical based synthetic materials, often in contradiction to official policy and this gives hope that environmentally responsible measures will become more widely adopted in the future. Manufacturers and distributors of ecological products have begun to escape from the 'green ghetto' and become accepted as part of normal building practice.

Resistance to this ecological innovation remains however. Even campaigners for greener solutions can be hostile to natural materials and fail to understand the importance of low impact solutions. The majority of men (and it is mostly men) working in this sector get caught up in thinking that the only answers is to be found in manmade, synthetic, 'high-tech' and mechanical solutions to all the problems. Often these solutions use more energy to create than they will save over the next 20 or 30 years, but their advocates are blind to this. This approach is preoccupied with saving *operational* energy and ignores *embodied* energy. Ignoring the energy consumed to solve the problems can make the problem worse not better.

Even more worrying is that many of the conventional solutions to energy efficient buildings, and houses in particular, are using technological solutions that are mistaken and may fail or cause serious problems in the future. Super-insulated and so-called passive house buildings, using synthetic manmade materials, could be creating health problems and are dependent on mechanical solutions to try and mitigate problems of condensation and dampness. Problems of indoor air quality and the toxicity of materials are swept under the carpet in building systems that, when tested, fail to come anywhere near meeting the energy standards that are predicted. This is a scandal and it needs to be exposed, though it will need further research and more detailed analysis of failures, beyond what was possible in this book.

What is particularly frustrating is that alternative and much better systems of construction using natural and renewable materials are available, and far more investment should be directed to developing these materials and systems. Much more needs to be done to support the production of low impact materials at a local level in both developed and developing countries. Unfortunately the emerging economies seem envious of expensive high-tech resource-wasting solutions in the West and see low impact approaches as turning the clock back. Large and powerful multinational companies, who consume a lot of energy producing synthetic materials, and their trade associations, have much more influence over government and international policies. Ultimately this is a political issue and governments need to introduce much more stringent environmental and health limits to ensure that benign methods and materials predominate.

The Renewable House Programme

Central to this book is an account of a programme funded by the UK Labour Government (2007–2010) to encourage the use of natural renewable materials in social housing construction; this became known as the Renewable House Programme (RHP). Twelve projects were funded with varying levels of subsidy, leading to the construction of approximately 200 houses. The book contains twelve case studies providing an insight into the pros and cons of using innovative natural renewable materials in mainstream construction.

The case studies give some indication of how architects, specifiers, clients, builders and insurers operate, in the choice of materials and construction techniques. The construction industry in the UK and most parts of the world tends not favour natural building solutions, so there were many problems coming to terms with an alternative approach. Technical problems are apparent but none were serious enough to completely undermine confidence in the materials and techniques. Despite the requirements of the special government funding to use renewable materials, particularly insulation, many of the projects substituted synthetic materials for part of the construction and one did not use any renewable insulation materials at all! On the other hand, many agencies and individuals involved were happy to use unfamiliar techniques and renewable materials and had surprisingly few problems in substituting them or including them in the designs and construction. Many lessons were learned from these projects, and while more will become apparent as monitoring and evaluation take place over the next few years, there is enough information to influence how the natural renewable materials market moves forward.

When this review of the case studies began in 2010 it seemed feasible to complete it within 18 months, as government funding requirements meant that the projects had to be completed by April 2010. However, at the time of writing (spring 2012), some of the projects were still under construction and some had only just started. The delays were largely due to issues other than the use of natural materials.

The expansion of natural building

Since *Natural Building* (Woolley 2006) and *Hemp Lime Construction* (Bevan 2008) were published, many more UK projects have been built using natural and renewable materials. Apart from numerous housing projects, there have been significant commercial, industrial and leisure buildings that have used hemp and other natural materials. Hempcrete construction, for instance, has been used in numerous food and wine storage warehouses and a large superstore in Cheshire for Marks and Spencer.

The difficulties and problems associated with introducing sustainable approaches to the mainstream construction and house building industry are wide-ranging. Thus, in addition to the 12 RHP projects, the book includes a chapter highlighting some other interesting housing projects that were not part of the RHP but have used innovative construction approaches both natural and synthetic petrochemical.

The book also includes chapters that deal with the many questions surrounding energy efficient building construction. These include the nature and range of natural materials available, supply chain and sourcing issues, legislation, building regulations, environmental policies and building physics. The science of natural materials is very different from that of synthetic petrochemical based materials, particularly in terms of thermal performance, moisture management and durability. Buildability, design and detailing issues also vary. Finally, there are the attitudes of all the different players towards natural materials and how they are reacting to energy efficient and innovative houses. The book concludes with an brief appraisal of the likely future for natural and renewable materials both in the UK and internationally.

The wider environmental agenda

Deeply embedded in the idea of using low impact materials, should be the aim of helping humanity survive the many environmental crises that face us. Yet it is disturbing how many people are in a state of denial about the real dangers. For the head-in-the-sand group, energy efficiency is simply seen as a way to cut running costs, whatever the environmental impact, or to display wealth through expensive and ostentatious renewable energy arrays and wind turbines. In a recent discussion with someone who wanted a new house designed, when asked if they were interested in an environmentally friendly design, they replied that they wanted the house to be energy efficient, but they didn't want it to be environmentally friendly! This is an indication of the major attitudinal problem that needs to be overcome before materials that are better for health and the planet are readily adopted by society.

One of the difficulties in advancing renewable and natural materials is that they can no longer be perceived as fringe to the main construction industry. Those who produce natural, renewable and alternative materials must have a sound economic basis for their products and must engage with normal capitalist business approaches to get their products to market. This has happened quite successfully in Germany and some other European countries, though the market share for environmental products is still quite small. Market pressures can lead producers into business relationships with investors and others where the priority is to make money and the environmental objectives are less important. The natural and renewable building sector is going through a tough time, due to economic recession and also they need to develop successful business models that do not undermine the environmental quality of their products. It is also hard to distinguish what they have to offer from many other 'greenwash' and flawed solutions to making buildings more energy efficient.

Another problem results from confusion over the word 'renewable'. Renewable materials have nothing to do with renewable energy. Generating renewable energy is not always a sustainable practice. Clearly alternatives to fossil fuel, coal, oil and nuclear energy are needed, but the manufacturing of photovoltaic cells that pollutes local watercourses and uses dangerous materials is part of a technology that uses manmade, not renewable materials:

> A solar panel factory in eastern China has been shut down after protests by local residents over pollution fears. Some 500 villagers staged a three-day protest following the death of large numbers of fish in a local river. Some demonstrators broke into the plant in Zhejiang province, destroying offices and overturning company cars before being dispersed by riot police. Tests on water samples showed high levels of fluoride, which can be toxic in high doses, officials said.
>
> (BBC News 2011)

Confusion is caused by mainstream businesses who claim almost every construction material and method is 'green' They pay for environmental assessment methods, certificates and standards that are diluted to the point where they become meaningless. When everything seems to be greenwash, it is easy to lose sight of those solutions that do work, and thus natural renewable building materials can be tainted by consumer cynicism about bogus claims. When some of the new energy efficiency technologies don't work, as well as they should, instead of identifying the flaws in the technologies, they blame the people in the buildings for being too stupid not to live in an environmentally friendly way! *People don't understand how to live in an energy efficient house*, they argue. A government-sponsored conference even discussed what was termed 'misuse of buildings' (ESRC 2009). It is clear that every householder will have to embrace the need to save energy and reduce CO_2 emissions, but solutions and technologies used to achieve this must be easy, simple to understand and user-friendly and safe.

There is no doubt that there is a need to change attitudes, but not just the attitudes of ordinary building occupants. It is changing the attitudes of the professionals, scientists, academics and envirocrats that is the real challenge. They have to be persuaded not to go running after the latest high-tech 'snake oil' solutions, but to carefully consider the environmental impact of what they do in a holistic way. Proposals should be ethical, responsible and based on good science. Only then will we begin to see genuinely sustainable ways forward. One of the reasons this doesn't happen is due to the way in which research is now funded and directed, much of it linked to industrial vested interests.

Government research funding in many advanced countries now expects a quick business return on their investment and this excludes research that is more thoughtful and critical. If you cannot find industrial sponsors and immediate users it is almost impossible to develop innovative solutions.

> The intrinsic value of intellectual enquiry and exploratory research is not a concept easily sold to the Treasury (nor, rather more worryingly to UK research councils). … University research must demonstrate strong potential for short term (socio)-economic impact for it to be considered worthy of funding.
>
> (Moriarty, 2011)

As a result, there is a lack of good quality independent research into sustainable housing and, in particular, building physics and materials science. The need for better building physics and science is discussed at some length with a critical account of current approaches.

I believe that RHP was poorly conceived and was an example of poorly thought through government policy and action. Civil servants seem to assume that if industry and housing developers are given a handout of a few million pounds, to be spent in a few months, something – anything – will come out of it. The lack of care in defining objectives, criteria and outcomes and the failure to allocate money with openness and fairness, followed by careful independent monitoring, is very disappointing and is dissected in Chapter 3.

However, a lot of useful experience and information has and will come from the RHP, despite its many flaws, and hopefully this book will have ensured that the appropriate lessons can be learned.

Chapter overview

In Chapter 1 the nature of renewable materials is explored in greater depth. Where do they come from, what are they made of and how do they get into the construction supply chain? The difference is explored between artisan and self-build materials such as earth and straw, and more highly processed and manufactured products such as wood fibre insulation boards. The difference between natural and synthetic materials also has to be understood and the environmental drawbacks of normal building methods are considered.

Chapter 2 gives more detail of the RHP with an account of each of the 12 case study projects.

Chapter 3 is an account of the RHP itself with details of how it came about and how it was funded and managed by government agencies.

Chapter 4 provides an analysis of the issues that emerged from the 12 case studies.

In Chapter 5 the policy context of energy and sustainability policy is examined in the UK, Europe and internationally, to see how this affects the use of natural and renewable materials in the market for insulation and other construction materials. The difference between energy in use and embodied energy is discussed, as this is central to the reason why even many environmentally progressive people ignore or are even hostile to the case for natural and renewable materials. The weaknesses of mainstream modern methods of construction and conventional proposals for the future development of housing and building are considered.

Chapter 6 is a discussion of building physics and science. Energy performance, moisture, durability, health and similar issues are considered. A critical evaluation of assessment, accreditation and labelling of materials and green buildings is central to this, and a review of some of the research in the field is provided.

Chapter 7 outlines other examples of projects outside the RHP, using (or in some cases not using) a range of alternative innovative approaches.

Chapter 8 examines the case for natural and renewable materials and looks at the prospects for them in the future.

References

BBC News Asia Pacific www.bbc.co.uk/news/world-asia-pacific-14968605 (viewed 19 September 2011)

Bevan R. and Woolley T. *Hemp Lime Construction* BRE Press 2008

Dale S. and Saville J. 'The Compatibility of Building regulations with Projects under new Low Impact Development Policies' (unpublished paper) 2012

ESRC seminar series mapping the public policy landscape how people use and 'misuse' buildings, 26 January 2009 http://www.esrc.ac.uk/funding-and-guid ance/collaboration/seminars/archive/buildings.aspx

Lammas Project http://www.lammas.org.uk/ (viewed 15.3.12)

Moriarty P. (2011) *Scientists for Global Responsibility (SGR) Newsletter* Issue 40 autumn 2011. p.15

Olsen R. *Handmade Houses: A Free-Spirited Century of Earth-Friendly Home Design*, Rizzoli 2012

Watkins T. *The Human House, Sustainable Design*. Karaka Bay Press, Auckland 2009

Woolley T. *Natural Building* Crowood Press 2006

1. Renewable and non-renewable materials

…many of us feel motivated to choose environmentally friendly products, even if they cost a little bit more. We know that products can be made from rare natural resources or from renewable raw materials, with or without unfair labour, with chemical input or from organic agriculture, with more or less energy based emissions. This is not a question of income but one of willingness.

(Welteke-Fabricius 2011)

In order to understand why natural and renewable materials are beneficial in mainstream building construction it is necessary in this chapter to explain what these materials consist of and to compare them with more conventional products. This book focuses largely on timber frame construction, insulation and board and panel materials. From these materials it is possible to construct many buildings that are required by society, even some multi-storey buildings. Environmental issues related to steel and concrete are not discussed in any detail here though they will be touched on in Chapter 6.

For many practitioners of natural building around the world, this would be quite a narrow perspective, as natural builders will use a wide range of resources, local green timber, earth, straw, bamboo and whatever else is to hand. This approach was covered in another book (Woolley 2006), and there are many organisations offering services, training and advice on natural building in the UK and throughout the world. In this book, the aim is to concentrate on natural materials being used in mainstream construction rather than handmade /self-build structures.

Natural and renewable materials can be made from biological sources such as hemp, flax, wood, straw, sheep's wool and so on. They can also be combined with benign or low impact materials such as lime and earth into composites. However, some natural materials also include synthetic additives that are intended to improve performance. A key issue here is the reasons for selecting such materials and also the reasons given for not

Low Impact Building: Housing using Renewable Materials, First Edition. Tom Woolley.
© 2013 John Wiley & Sons, Ltd. Published 2013 by John Wiley & Sons, Ltd.

selecting them. There is a great deal of prejudice against natural or unusual materials and in conversation 90% of people also say that such materials are 'too expensive', even though this is not always the case and is usually based on ignorance. Many people also fear that such materials are not robust and long lasting.

However, there are many people, professionals and builders who overcome these prejudices and have been willing to give natural and renewable materials a chance, in preference to manmade synthetic products, even when they do cost a little more. This is even the case in projects where there are cost constraints, such as social housing. One key to selection is the level of commitment to doing the right thing for the environment.

Synthetic, manmade materials

Most construction materials used today involve a great deal of energy and much environmental damage to produce. They must be quarried, processed, subjected to heat or treated with a range of chemicals. Very often they are derived directly or indirectly from petrochemical sources, and polluting emissions are frequently a by-product of the manufacturing process. For the purposes of this book, these materials will be referred to as synthetic materials. Often such products are also referred to as 'manmade', but this is confusing as some of the natural renewable materials discussed here are also manmade. The word *synthetic* is used to contrast with the word *natural*, but as with so much in the English language there are problems of definition. Mineral wool insulation, for instance, is sometimes referred to as a *natural* product as it is made from naturally occurring rock. However, the process of melting the rock and then binding it with chemical glues is far from natural and can safely be referred to as synthetic. On the other hand, many natural insulation materials such as sheep's wool or hemp may also have manmade glues and binders and other chemicals added to them to make them perform better. However, many natural materials use natural glues, resins and binders or simply water. Other terms such as *ecological* and *bio-based* are also used to describe natural renewable materials.

There is also a growing body of materials made from recycled materials such as glass and plastic that many regard as environmentally acceptable. These recycled materials are even referred to as renewable as there seem to be unlimited amounts of waste materials in our throwaway society. However, some recycled materials require significant amounts of heat and chemical processes to convert them. An environmental judgement, based on scientific evidence and independent certification, when this is available, has to be made about the impact of these processes before deciding whether such materials are acceptable. In order to understand the distinctive characteristics of natural, renewable materials, we first have to understand the limitations of synthetic products.

The key difference between natural and synthetic materials is the concept of renewability. Once a load of rock has been melted and spun into mineral wool insulation it cannot easily be returned to the earth and certainly cannot be grown again so it cannot be *renewed*, and its CO_2 emissions, from manufacturing, cannot be recovered.

However, many companies make strong environmental claims in favour of non-renewable products. For instance Rockwool says that its stone-based insulation product is '*sustainable*'.

> Rockwool is an environmentally conscious company with a long track-record of producing, according to independent assessments, *one of the most sustainable insulation products available*. During its long lifetime, a typical Rockwool insulation product saves more than 100 times the energy invested in its manufacture, transport and ultimate disposal. Therefore, Rockwool insulation is one of the most practical, cost-effective and environmentally efficient ways that homeowners and organisations can reduce their energy consumption and improve their carbon footprint. Created from natural and recycled products, Stone wool is made by melting *naturally occurring* volcanic diabase rock and recycled briquettes, made with carefully selected by-products from our own and other industries. Our high-tech production process employs filters, pre-heaters, after-burners and other cleaning collection systems to ensure an environmentally responsible approach. (emphasis added)
>
> (Rockwool 2011)

There is little doubt that stone based insulations can be useful products, particularly because of their fire safety characteristics, though many natural renewable products also have good fire resistance performance. The aim here is not to suggest that they should never be used, as they might be the best material for a particular job. However, the specifier is confronted with a simple choice when considering the use of renewable or synthetic products and needs to question some of the *sustainability* claims for such products. For instance Rockwool states on its website; 'Rockwool is 97% recyclable', though it is not clear what happens to the mysterious 3% that is not recyclable. It also states correctly that something being recyclable does not mean that it is actually recycled.

Stating that rock wool is one of the most sustainable products available is based on a flawed definition of sustainability. In order to be sustainable, based on the Brundtland definition (Brundtland 1987), requires human activity not to compromise future generations, so non-renewable materials (that use a great deal of fossil fuel energy for manufacture, and resources that cannot be renewed) should not be referred to as sustainable. Stone wool insulation may help with energy efficiency but it is the energy used in the short term, to manufacture the material, that is doing the greater damage to the environment. To be regarded as sustainable, materials should be largely free of added toxic chemicals and be able to be disposed of safely. Stone wool products may not meet this standard.

There may be an argument for the use of high embodied energy or petro-chemical based products used in small quantities, such as aluminium or plastics, when nothing else will do the job. This is a social policy or political decision, but if a manufacturer like Rockwool says its product is the 'most sustainable', the average specifier seems to believe it, without investigating the claim any further.

It is possible that stone wool products can be recycled if the building containing the materials is carefully dismantled so that the insulation can be taken out and reused, but this rarely happens in practice. Synthetic fibre insulations often become dirty and damp and fall apart if disturbed and this makes reuse almost impossible. More commonly, synthetic insulations end up as waste in landfill. Mineral fibres do not biodegrade into the earth. Also, the off-cuts and general mess on building sites can lead to a significant amount of new insulation material going to waste and landfill.

Questioning claims about recycling

Most of the manufacturers of synthetic insulation materials make claims about the role of recycled content in their materials to claim a good environmental performance. They state that they can recycle all recovered material in their factory but never give figures, so it makes one suspect that these claims may be misleading. There are a few synthetic products that are largely made from recycled materials but it is often hard to distinguish these from other products where perhaps only a tiny proportion of the material is from recycled sources.

Black Mountain Ltd, one of the leading UK manufacturers of natural insulations, claimed on its website in 2011, that mineral fibre insulation was not recycled and that manufacturers of these products were wrong to claim that this was the case.

> Sheep's wool is biodegradable and therefore can be composted into the ground to enrich the soil and remain part of the earth's natural cycle. Sheep's wool insulation can be recycled or incinerated to produce additional energy, whereas man-made mineral fibre materials currently have no practical recycling system in place and can only be properly disposed of into landfill sites.
>
> (Black Mountain 2011)

A complaint was made about this to the Advertising Standards Authority (ASA) by the Mineral Wool Insulation Manufacturers Association (MIMA) but the ASA found in favour of Black Mountain, as they said that MIMA did not provide any solid evidence of recycling.

> The Mineral Wool Insulation Manufacturers Association (MIMA) challenged whether the claim was misleading and could be substantiated, because

they understood that mineral wool insulation could be recycled. We noted that the MMMF (Man Made Mineral Fibre) manufacturers website MIMA referred to, stated that the manufacturer encouraged the return of their product for recycling where it was in the form of construction off-cuts or reclaimed from refurbishment or demolition work. However, we considered that that statement did not in itself constitute evidence that that particular manufacturer recycled significant quantities of end of life MMMF, nor that there was a generally used system in place for the recycling of significant quantities of end of life MMMF. We concluded ... that there was not a generally used system in place for recycling significant quantities of end of life MMMF.

(ASA 2011)

While site management practices have improved significantly in recent years and waste is separated into different skips to assist recycling, insulation off-cuts rarely end up being recycled. Despite the existence of WRAP (Waste and Resources Action Programme) which was established by the UK Government in 2000, to promote recycling of materials, no robust standards for measuring recycled content of construction materials has been established. Environmental management standards, often quoted such as ISO 14001, are largely tick box exercises.

The principal limitations to recycling insulation materials is the difficulty of processing the material, particularly in the case of fibre glass and polyurethane foam insulation. For example although the recycling of fibreglass is technically feasible, the practical issues are significant i.e. noxious emissions are produced from the organic binder when remelting the fibres. It has also been identified that the lack of sufficient recycling facilities and associated infrastructure are limiting the recycling potential of insulation, although *these criticisms are refuted by the manufacturers*. (emphasis added)

(WRAP 2012)

Some synthetic fibre insulations are made, in part, from recycled materials such as waste glass. A glass based mineral wool product, produced by Knauf, called ECOSE is marketed as more environmentally friendly than conventional glass fibre due to its claimed recycled content. The product is coloured brown rather than the normal yellow or pink.

The natural brown colour represents a level of sustainability and handling never achieved: Manufactured from naturally occurring *and/or* recycled raw materials, and bonded using a bio-based technology free from formaldehyde, phenols, and acrylics and with no artificial colours, bleach or dyes added
* *Contributes to improved indoor air quality compared to our conventional mineral wool*
* *Reduces impact on environment through lower embodied energy*
* *Reduces pollutant manufacturing emissions and workplace exposures*

- *Improving the overall sustainability of buildings in which they are incorporated* (emphasis added)

(Knauf 2011)

What is interesting about Knauf's marketing is that they imply in the above statement, that other products may have problems in terms of indoor air quality and are environmentally less attractive. They also sell a product called 'earthwool' which could give the impression to poorly informed people, from its name, that this is a natural product derived from earth rather than glass (Knauf 2012).

While the ECOSE product may be based on glass cullet (recycled glass) Knauf's does not always state what the formaldehyde free binder is made of. Formaldehyde is a known carcinogen but it is still found in many building products including some kinds of glass-based insulation. The Earthwool health and safety data sheet states that the materials used are vitreous fibre (mmvf), alkali and alkaline earth ($CaO + MgO + NaO + K_2O$), thermo set, inert polymer bonding agent derived from plant starches (Earthwool 2010).

The insulation materials that are made from recycled sources such as glass *may* be about 60–80% based on recycled materials, though not all are. Environmental analysis of such products has to consider both the source of the material – especially that which is not from recycled sources – the amount of energy used in manufacture and any chemicals that are added. Some recycled products such as Corning's 'Foamglass' have achieved 'Natureplus' certification and are regarded as relatively environmentally benign (Foamglass 2012). However, other recycled materials still present environmental risks. This presents consumers and specifiers with a set of choices, highlighted in Table 1.1. Deciding whether to use materials based on renewable or recycled materials may ultimately be a complex and subjective choice. Some natural insulation materials may also include recycled material such as waste wool or recycled wood fibre but it is important to take into account all the other factors listed in the Table 1.1 when considering material choice.

There have been a significant number of judgements against mainstream insulation companies about advertising claims...here is an example:

Monday, 21 February 2011
Rockwool fire ads held unlawful
Building solutions manufacturer Kingspan Group plc has just won a trade mark and advertising dispute against Rockwool Limited. According to a press release from Wragge & Co., who acted for the victorious company, Mr Justice Kitchin, in the Chancery Division of the High Court (England and Wales) found that a series of Rockwool demonstrations and video recordings, which compared the fire performance of Kingspan and Rockwool products, was misleading and failed to comply with the Misleading and Comparative Advertising Directive. The judge also ruled that Rockwool took unfair advantage of Kingspan's trade marks, causing damage to its reputation.

(Marques 2011)

Table 1.1 Comparing natural and synthetic materials

	Natural renewable	Synthetic
Energy used in manufacture (embodied energy)	Usually low but energy is used in processing	Can be high, e.g. from melting
Added chemicals	Glues are added but are claimed to be low impact	Some products involve toxic glues, formaldehyde
Robustness	Some natural insulations claim to be highly robust	Some synthetic products are very robust; others can fall apart quite quickly
Ability to handle moisture	Some natural insulations are able to handle moisture very well, but some can degrade if not able to dry out	Most synthetic insulations are unable to absorb moisture; some fall apart as a result of wetting, others are unaffected
Moisture buffering	Many natural insulations can help to regulate humidity	Most synthetic insulations do not have this ability
Breathability	Most natural materials are breathable and moisture permeable	Some synthetic materials are breathable but most are not
Indoor air quality (IAQ)	Most natural insulations help with good IAQ, some products like sheep's wool, claim that it absorbs formaldehyde	Either neutral or negative on IAQ
Recycling	Limited knowledge of recycling so far but some include recycled and waste materials. Best if not in composite form	Some products are based on recycled resources but very little evidence of the finished product being recycled
End-of-life disposal and pollution	Natural materials can decay back into the earth	Synthetic materials can be classified as hazardous waste
Ozone depletion	No or low negative effect	Many synthetic products, even from recycled sources, use chemical blowing agents
Thermal mass	Most natural materials contain varying levels of thermal mass, which improves thermal performance	Most synthetic materials do not contribute to thermal mass
Durability	Most natural materials are much more durable than is assumed and can survive wetting	Many synthetic materials are not as durable as is assumed though some are much more than others
Acoustic performance	Most natural materials have a superior ability to absorb sound	Some synthetic materials have good sound absorbency but most do not

Resource consumption problem with synthetic materials

There is little doubt that it is environmentally beneficial to use recycled resources such as waste glass. When we go to the bottle bank we want to believe that this material is going to be used for something and not end up in landfill. However, using rock and stone is a different matter. The cement and concrete industry sometimes argue that, as the planet is made of rock, there is plenty to go round! This rather ignores the disruption caused by digging big holes in the ground with massive excavators and explosions, often in environmentally beautiful or sensitive areas! For instance, one multinational cement company, Lafarge (ex Redland Aggregates), wanted to demolish an entire mountain on a Scottish island, creating a 'super quarry' (McIntosh 2012). There have been countless environmental campaigns against quarries, and while rock may not be regarded as a scarce resource, control of extraction is a key environmental criteria (Earthfirst 2011).

Rockwool go one stage further than saying there is an unlimited supply of stone by arguing that, as their raw material is volcanic stone, it is almost a renewable material because of regular volcanic eruptions! They say, 'Thanks to volcanic activity 38,000 tonnes of new diabase material is created every year more than they use'(Rockwool 2012). Of course they don't use this new volcanic material for insulation, stating instead that their source is 200 million years old stone in 'Ireland' (op. cit.). Rockwool is manufactured (at the time of writing) in Bridgend, South Wales, from basalt stone, quarried in Northern Ireland and shipped from Belfast to South Wales. The bedrock of the basalt quarries is not far away from the Giant's Causeway world heritage site. This basalt is about 60 million years old (not 200 million) and certainly not as a result of recent volcanic activity!

Quarrying aggregates in Northern Ireland has been a financially attractive option as the Northern Ireland Government waived the EU Aggregates Levy, thus reducing the price of the material. Quarries in the province have been paying 40p per tonne under the Levy exemption, whereas UK mainland producers had to pay £2.00 per tonne. A legal judgement in 2010 declared that the waiver of this levy was illegal but the matter still hasn't been resolved at the time of writing (AGGNet 2012).

The issue of resource consumption is a critical factor when sourcing environmentally friendly materials. Very often designers and specifiers are unaware of the origin of materials, as their main preoccupation is with getting the building built. Bioregional and WWF argue for local sourcing of materials in their One Planet Living standard.

> Using sustainable and healthy products, such as those with low embodied energy, sourced locally, made from renewable or waste resources…
> (Bioregional 2012)

But this can be interpreted as the nearest supplier rather than the actual source of the materials. The origins of materials have to be traced beyond where they are manufactured or stored. For this reason local sourcing of materials should not be regarded as a very useful environmental criterion and it can often be greenwash, unless the materials are literally obtained from the site or nearby. Standards like One Planet Living give general guidance but do not require a full carbon footprint and analysis of embodied energy, so it allows developers and builders to suggest that they are being

Figure 1.1 Basalt quarry in Northern Ireland (source http//www.stonedatabase.com/). Reproduced by permission of Stone Conservation Services, Consarc Design Group Ltd.

green by making vague assertions about 'local sourcing'. If materials such as earth are dug up on the site or timber felled from surrounding woodland or straw from adjoining fields, then this is a valid form of local sourcing and there are excellent projects that have put this into practice. Obtaining a material from a nearby builder's merchant is not local sourcing!

If we are serious about safeguarding the planet for future generations we should try to limit the use of non-renewable materials. This is one of the strongest reasons for using bio-based, natural and renewable materials.

Renewable materials – insulation

Insulation materials made from hemp and sheep's wool are renewable because the hemp can be grown again and the sheep sheared again next year. As most of the natural and renewable materials are quite new to the industry, there is little evidence of the extent of recycling so far, but some natural materials can include recycled content. The issue becomes a little more complicated with wood based products because timber, while being a renewable material, cannot be replaced on an annual basis, as trees take a lot longer to grow. Also some wood fibre products are made from wood waste but this is not so much recycling as using a by-product of another wood processing activity. In some products wood fibre and wood chipboards may be made from virgin timber, but with other products they can be made from recovered wood. Some products are made from mixed sources.

Natural and renewable natural materials have a number of advantages over synthetic products such as those discussed above, even if they are made from recycled materials. This is because natural renewable materials generally have a much lower embodied energy and they are significantly better in terms of health and indoor air quality, as they are made with less toxic materials. Similarly they have a much lower pollution risk during manufacture and when disposed of at the end of life. Perhaps most significant of all is the characteristic of plant based materials as having absorbed CO_2 during growth, which is known as *carbon sequestration*. Sheep's wool does not have this advantage, as sheep can also be blamed for methane emissions, though this is not as serious as from cattle (Fairlie 2010).

Carbon sequestration and embodied energy

Carbon sequestration has given natural renewable materials an edge over synthetic materials as they can be seen as 'carbon negative'. However, carbon negative is not a very helpful term – carbon positive would sound better! Calculating how much CO_2 is locked up in a natural product is a controversial area and there are no internationally accepted standards for this yet. However, it is argued by some that locked in CO_2 can be seen as offsetting the energy used to produce a material. Not all environmentalists agree with this view. Materials like hemp and timber will have used some fuel in harvesting, processing and transport and frequently natural products arrive on site wrapped in plastic bags so they are not fossil fuel free. However, despite this, the overall environmental burden is reduced by the fact that plant based materials have locked up carbon when growing which synthetic materials can never do.

Despite the CO_2 reductions afforded by sequestration, embodied energy databases frequently show higher levels of energy use and carbon emissions for some natural products and much lower levels for some synthetic products. This is because very few databases draw on information from their own original research, but instead reproduce claims from other sources. For instance the ICE database from Bath University (Bath 2012) give the following embodied energy figures on its summary page:

Mineral Wool at 16.6 MJ/kg
Fibreglass/Glasswool at 28 MJ/kg,
Flax at 39.5 MJ/kg.

Anyone looking superficially at this would draw the conclusion that natural insulations have a higher embodied energy than synthetics. First of all this is strange as there are almost no flax insulation products on the market (the only one readily available is a mix of flax and hemp) and yet the ICE database does not list other more common natural products. It should be obvious that a product that involves melting solid rock at over 1500 °C uses more energy than a crop based product like flax. In some cases rock wool products are heated using waste incineration, so possibly avoiding a high score for using fossil fuels. If you are unable to interrogate the build-up of figures in embodied energy databases it is important to remain sceptical about what is published. What is good about the Bath database is that details of the original source are given on a spreadsheet so the source can be checked. In this case of flax versus rockwool, the figures come from a Danish study that has hundreds of citations due to its conclusions that rockwool had the best LCA rating (Schmidt et al. 2004). The methodology used by the authors of this study provide a useful insight into the way in which LCA results can be determined by the assumptions used.

There is the danger that users of such databases simply look at the simplified published figures without looking to see where they came from, which means that commercially driven research takes on an unwarranted authority.

Performance and Durability of natural materials

Natural materials perform very differently to synthetic products. They can be more robust, provide better energy performance and cope with moisture and humidity. Ironically this is the one aspect most quickly discounted by those hostile to natural materials as there is an assumption that synthetic products will inevitably be more robust and effective. There is a growing body of practical experience and scientific evidence that shows that natural materials can have a better performance than synthetic materials. Unfortunately standards and regulations can be stacked against natural materials and examples of this are discussed in later chapters.

Breathability and moisture permeability are crucial issues in well-insulated buildings as there is increased risk of humidity and condensation, as discussed in more detail in Chapter 6 . Natural insulations are able to 'breathe' and vapour can pass through the material. Rock and glass fibre products can also be regarded as breathable though some are classified as semi-permeable. Other synthetic insulation boards made from polyurethane, polystyrene etc. have very limited ability to breathe and handle moisture.

Natural insulations can retain their thickness better than some synthetics and can recover more quickly if they get wet. Finally natural materials also possess thermal mass and the ability to store heat and react to building conditions in a dynamic way. The ability to store heat can make a significant difference to improved insulation and thermal performance. Natural materials will vary in this respect quite significantly but all are much better in this way than synthetic materials, which possess almost no heat storage capacity. Table 1.1 summarises these issues.

Natural renewable materials commercially available

We will now look at the main natural renewable materials commercially available for mainstream construction.

Hemp, hemp lime, hemp 'concrete' or hempcrete

Hemp fibre is used to make insulation quilts and boards. Sometimes it is mixed with flax or wood fibre. Industrial Hemp is similar to marijuana or cannabis but with minimal drug content. Hemp is widely grown throughout Europe, and many other parts of the world and, it is claimed, has over a 1000 uses (Robinson undated; McCabe 2010). Apart from oil and seed for food production, hemp is used for clothing, automobile interiors and a wide range of bio-plastic composites. Growing Hemp often needs permission from the authorities because of concern about illegal drugs, and although most countries allow the growing of hemp, in the USA and some Muslim countries strong prejudices remain. Hemp is relatively easy to grow and is used as a break crop in agriculture. The hemp fibres and shiv (straw) are high in lignin and the shiv is also high in silica.

Hemp is a very strong and tough plant and needs special processing. The fibre has to be stripped from the shiv. The leftover shiv or hurd (the woody core or straw) after the more valuable fibre has been stripped, can be mixed with a lime binder to create a solid but lightweight insulating concrete (Bevan and Woolley 2008).

It is a common question why wood chips, miscanthus or jute or other plant fibre is not used instead of hemp. Such questions usually indicate that the questioner has a prejudice against hemp because of its cannabis connection. Experiments using other alternatives have not been very successful as the plant fibres lack the strength and moisture handling capacity of hemp. Some products mixing cement with wood chips do exist, but they do not provide the insulating properties of the hemp and lime composite. Mixing the shiv with a lime binder creates an insulating, breathable solid wall system which features strongly in the case studies in this book. Water is added to the hemp and lime, and the mix can be cast like concrete between shuttering, sprayed, used as an insulating plaster or made into blocks. It is very important to use the right proportions of material, the right mix of lime binder and not too much water. The mix when cast is strong enough for the shuttering to be removed almost straight away, though it is usually left in place for 12–14 hours. It then takes a few weeks to dry and as the lime carbonates it becomes stronger over a period of months. Plastering and finishes such as painting must be left until the wall is reasonable dry. Hempcrete, as it is sometimes called, has been used in roofs and floors though its normal use in the UK is in walls.

Hemp fibre insulation

A wide range of hemp fibre insulation products are available from companies throughout Europe, with France, Germany and Poland being the main sources. The growing, processing and manufacturing of hemp for industry is now big business, and materials for construction using hemp are only a small part of the market. The European Industrial Hemp Association (EIHA 2012) is holding its 9th international conference in 2012, covering hemp seed as an anti-ageing dietary supplement to soaps, foods, medical treatments as well as polymer composites, particle boards and shiv for building. Hemp fibre insulation is made in several ways. Sometimes it is blended with flax, wood or cotton waste and usually polyester fibres are also added (usually about 15%). Hemp fibre insulation can be made using other natural additives, but commercially polyester seems to be preferred. The hemp fibre insulation can be used as a direct substitute for glass fibre or low density stone wool. The fibres are treated with a fire retardant, usually a borate or phosphate based compound. Manufacturers usually play down the polyester and flame retardant components as this takes away from the otherwise natural and organic nature of the materials. Both borate and phosphate fire retardants raise difficult environmental issues and the long-term aim will be to avoid the use of such materials.

Flax

Flax is sometimes confused with hemp but is quite different. Flax is used to make linen clothing and is also a food crop (linseed also known as flax seed).

Flax is not as tough as hemp but it can also be used for insulation, though it is more commonly mixed with hemp. Flax boards and other composite products are available but not as common as hemp products. Insulation products such as 'Breathe' are made in Denmark from blending hemp and flax (Breathe 2012).

Straw and straw composite boards

The shiv or straw from hemp and flax is referred to above, but generally straw is normally regarded as the waste material from wheat, barley, oats, rice and other cereal crops. Straw can be baled into oblong bales in the field and these can be used in strawbale building. This is often referred to in the UK as hay bales, but it makes little sense to use hay for this purpose as it is a food material and may decay more rapidly than straw. Strawbale building can be found all over the world, but particularly in the USA and throughout Europe (Strawbale EU 2012; Strawbale Construction 2012). Strawbale building has largely been seen as a form of construction for amateur self-builders but there are a growing number of buildings built by mainstream contractors (see Chapter 7).

There are numerous organisations promoting and studying strawbales and straw as a building material (Ecobuildnet 2012; The Last Straw 2012, GSBN 2012) and considerable knowledge and scientific data is now available. Strawbale building has been incorporated into building codes in some parts of the USA, though there seems to be a constant struggle against prejudice about straw (DCAT 2012).

In an effort to produce a more highly engineered strawbale project, the Modcell off-site system has been developed and is being used for one of the case study projects. This has attracted research funding, and a test building has been constructed at Bath University (Balehaus 2012).

Cereal straw can also be combined, as with hemp and wood fibre, into boards and panels. Strawboard was very common in the 1960s and 1970s and was widely used but gained a bad reputation when it was used in situations where it got wet and could not dry out, resulting in rot. Despite this, many buildings that incorporated Stramit boards are still around today, and in recent years the manufacture of strawboards has returned in Sweden and Australia. The straw is compressed with heat and bound together by the natural internal resins without added glues. Stramit is the Swedish word for straw.

Sheep's wool

Sheep's wool insulation is currently made in the UK, though a number of products are imported from other European countries. It has become well established in the UK market through the pioneering work of 'Thermafleece' in Cumbria established in 2001 (Thermafleece 2012). Thermafleece, based in Cumbria offers a range of products including hemp and recycled plastic insulation. Black Mountain sheep's wool insulation, is made in North Wales. However, the initial processing and some manufacture of sheep's wool insulation is carried out in Yorkshire where wool manufacture dates back to the 18th century.

The marketing of sheep's wool tends to emphasise the benefits to local farmers but most wool is bought through the British Wool Marketing Board, or imported, and thus the source cannot always be determined as market forces are always changing. It is best to quiz the manufacturer and supplier about this. Wool insulation may be made with a polyester binder but some makes do not use this. The insulation effectiveness can be altered by the manufacturing process. The wool is subject to fairly aggressive cleaning, and fire and pest retardant chemicals such as sodium borate (borax) are normally added. Sheep's wool is hygroscopic, handling moisture very well and is also able to absorb toxic chemicals such as formaldehyde. It is not a good idea to use fleeces straight from the farm, as is sometimes suggested, as wool can be very dirty, smelly, contaminated with sheep dip and subject to insect infestations. There have been stories of moth infestation associated with sheep's wool insulation but little solid evidence of where this has occurred. In the long term, 'borax' treatment may be inappropriate as it is regarded by some as toxic and alternative treatments are being developed.

Bamboo

Bamboo has recently been described as 'green gold'. Production and use of bamboo is booming as its advantages become more widely understood. Bamboo can rival hemp for having even more uses. The current world

Figure 1.2 Black Mountain factory, North Wales wool processing

Figure 1.3 Black Mountain factory

market is $10 million but this is growing rapidly. Unfortunately bamboo is already being traded on the commodity and futures markets and this may distort its potential as financiers and dealers try to use it to make trading profits (Ecoplanet 2012). Bamboo also rivals hemp as one of the fastest growing plants, and is thus ideal as a renewable material. It can be used as a structural material and is also converted into a wide range of composite products such as flooring. So far bamboo is not widely used in Western temperate countries in building construction but is an excellent substitute for slow growth timber in many poorer developing countries where the climate is ideal for growing bamboo. It has been used in Japan and China for centuries and is also common throughout Asia. It is also becoming more important in South and Latin America. Bamboo can be grown in more temperate climates but is usually imported. Prefabricated bamboo houses are available (Bamboo 2012). There is a substantial literature on bamboo in architecture and building (Worldbamboo 2012). Bamboo can be used as round poles or split. It is even possible to use it to make corrugated sheet material.

Cork

Corkboard and insulation is one of the most natural of products, stripped from the cork oak tree (Quercus suber) in countries such as Portugal, and it can be used for excellent thermal and particularly acoustic insulation. Cork insulation is made with granules of cork that are steam treated so that they bond together using natural resins in the cork. It is used as an alternative to stone wool in some proprietary external insulation systems, even combined with synthetic petrochemical based materials. Cork is also used as a wall lining material. Cork is usually more expensive than synthetic insulations and has become less commonly used in recent years as other renewable and low impact materials have become available. However, it is a material with excellent properties and is always worth considering where other materials are not suitable (Corklink 2012).

Wood

Timber is the most familiar renewable material. Responsible forestry should ensure that any timber felled is replaced with multiple replanting – but trees take many years to grow. Thus while wood is a renewable material it cannot be replaced as quickly as materials such as hemp and bamboo. Timber should be regarded as one of the most precious and valuable resources on the planet. Forests and woodland should be retained and sustainably managed so that timber is not clear-felled but thinned as part of proper management. Timber is used for many low value uses such as paper production and fuel. Paper can be made from hemp and biofuels should only come from short rotation cropping and thinning so as to save timber for higher value uses.

Forest Stewardship Council (FSC 2012) certification provides some guarantee that responsible forestry practices are being followed but there is a great deal of confusion about FSC certification. Timber sold for building construction is usually referred to as FSC certified, but this usually means from an FSC source. Timber suppliers, joinery and timber frame companies and contractors should all have what is known as chain of custody certification – very few do. PEFC is another certification standard, often referred to as equivalent to FSC, but PEFC is run by the timber industry whereas FSC is independent (FSC 2012; PEFC 2009).

If timber is to be regarded as a renewable material it should be FSC certified and preferably locally sourced. Architects like to use cedar cladding for instance; one of the case studies in this book has used this material. Most supply companies claim to offer cedar 'with FSC', but there is a lot of cedar being sold that is not certified. Cladding using locally sourced FSC certified larch or Douglas fir is generally viewed as more environmentally acceptable.

Because timber is a precious resource this wonderful material should be used sparingly. The natural warmth of timber has a beneficial effect on people in buildings and thus it should be used in such a way that the timber can be seen and appreciated. Far too many buildings contain large amounts of timber that are unnecessary, such as large sections for floor and roof structures. As demands for greater insulation thickness are made, additional timber is used to create deeper frames, again wasting timber. Double stud frames and large timber sections are used simply to give greater thickness of insulation. Careful design can avoid this. Composite timber products such as I-beams are much more economical and can make use of poorer quality timber. Other products such as LVL, glu-lam and cross-laminated timber make better, more economical use of timber resources but some are concerned about the glues that are used. Conventional glues in composite timber products have contained varying levels of formaldehyde which is classified in some countries as carcinogenic.

Glues based on isocyanates, phenols, PVA and melamine can also contain formaldehyde but some do not. Composite timber manufacturers are rarely open about glues and so the specifier has to query the constituents.

There is also a wide range of timber products made from shavings, sawdust and wood waste, chipped and recycled timber. Some of these products may be made using natural binders, water, heat and pressure but also glues. Woodwool boards, made in Italy, Sweden, Austria and India, once widely used are also becoming more common again. These are mostly bound with Portland cement but more environmentally friendly products use magnesium and calcium silicates.

Timber composites and wood fibre

Wood fibre is the generic term for a wide range of products, which include rigid boards, semi-rigid boards and insulation batts. Most people in the construction industry will be familiar with a wide range of composite wood panel products such as MDF, chipboard, wafer board and plywood. While there are negative environmental and health impacts of glues, even the natural lignins in timber can cause pollution problems (Sierra-Alvarez 1991).

The Masonite Factory near Carrick on Shannon in Ireland, where environmentalists opposed planning permission and have raised concerns about a range of pollution emission risks, was prosecuted by the Irish Environmental Protection Agency in 1997 (EPA 2012). Wood fibre products, on the other hand, can be environmentally benign, compressed using water which releases natural resins. It is important to distinguish between environmentally friendly wood fibre products and those made with synthetic additives and glues. Pentachlorophenol (PCP) and copper chrome arsenic (CCA) are highly dangerous toxins that have been used in timber for many years (Jagels 1985) but are now being replaced with less dangerous materials.

There is a wide range of wood fibre products, from relatively stiff boards to floppy insulation batts. This range of products can meet many building needs from roof sarking boards, boards that can be rendered and used in external renovation, laid on floors for acoustic separation and as sheathing boards in timber frame construction and so on. In lightweight timber frame construction, wood fibre products have the additional benefit of providing some thermal mass to the build-up. Some manufacturers have introduced a range of environmentally friendly wood products that are largely or completely free of added chemicals.

Hofatex, who make a range of wood fibre insulating boards, for instance, claim to use an 'ecological glue', made from a modified starch, having previously used polyvinyl acetate (PVA). Its factory initially established in 1951 in Banska Bystrica is by the side of the Bystrica River in Slovakia. They treat the incoming softwood chips using a thermo-mechanical process and the fibre is mixed with water and then dried. They do admit to adding paraffin, however:

> Hofatex® wood-fibre boards include only natural materials which cause no health problems. They are predominantly (up to 98%) comprised of wood fibres. Only natural substances such as paraffin and natural starch are added to improve some of the properties. As opposed to most fibre insulation materials, they contain no carcinogenic formaldehyde. To increase water resistance, a natural hydrophobiser is added to some of the boards (Hofatex® UD and Hofatex® System). This is not just a surface treatment; this hydrophobiser is added when the fibre suspension is created, i.e. the entire thickness of the boards have greater water resistance and consequently on both sides. The wet process for producing Hofatex wood fibreboards removes from the wood all the aromatics which attract insects and pests. Conversely, the final product has an approximately 7-8% humidity content. From a biological point of view, wood-destroying insects are attracted to softwoods with a humidity content of above 15%.
>
> (Hofatex 2012)

Pavatex is leading manufacturer of a wide range of wood fibre insulation and board products, some of which were used in the RHP case study

Table 1.2 Examples of natural manufactured insulation and related products available in Europe

This list of natural products available in 2010 is included to give an idea of the range of products that have been available in recent years. This list will be out of date almost immediately as some products disappear and other new ones are introduced. However, many architects and specifiers are not aware of how many different products do exist.

Breathe hemp flax insulation

Isonat wood fibre and hemp

HDW Stopfwolle

Hanf-Lehm-Steine hemp-clay bricks

HDW Faserschuettung hemp fibre insulation

Einblasdaemmung hemp blown-in insulation

Canafloc hemp insulation

Cannabric

Stopfwolle hemp insulation

Hanfstopfwolle hemp insulation

Hanfdämmschüttung hemp pellets for fillings

Hanfeinblasdämmung hemp blown-in insulation

Canaflex

Daemwool Schafwoll Dämmatten (30–240 mm) wool insulation

Alchimea wool insulation

Sheep Wool Insulation Ireland

Thermafleece sheep's wool

Thermafleece hemp

Thermo hemp / Thermohanf hemp insulation

Black Mountain sheep's wool

Black Mountain natural hemp insulation

Isolena

Woolin

Flachshaus insulation panel DP flax

Flachsdämmatten flax insulation mats

Steico Flex

Steico Therm

Steico Roof

Steico Floor

Steico Zell

Gutex fibreboards

Hofatex wood fibre boards

HolzFlex® Protect

HolzFlex® Mais

Flexible insulation board with a textile bonding fibre made of cornstarch

HolzFlex® standard

Pavatex wood fibreboards

Isolair

Pavatherm and Pavatherm HB

Pavaflat

Diffutherm

Pavaclay

Pavadentro

(continued)

Table 1.2 (continued)

Pavapor
Pavaboard
Pavastep
Pavatex
Pavaself
Isofloc blown-in insulation
(recycled newspaper)
FlexCL board type cellulose insulation
FineFloc blown-in
Climacell blown-in Insulation (recycled newspaper)
Däemmstatt's CI 040 blown-in insulation, fillings, with and without borates
Klimafloc blown-in insulation, fillings, with and without borates
AgriCell BW blown-in insulation (cellulose)
Extruded rye filling or blown-in (used for all hollows, also for floor insulation)
Schilfrohrleichtbauplatte WLS 055 (20 & 50 mm)
Reed lightweight panel
Hiss Reet Platte reed panel
Hiss Reet Granulatplatte
KORK Dämmplatte WLS 040 (40–200 mm) cork panel

projects. Pavatex is based in Cham and Fribourg on the Saane River in Switzerland. The company began work in 1936 and uses a wet process relying on natural lignin in the wood for bonding though a small amount of bitumen (2%) is added to some of their products. Latex for waterproofing is added to the roofing products to provide rain protection during construction. The fibres are pressed using heat in a process illustrated on their website (Pavatex 2012). Softwoods, spruce and fir timber are used. Water is recycled on site and the heat for drying comes from burning wood waste in a plant on their sites.

Another company making wood fibre and also hemp boards and insulation is Steico, which was founded in 1986 as Steinmann & Co., with headquarters in Feldkirchen near Munich, now producing materials on two sites in Poland, Czarnków (north of Poznan) and Czarna Woda (near Gdansk). They also have a base in Casteljaloux (near Bordeaux, France). Steico offers a wide range of products including engineered timber structural components (Steico 2012).

There are other companies making wood fibre products in several European countries but the reason for looking at these companies in detail is to question why such an industry has not developed in UK and Ireland. In Ireland, the government has invested heavily in supporting a large MDF factory in Clonmel and the Masonite factory in Carrick on Shannon but it has not supported the development of environmentally friendly low impact wood fibre materials production. Similarly other composite and solid wood products are all imported into the UK and Ireland when they could easily be made locally.

There are a wide range of natural insulation products available and it is not possible to describe them all. Table 1.2 shows a list of some trade names of products; while such a list will be out of date as soon as it is produced, it does give an indication that there are far more products than most people realise.

Solid timber

Glu-lam and laminated veneer lumber (LVL) beams offer an attractive alternative to steel and concrete for the structure of buildings, providing concerns about glues are addressed. Often long spans can be achieved with light-weight material using composite joists made of smaller sections of softwood timber. An interesting further development is the use of cross-laminated solid timber panels (CLT) that are prefabricated and can provide floors, walls and roofs as well as structural elements of a building. This is regarded by some as a valuable use of timber as lower quality timber can be used in smaller sections. The Inverness case study in the RHP has made use of solid timber panels. Solid timber panels have been used to construct an eight-storey building with 41 apartments, Bridport House in Hackney North East London. The CLT structure was built in 8 weeks by Eurban with CLT panels from Austrian Company Stora Enso (TTJ 2012).

In an attempt to develop solid timber construction without glues an Austrian company, Brettstapel, has developed a glue free solid timber panel that is held together with dowels. A small number of Brettstapel projects are completed or planned in the UK (Brettstapel 2012).

Conventional timber framing simply uses treated timber studs usually with a sheathing board for racking resistance made of chipboard or some other timber composite board. Timber structurally insulated panels are available but these generally use petrochemical based insulation materials. The mainstream timber frame construction sector has sadly done little to

Figure 1.4 Bridport House, Hackney, solid timber panel multi-storey construction

adopt natural renewable materials. While UKTFA (2012) does explain the benefits of what it calls a 'fabric first' approach, claiming that timber frame saves 0.8 tonnes of CO_2 per m^3 in comparison to other materials, they dodge issues like thermal mass and the environmental impacts of synthetic insulation materials. They have done little to support innovation in timber frame. However, a UK based alternative approach to timber construction has been developed in Wales by Elements Europe, where a low energy house has been constructed in box sections from local spruce: the Ty Unnos project. Insulation used so far has been rockwool and cellulose recycled newsprint, but Ty Unnos say that other more natural insulations could be used (more details in Chapter 7).

Low impact materials

Earth

Unfired earth is an important material that can be used in low impact construction. Earth is not a renewable material, as once dug up from the ground it does not grow again! However, earth can be returned to the ground without environmental damage in most cases. Unfired earth can be used in rammed earth walls and cob walls (where it is mixed with a small amount of straw) and unfired earth bricks. Unfired earth products and construction methods have a very low embodied energy unless the earth is transported from some distance. Subsoil earth can often be excavated on site as part of normal earth moving for foundations. Earth can also be mixed with hemp and other plant based materials to create blocks etc. (Woolley 2006). In some developing countries it is common to use cement stabilised earth as practitioners have been convinced by the cement industry that unfired earth is not strong or robust enough. In many cases it is not necessary to add cement to unfired earth.

It is not proposed to discuss earth construction in depth here as none of the case study projects used earth and this book is focused on renewable materials. There are some excellent books on earth construction such as Minke (2000) and Morton (2008). There is also a UK earth building association, (EBUK 2012). Earth building can be useful as a form of thermal mass in a building; it can also enhance the appearance, as earth walls can be beautiful. Earth is also hygroscopic and can absorb moisture.

Lime

Building lime is also an important part of natural building. Lime can use as much energy to produce as cement, and quarrying and burning can contribute to carbon emissions much as cement, which is also made from limestone. On the other hand it has many beneficial effects that cement does not have, and lime, once in place in a building, absorbs

CO_2 from the atmosphere in a process known as carbonation. As the lime carbonates, it gains strength, but it still remains breathable and flexible in walls, unlike cement and concrete. Lime has natural waterproofing and biocidal preservative properties so, when used with timber and other natural materials it can help to preserve them. If it is necessary to have a breathable wall then lime renders and plasters will assist with the breathability.

Lime has been used for centuries, and old limekilns can be seen in many parts of the UK and other parts of the world. Today there are a variety of limes available and it is important to use the correct one for the job. Lime technology has been kept alive because of the need to use the correct lime in historic building conservation but it has also become much more popular in modern new-building and renovation. Lime also provides the basis for many new render systems and insulating plasters. A specially formulated lime binder has been developed for use with hemp and this has been used in the case study projects in this book. Other lime mixes have also been used with hemp though not always successfully, as the wrong lime has been used in some cases.

Again a detailed discussion of lime is outside the scope of this book. There are useful guides to building with lime (Holmes 2002; McAfee 2009) and lime mortars (Yates 2008) but there is still a need for a comprehensive book on lime in new building construction.

References

AGGNet (2012) The Aggregates and Recycling Information Network http://www.mqr.info/news/baa-defeats-uk-government-in-eu-court (viewed 16.2.12)

ASA Advertising Standards Authority http://www.asa.org.uk/ASA-action/Adjudications/2011/5/Black-Mountain-Insulation-Ltd/TF_ADJ_50476.aspx (viewed 10.11.11)

Bamboo (2012) http://www.bambooliving.com/ (viewed 12.2.12)

Bath University 2012 http://www.bath.ac.uk/mech-eng/sert/embodied/ (viewed 12.1.12)

Balehaus (2012) http://www.bath.ac.uk/features/balehaus/ (viewed 12.1.12)

Bevan R. and Woolley T. (2008) *Hemp Lime Construction*, BRE HIS Press

Bioregional and WWF, One Planet Living. http://www.oneplanetliving.org/index.html (viewed 28.2.12)

Black Mountain Ltd (2011) www.blackmountaininsulation.com/Wool%20Brochure%20 (viewed 23.4.12)

"Breathe" (2012) http://www.hemptechnology.co.uk/insulation.htm (viewed 24.4.12)

Brettstapel (2012) http://www.brettstapel.org/Brettstapel/Projects/Projects.html (viewed 24.4.12)

Brundtland *The Report of the Brundtland Commission, Our Common Future*, Oxford University Press 1987

Corklink (2012) http://www.corklink.com (viewed 3.04.12)

DCAT http://www.dcat.net/resources/index.php (viewed 16.2.12)

Earthfirst https://earthfirst.org.uk/actionreports/content/rossport-round (viewed 24.10.11)

Earthwool COSHH Glass Issue Safety Data Sheet KI_DP_101 – UK (en) http://www. knaufinsulation.co.uk/PDF/MSDS-KI_DP_101_UK_Glass_ECOSE_EN.pdf (viewed 6.5.10)

EBUK http://www.ebuk.uk.com/ (viewed 29.3.12)

Ecobuildnet (2012) http://www.ecobuildnetwork.org/ (viewed 16.2.12)

Ecoplanet (2012) http://ecoplanetbamboo.com/about-us (viewed 12.2.12)

EIHA (2012) http://www.eiha-conference.org/ (viewed 30.3.12)

EPA (2012) www.epa.ie/licences/lic_eDMS/090151b2802a3895.pdf (viewed 14.11.11)

Fairlie S. (2010) *Meat: A Benign Extravagance*, Permanent Publications, Hampshire

Foamglass (last viewed 28.2.12) http://www.foamglas.co.uk/building/products/ environmental_statement/

Forest Stewardship Council (2012) www.fsc-uk.org/ Also Architects and Timber Specifiers http://www.fsc-uk.org/?page_id=22 (viewed 11.4.12)

GSBN http://sustainablesources.com/mailman/listinfo.cgi/gsbn (viewed 16.2.12)

Hofatex 2012 http://www.hofatex.eu/en/products/walls/hofatex-therm-dk (viewed 29.2.12)

Holmes S. and Wingate M. (2002) *Building with Lime* ITDG

Jagels R. 'Health hazards of natural and introduced chemical components of boat-building woods.' Am J Ind Med. 1985, 8(3):241–51)

Knauf Insulation http://www.knaufinsulation.co.uk/sustainability/ecose%C2%AE_ technology.aspx#ixzz1hjJMcRyr (viewed 27.12.11)

Knauf Insulation http://www.knaufinsulation.co.uk/earthwool.aspx (viewed 28.2.12)

Marques (2011) 'Rockwool fire ads held unlawful' http://www.marques.org/class46/ default.asp?D_A=20110221 (viewed 15.4.11)

McAfee P. (2009) *Limeworks*, Associated Editions

McCabe J. (2010) *Hemp What the World Needs Now*: Carmania Books, Santa Monica, California

Mcintosh A. http://www.alastairmcintosh.com/articles/2004-ecos-lafarge.htm (viewed 28.2.12)

Minke G. *Earth construction handbook*, WIT Press, 15 July 2000

Morton T. (2008) *Earth Masonry Design and Construction Guidelines* IHS BRE Press

Pavatex http://www.pavatex.ch/herstellung.aspx (viewed 28.2.12)

PEFC (2009) FSC summary report – Comparative analysis between the controlled wood requirements and PEFC, PEFC Germany and SFI: FSC International Center first edition, October 2009, Forest Stewardship Council AC

Robinson R. (undated) *The Hemp Manifesto: 101 Ways That Hemp Can Save Our World*, Park Street Press, Rochester

Rockwool http://www.rockwool.co.uk/homeowner/why+stone+wool-c7-(URL includes final hyphen) (viewed 28.2.12)

Rockwool http://www.rockwool.co.uk/sustainability/sustainability (viewed 24.10.11)

Schmidt A., Jensen A., Clausen A.A., Kamstrup O. and Postlethwaite D.A., 'Comparative Life Cycle Assessment of Building Insulation products made of Stone Wool, Paper Wool and Flax', International Journal of LCA 9 Parts 1 and 2 2004

Sierra-Alvarez R., Lettinga G. 'The methanogenic toxicity of wastewater lignins and lignin related compounds', Journal of Chemical Technology and Biotechnology Issue Wiley Blackwell Volume 50, Issue 4, pages 443–455, 1991)

Steico (2012) http://www.steico.com/en (viewed 12.4.12)

Strawbale Construction http://strawbale.sustainablesources.com/ (viewed 16.2.12)

Strawbale EU (2012) http://www.strawbale-net.eu/ (viewed 16.2.12)

The Last Straw http://thelaststraw.org/ (viewed 16.2.12)

Thermafleece (2012) (http://www.thermafleece.com/products (viewed 12.5.12)

TTJ (2012) http://www.ttjonline.com/story.asp?storycode=68366 (viewed 20.4.12)

UKTFA (2012) http://uktfa.com/fabric-first/ (viewed 20.4.12)

Welteke-Fabricius, Uwe: Speech at the launch of the Alliance for Sustainable Building Products, Grand Committee Room, Westminster, London, 16 November 2011

Woolley T. *Natural Building*, Crowood Press 2006

World Bamboo (2012) http://www.worldbamboo.net/ (viewed 12.2.12)

WRAP Waste and Resources Action Programme http://www.wrap.org.uk/construction/construction_materials/insulation/insultation_limits.html (viewed 28.2.12)

Yates T. and Ferguson A. *The use of lime based mortars in new build*, NHBC Foundation 12 December 2008

2. Case Studies: twelve projects in the Renewable House Programme

The UK Labour Government of 2007–2010 provided £6.7 million through the Department of Energy and Climate Change (DECC) to encourage the use of natural renewable materials in social housing construction through the Renewable House Programme (RHP). Twelve projects were funded contributing to the construction of approximately 200 houses. The process by which the programme was set up and administered is discussed in detail in Chapter 3. This programme provided an opportunity to see how natural, renewable materials could be used in mainstream social housing projects.

According to a section of the DECC website (accessed in 2010 but since removed) the funding was to build low carbon affordable homes using 'innovative highly insulating *renewable* materials'. The scheme was to demonstrate the viability of the materials and act as a spur for the renewable construction materials industry. However, one of the projects did not use renewable insulation materials and others used synthetic insulation materials in substantial elements of the schemes. This apparent breach of the grant conditions was justified in some cases by claims that DECC had not explicitly stated that renewable insulation materials should be used and that the use of timber frame and timber windows was sufficient. The DECC website, however, made it very clear:

> 'Only homes … that use a very high proportion of construction materials from renewable sources such as timber frame, natural insulation and timber windows are eligible for funding.
>
> (DECC 2010)

The DECC funding only provided a little extra money in most cases, with the majority of finance coming from elsewhere such as housing association grants. However, in the case of the Diss project, the grant appears to have paid for most of the scheme. The list of projects shown in Table 2.1 gives an overview of the programme and each case study is then discussed in more detail. The amount of funding shown for each project was based on

Low Impact Building: Housing using Renewable Materials, First Edition. Tom Woolley.
© 2013 John Wiley & Sons, Ltd. Published 2013 by John Wiley & Sons, Ltd.

Table 2.1 RHP case study projects (The grant figures and numbers of houses listed here were supplied by DECC and may differ from those reported in the case studies below)

Developers	Location	No. of houses/ units	RHP Grant £	Insulation materials	Page number
United Welsh Housing Assoc	Abertridwr, Wales	8	220k	sheep's wool	29
Oaklee Housing Association	Carnlough Antrim, NI	12	110k	Hemcrete, sheep's wool and cellulose	35
Cottsway Housing	Blackditch Oxford	16	320K	Hemcrete and sheep's wool	40
Network Housing Group	Callowlands, Watford	16	320k	Hemcrete and synthetic foam	44
Joseph Rowntree Trust	Domary Court Huntingdon Road York	6	160K	Hemcrete and fibreglass in roof	49
Albyn HA	Scotland Inverness	2	75k	wood/hemp fibre and solid wood	55
Flagship Housing & CZero	Long Meadow Denmark Lane, Diss, Norfolk	114 planned only 29 built	3 million	Hemcrete and hemp fibre	59
Lilac Co-operative	Leeds	20	420K	Modcell strawbale system, no details of other products yet	64
North Herts Homes	Letchworth Tomorrows Garden City	46(60)	920k	Hemcrete and Pavatex wood fibre	68
Four Housing Group	Reed Street South Shields	21	320k	Pavatherm wood fibre and stone wool in roof	76
Greensquare & Hab Oakus/ Kevin McCloud	Swindon The Triangle	42	840k	Hemcrete and sheep's wool	80
Kingdom HA	Scotland Pittenweem Fife	1	35.4k	appears not to have used any renewable insulation materials except timber frame and windows	88

figures supplied by DECC and there may have been some variation in the final amounts allocated.

Another grant condition on the DECC website was that the homes had to start on site in the 2009/2010 financial year and, as a result, several projects were rushed into, in order to meet the deadline of April 2010. The majority of the other projects, however, proceeded at a more leisurely pace and construction was in progress or only just started in 2012.

Information on each project was gathered through a series of email and telephone exchanges with the housing associations or developers, architects and builders. With a few exceptions, everyone contacted was very helpful and prompt in supplying information. The original list of approved projects provided by DECC (including grant figures and numbers of houses) was inaccurate and it took some time to track down all of the project contacts, with the help of the Homes and Communities Agency. Initial telephone and email information was then supplemented by further queries both by email and during site visits. In every case the builders were very accommodating in arranging site visits, even when they were very busy. Some of the architects were particularly helpful in sending photographs and updates on the progress of projects.*

---

*There may be some contradictions in information about grant finance and numbers of houses in the following case studies because different information was provided by different organisations.

Abertridwr: Y Llaethdy South Wales: sheep's wool insulation

Type	8 two-storey flats, CSH Level 4
Location	Abertridwr, Y Llaethdy South Wales
Builder/developer	Greenhill Construction for United Welsh Housing Association
Material	Timber frame, hempcrete
Insulation	Sheep's wool
Grants	£200,000 (RHP)

This scheme was completed in autumn 2010 for the United Welsh Housing Association. The project was already under way when a grant became available from the DECC RHP to use renewable materials and so the insulation specification was changed to incorporate sheep's wool. The builder-developer, Greenhill Construction, and their architectural technician/designer, Byron Way, were very helpful in providing information about the project.

The aim was to build Code Level 4 apartments, part of a larger development with a number of other conventional houses built using masonry and fibreglass insulation. The renewable grant went towards part of the development, eight two-storey flats in a courtyard.

It had originally been planned to build the apartments with timber frame so it was possible for details to be changed at the last minute to incorporate renewable insulation to justify the renewable materials grant. The builder said that they would normally have used Kingspan PUR in the walls with fibreglass in the roof space.

The timber frame suppliers did not have anything to do with the supply or installation of the insulation as they supplied an open frame and the builder added the insulation on site. Greenhill Construction explained that they substituted sheep's wool in the walls and roof without any real change in the detailing. The sheep's wool was sourced through a builder's merchant, Encon, and it was suggested that this was from Black Mountain (BM) in North Wales. Unfortunately, there were no photographs of the construction process showing sheep's wool being installed and there was no firm evidence of which sheep's wool product had been used. The Encon depot that had supplied the insulation was contacted by phone but they initially denied ever having heard of sheep's wool insulation, but when pressed said that they had supplied some a few years ago but did not stock it anymore as 'there was no demand'. Encon Insulation Ltd is a specialist merchant who supply insulation materials and they certainly show Black Mountain and Thermafleece sheep's wool on their website (Encon Insulation 2012).

Greenhill construction did not indicate any problems in using the sheep's wool though they suggested it would normally be too expensive. The builder kindly provided financial details and they indicated spending £7,602 on the sheep's wool insulation. Based on an estimation that approximately 1000 m^2 of insulation had been used, this suggested a cost of £7 per m^2. Comparing this cost with current insulation prices (Insulation Price 2012) this does not seem excessive.

Significant emphasis was placed on the provision of renewable energy in this scheme with an NIBE air source heat pump system and photovoltaic panels on the south facing roofs. Triple glazed timber windows were also used. The bulk of the resources provided by the £200,000 grant went on the renewable energy element of the scheme and the Welsh Government decided that this was allowed as part of the renewable grant scheme.

The standard of finish on the scheme was quite high and cedar boarding was used for external cladding. Clearly the timber frame, timber windows and cedar cladding could be regarded as renewable materials but the amount of grant for the sheep's wool was only a small proportion of the £200,000 available. In response to a freedom of information (FOI) request the Welsh Government stated that they had agreed with DECC that 'photovoltaic panels were eligible for the funding in order to achieve a Code Level 4 standard' (Welsh Government 2012).

The project was visited on a very cold day in November 2010 and access was available to one occupied ground floor apartment, which was extremely well heated, if not overheated. The tenant seemed very satisfied but had not been in the flat for long enough to appreciate the heating costs. The amount of space required for the renewable energy equipment seemed high compared with the very small area of the flat.

The wall build-up detail, Figure 2.2, includes OSB timber sheathing board on outside of frame with a 'high performance' metallised breather membrane on the outside. An impermeable polythene high-density membrane was used on the inside of the insulation. This is not a detail that would normally be recommended by natural insulation manufacturers but there is much debate about what would be regarded as best practice to avoid problems with interstitial condensation. On the other hand building control officers and energy assessors can sometimes insist on impermeable barriers saying that this, if installed properly, would contribute to a good standard of airtightness. At the moment there is little scientific data available on the performance of such a detail so the risk of interstitial condensation is unknown. Most ecological designers

Table 2.2 Abertridwr Energy data

Abertridwr energy data
The designed airtightness: level 3
TER reduction: 44–69%
Roof design values: 0.1
Floor: 0.11 to 0.16
Walls: 0.16

(Note: figures from Byron Way)

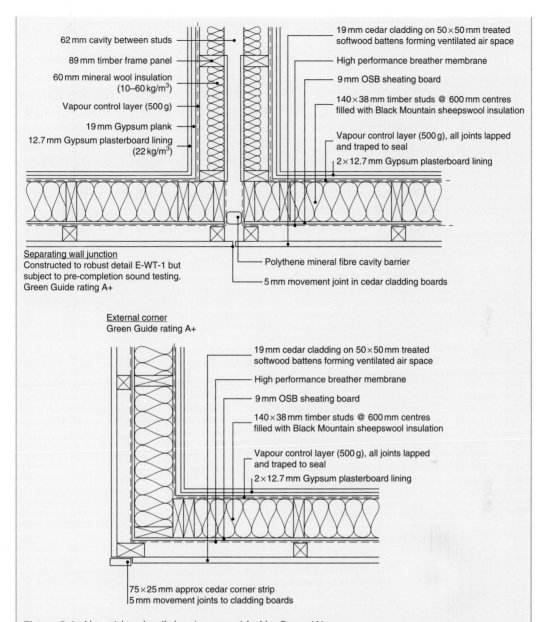

62 mm cavity between studs

89 mm timber frame panel

60 mm mineral wool insulation (10–60 kg/m³)

Vapour control layer (500 g)

19 mm Gypsum plank

12.7 mm Gypsum plasterboard lining (22 kg/m³)

19 mm cedar cladding on 50×50 mm treated softwood battens forming ventilated air space

High performance breather membrane

9 mm OSB sheating board

140×38 mm timber studs @ 600 mm centres filled with Black Mountain sheepswool insulation

Vapour control layer (500 g), all joints lapped and traped to seal

2×12.7 mm Gypsum plasterboard lining

Separating wall junction
Constructed to robust detail E-WT-1 but subject to pre-completion sound testing. Green Guide rating A+

Polythene mineral fibre cavity barrier

5 mm movement joint in cedar cladding boards

External corner
Green Guide rating A+

19 mm cedar cladding on 50×50 mm treated softwood battens forming ventilated air space

High performance breather membrane

9 mm OSB sheating board

140×38 mm timber studs @ 600 mm centres filled with Black Mountain sheepswool insulation

Vapour control layer (500 g), all joints lapped and traped to seal

2×12.7 mm Gypsum plasterboard lining

75×25 mm approx cedar corner strip
5 mm movement joints to cladding boards

Figure 2.1 Abertridwr detail drawings provided by Byron Way

would prefer to use breathing materials throughout, though it is normal practice to have less permeable material on the inside with greater permeability towards the outside. A breather membrane would work just as well as an impermeable one in terms of airtightness.

The Code assessor for the scheme was also the designer, Byron Way. SAP calculations were carried out by BEM Ltd. (The Welsh Assembly has now required all new housing, including private houses, to be subject to the Code for Sustainable Homes and this is enforced through the planning process).

The figure of 0.16W/m²K was an ambitious U-value target for sheep's wool, with a wall thickness of 140mm, but no test results were made available to see if this had been achieved in practice. Black Mountain, in their technical leaflet, (Black Mountain 2010) quote a U-value of 0.4 for 100mm thickness. Foil backed boarding is assumed to improve U-values but there is some debate about this. Staff at Cardiff Metropolitan University will be carrying out monitoring work and this may indicate how good a standard was achieved.

This project shows that it was feasible to substitute sheep's wool for a synthetic material without any apparent difficulty. It is unlikely that the design U-values could have been achieved with fibreglass and mineral wool but it is possible that a better insulation standard would have been claimed for PUR.

Table 2.3 Abertridwr finances

Funding details	Grant approx. £200,000	Timber cladding £31.900	Timber frame £41,600
	Black Mountain sheep's wool insulation to roof or walls £7,602	PV panels £61,200	Jeld Wen (Melton Mowbray) FSC Timber windows and doors £54,152

Table 2.4 Abertridwr organisations

Abertridwr: 8 units

United Welsh Housing Association Y Borth, 13 Beddau Way, Caerphilly CF83 2AX (029) 20858178

Green Hill Construction Ltd
Darran Watts Director
http://www.green-hill.co.uk/

Byron Way MCIAT: Sustainable Building Science
Chartered Architectural Technologist & Code Assessor
20 Hawthorn Road, Nelson, Caerphilly, CF46 6PB
www.sustainable-building-science.com

BEM Building Energy Performance Ltd:
7 Roundabout Court, Bedwas, Caerphilly, Mid Glamorgan CF83 8F

Figure 2.2 Abertridwr: Y Laethdy Terrace

Figure 2.3 Abertridwr: elevation showing PV cells on roof

Figure 2.4 Abertridwr: cedar cladding detail

Figure 2.5 Abertridwr: under construction. Reproduced by permission of Green Hill Construction Ltd.

Drumalla House, Carnlough, County Antrim: Hemcrete and sheep's wool

Type	11 houses (10 two-storey semi-detached houses, 1 wheelchair bungalow), CSH Level 4
Location	Drumalla House, Carnlough, County Antrim
Builder/developer	MSM Construction Ltd. for Oaklee Housing Association
Material	Timber frame, hempcrete walls, PV panels, mechanical ventilation heat recovery systems
Insulation	Sheep's wool
Grants	£110,000 (RHP)

This project was built using timber frame and hempcrete walls, with sheep's wool in the roof, for Oaklee Housing Association. Cellulose insulation was also added in certain positions. The scheme had already been designed and detailed when funding became available from the RHP. The grant was administered in Northern Ireland by the Department of Social Development, and the scheme was expected to achieve Level 4 of the Code for Sustainable Homes. The project has won a Green Apple bronze award for Oaklee Housing Association in November 2011 and several other awards subsequently. It was officially opening by Northern Ireland Assembly Minister, Nelson McCausland, on 30 September 2011.

Eleven houses were built consisting of:

10 × 3-person, 2-bedroom 2-storey semi-detached houses

1 wheelchair bungalow

The details of the scheme were changed from a conventional insulation system to the use of hempcrete in the walls when the grant became available. Work had already started on site and the timber frames had been ordered. Magnesium silicate boards were used as permanent shuttering for the hempcrete, but Heraklith Wood wool boards were used as shuttering around the windows to provide a better key for rendering. Sheep's wool insulation was used in the loft space. Some sprayed cellulose insulation was also used in part of the scheme where it was considered difficult to place hempcrete. Triple glazed windows, photovoltaic panels and mechanical ventilation heat recovery systems (MVHR) were used and an airtightness level of below 3 was achieved.

The homes were fitted with visible energy meters to be monitored by the Association's own energy officer in liaison with tenants. Tenants have also been provided with a comprehensive home user guide, which includes tips on how to conserve water and energy. Information on the environmental features of the properties was included in the handover talks.

The builders were MSM Construction Ltd of Portadown, Northern Ireland, who had not previously had any experience with hemp lime or other eco-materials. Lime Technology trained the builders in the use of the new system and they decided to do their own casting of the hempcrete walls. On the training day, they brought in quite a few of their operatives and there seemed to be a very positive response to the unfamiliar form of construction. The contractors indicated that hempcrete walls were installed without too much difficulty. They managed to find a local hire company that provided a horizontal pan mixer for mixing the lime binder and hemp shiv. The hempcrete mix was then placed by hand. Some of the hempcrete, once cast, had to be cut away for services installation but this did not appear to cause any major problems (Figure 2.10). No problems were reported with the loft insulation.

Detailing of the roof and at the head of the wall might have been given more consideration but so far there is no evidence of any problems. Airtightness results were satisfactory.

Table 2.5 Carnlough organisations

Carnlough – Oaklee Housing Association: 11 houses

10 × 3p2b houses (70–75 m²) (5 sets of semis)
1 × wheelchair bungalow (90–95 m²)

Oaklee Housing Association 37–41 May Street, Belfast, BT1 4DN

Contractor MSM Contracts Ltd, Unit 45a, Seagoe Industrial Estate, Portadown, County Armagh BT63 5QE

Architect: Knox Clayton Architects, Lisburn.

QS: Michael Magee, Brian Canavan Associates, Coleraine.

Engineers: Albert Fry Associates, Belfast.

M&E: John Conlon & Paul Hillan – BSD Belfast.

CSH: FW Consulting Belfast.

NI Department of Social Development (DSD)
Lighthouse Building, 1 Cromac Place, Gasworks Business Park, Belfast BT7 2JB

Figure 2.6 Carnlough: houses under construction showing permanent shuttering board in place before hempcrete is cast

Figure 2.7 Carnlough: contractors staff training on using hempcrete

Figure 2.8 Carnlough: hempcrete before render applied

The cost of scheme was £1,232,000, though a figure of £1.5 million was referred to in later press releases. The grant received from the RHP was £110,000.

Figure 2.9 Carnlough: wall head detail showing uncertainty on finishing the hempcrete where it meets the roof

Figure 2.10 Carnlough: wall detail where opening has been cut for electricity services

Figure 2.11 Carnlough: finished houses

Figure 2.12 NI Assembly Minister, Nelson McCausland, at the official opening. Reproduced by permission of Rory Moore Photography, www.rorymoore.com

Blackditch, Stanton Harcourt, Oxfordshire: Hemcrete and hemp fibre insulation

Type	16 'affordable' houses, CSH Level 4
Location	Blackditch, Stanton Harcourt, Oxfordshire
Builder/developer	E.G. Carter for Cottsway Housing Association
Material	Hempcrete, stone facing, FSC certified triple glazed timber windows and doorsets, PV panels
Insulation	Black Mountain hemp fibre
Grants	£800,000 (Homes and Communities Agency Social Housing Grant), £88,000 (DECC Low Carbon Buildings Programme), £320,000 (DECC RHP)

This development, by Cottsway Housing Association, of 16 'affordable' houses, is on the edge of a rural Oxfordshire village; it was designed to meet Level 4 of the Code For Sustainable Homes. The houses have been rented to housing association tenants and not sold as affordable homes.

The scheme consists of a mix of dwelling sizes:

$$2 \times 1\text{-bedroom 2-person flats}$$
$$1 \times 2\text{-bedroom 4-person flats}$$
$$6 \times 2\text{-bedroom 4-person houses}$$
$$6 \times 3\text{-bedroom 5-person houses}$$
$$1 \times 4\text{-bedroom 6-person houses}$$

The development was largely led by the construction company E.G. Carter, (head office in Gloucester but active throughout the Midlands and southern England). Architects Kendall Kingscott, from Bristol, were involved in obtaining planning permission and basic design work but do not appear to have been much involved in the site work, which was largely the responsibility of Carter.

The design of the scheme reflects the influence of the Prince of Wales (the Poundbury effect) in that a neo-vernacular or 'traditional' look was adopted in an attempt to blend in with the adjacent village with a number of historical and vernacular houses and cottages. Stone facing was used with some rendered walls.

The neo-vernacular appearance is somewhat marred by the PV panels on the roofs but the use of stone facing with hempcrete makes it different from many other schemes using hemp lime construction.

The scheme was due for completion early in 2011 but was not finished when visited in March 2011. The project was formally opened by the Prime Minister David Cameron, who is also the local Member of Parliament for West Oxfordshire, on 21 June 2011.

The principal renewable material and method of construction was hempcrete for the walls. This was installed by R. Curtis Building & Groundwork Ltd of Swindon, who attended training at Lime Technology. Steep roof pitches with dormers and loft spaces were designed with a

projects. When visited, about 60% of the hempcrete had been placed and appeared to be progressing well (Figure 2.18).

As the buildings have flat roofs it was decided to use synthetic insulation for the roof build-up. A rigid polyisocyanurate (PIR) sheet material called EcoTherm was evident on site though Crownloft fibreglass was also mentioned. Synthetic insulation PIR was also used for wall panels in the entrance porches in place of hempcrete. The porches and other wall sections were designed to have a timber rainscreen, and the insurers, LABC Warranty (LABC Warranty 2012) would not accept a timber rainscreen onto hempcrete as they said there was no approved detail for hempcrete behind rainscreen cladding.

Timber rain screen cladding had been used with hemp lime at Letchworth without any apparent difficulty. Hills the builder suggested that, as the cladding fixings passed all the way through the hempcrete to the timber frame, the insurers were concerned about a potential risk of moisture or rain soaking back into the building from these cladding ties. The builders said that the proposed system of rainscreen cladding over hempcrete had been previously used by them on a scheme in Hillingdon in 2011 without any problem (Hillingdon 2012).

It is not clear if LABC Warranty had considered the implications of the junctions between hempcrete and synthetic PIR insulation panels and how airtightness at the junctions would be resolved. The issue of warranties is discussed in Chapter 4.

The original architect design drawings for Callowlands indicated the use of Trespa panels for the rain screen. Trespa panels are coloured high compression laminates made from wood fibre and thermosetting resins, but this was replaced with Rockpanel Rockclad, which is a board made of compressed rockwool. The project, while demonstrating the use of a renewable material for the bulk of the walling, also used a significant level of synthetic products.

Table 2.7 Callowlands organisations

Callowlands, Network Housing Group – 16 houses

Network Housing Group, Olympic Office Centre, 8 Fulton Road, Wembley HA9 0NU
www.networkhg.org.uk

Airey Miller Partnership LLP (project managers)
Kelsey House, 77 High Street, Beckenham, Kent BR3 1AN
www.aireymiller.co.uk

Contractors: Hill Partnerships Ltd, The Power House, Gunpowder Mill, Powdermill Lane, Waltham Abbey, Essex EN9 1BN
http://www.hillpartnerships.co.uk

Design Architects: PCKO Architects 45–51 Lowlands Road, Harrow-on-the-Hill HA1 3AW (Replaced by Frank Reynolds Architects working for Hill the Contractors, 14 Clerkenwell Green EC1R 0DP)

Hemp Lime placement, Gunite Group/Limecrete Company, Endeavour House,Compass Point, St Ives, Cambridge PE27 5JL www.gunite.co.uk

Figure 2.18 Callowlands: three-storey block under construction

Figure 2.19 Callowlands: hempcrete when scaffolding starts to come down. Reproduced by permission of Luke Brooker MSc, The Airey Miller Partnership.

Figure 2.20 Callowlands: synthetic foam insulation was used for the porch and window surrounds instead of hempcrete. Reproduced by permission of Luke Brooker MSc, The Airey Miller Partnership.

Figure 2.21 Callowlands: different coloured bands on the hempcrete show variation in drying out. Reproduced by permission of Luke Brooker MSc, The Airey Miller Partnership.

Figure 2.22 Callowlands: LABC warranty sign

Domary Court, York: Hemcrete

Type	6 houses (4 two-storey, 2 shared single-storey bungalows), CSH Level 4
Location	Domary Court, York
Builder/developer	Joseph Rowntree Housing Trust
Material	Tradical hemcrete walls, timber frames
Insulation	Fibreglass
Grants	£160,000

This small development of six houses was one of the earliest to be completed under the RHP. The Joseph Rowntree Housing Trust (JRHT) owns over 2,000 houses in and around York and throughout Yorkshire. One of the charitable foundations, founded by the chocolate business, the JRHT is linked to the Rowntree Foundation and Charitable Trust (Rowntree 2012). It is well placed to develop small schemes as it owns land in the area and has experience of developing small projects. In the case of this project a small corner site had been occupied by a care home, close to a river. The existing buildings were demolished and the site boundaries altered, after some negotiations with the planning authority, due to its proximity to a river and nature conservation area.

The scheme consists of a terrace of four conventional two-storey houses and two shared single-storey bungalows at either end of the site for special needs tenants. The bungalows were built with generous sized rooms and flexibility so that the loft can be converted in the future as a flat for a special needs helper and also rooms could be reconfigured or the shared bungalows split into two dwellings. Designs are modest and simple but fit well into the context with a reasonable amount of external space and off-street parking.

JRHT had previously been interested to trial hemp lime construction, and the grant gave them an opportunity to use these materials. Timber frames with a permanent shuttering on the inside, with Tradical Hemcrete for the walls and a Baumit render externally, the same form of construction as in several of the other case studies.

The scheme was designed to meet Level 4 of the Code for Sustainable homes and includes PV panels and high efficiency gas boilers. High standard Rationel windows were used. The houses were designed by local, BSB Architects and built by a builder from Doncaster that is now part of the much larger Mansell Group.

Surprisingly, instead of using renewable materials for the roof insulation, glass fibre was used in the lofts. JRHT seems to have focused mainly on the use of hempcrete in the walls and so it is possible that the synthetic loft insulation was chosen by the builder. The Homes and Communities Agency, which funds social housing schemes, indicated that applicants were expected to use renewable materials but there did not seem to be any checks on the specifications when schemes were approved. Given the DECC's intentions for a high proportion of insulation materials to be from renewable sources, the JRHT were asked why they had selected fibreglass and they replied that the use of hemp or sheep's wool was an 'aspirational requirement' on the part of HCA/DECC.

Given the potential health benefits of living in houses built of natural materials it seems strangely inconsistent to then use a material about which there are health concerns. Loft insulation carries the highest risk of particulate contamination because occupants can enter the loft through a hatch and disturb the insulation, distributing the fibres throughout the house. Some people are hypersensitive to fibreglass and suffer from severe itching where it is present. The particular make of fibreglass was not clear as there was no label on the packaging seen on site (Figure 2.23). However, there is no evidence that any of the occupants of Domary Court have experienced any problems with ill effects from fibreglass. While fibreglass is considered by some bodies in the USA to be a cancer risk, this remains controversial in Europe.

> It is generally accepted that, in certain situations, fibreglass insulation has the potential to cause physical harm. Small particles that come into contact with skin can lodge in pores and cause itchiness, rashes and irritation. When inhaled, particles can cause coughing, nosebleeds, and other respiratory ailments. Very fine airborne particles are capable of becoming deeply lodged in the lungs and are believed by many to cause cancer and other serious afflictions. The US Occupational Safety and Health Administration (OSHA) considers this threat to be serious enough that it requires fibreglass insulation to carry a cancer warning label.
>
> (InterNACHI 2012)

It is disappointing that JRHT did not adopt a more holistic approach with this scheme as they have been willing to pioneer and experiment with a range of innovative projects. While using hemp and lime at Domary Court this does not indicate a move towards natural materials in other projects. Other recent JRHT schemes have been constructed to a good energy standard as part of their sustainability policy (JRHT 2010). The houses at Temple Avenue had been constructed by December 2010, one for sale and one for rent. These are claimed by JRHT to reduce heating costs by 40%, one using SIP panels with petrochemical based synthetic insulation, the other using lightweight concrete blocks with a thin mortar bed.

The architects, Brown Smith and Baker for the Domary Court scheme, had not specified hempcrete before, and the designers explained that they relied on advice from Lime Technology in terms of construction details and predicted energy performance. None of the other professionals involved, or the building contractor, had used this construction method before but the contractor sent some of their employees for training at Lime Technology.

Despite their lack of experience, the building process went quite smoothly and the only problem evident was that the hemp lime walls were slow to dry out. Some minor staining was evident when the project was visited in March 2011 and the final application of the external render on some outside walls was delayed until they were satisfied that the walls were dry enough. From what could be seen, in the visit, the staining was limited and the drying out seemed to be much less problematic than in some of the other schemes, despite the bad winter weather of 2011. In March 2011, the houses were almost complete and the occupants were about to move in. In November 2011 it was reported by JRHT that the occupants were very happy, with no complaints.

JHRT were told that there was no money for monitoring the project but, as they have a long-standing relationship with Leeds Metropolitan University (LMU), they were able to secure funding for building performance evaluation from the Technology Strategy Board, and LMU reported on the initial findings of this work in York on 29 Nov 2011.

A considerable amount of data will be available from the work by LMU, and their monitoring has been done in two stages. The results will be published by either LMU or the Technology Strategy Board and so it was not possible to access this data and in any case, their work was not complete. However, it is possible to report on the general conclusions presented at the meeting in York.

LMU carried out a range of tests on the houses, airtightness, thermal imaging, heat flux meters, ventilation and MVHR assessment etc. Airtightness results were disappointing, they said. No exemplary airtightness target had been set in the design so LMU had to compare results with normal targets. All the houses were well within building regulations targets but there was evidence of unnecessary air leakage. This was largely due to what LMU referred to as normal problems that would be found on many different housing projects and were not related to the hempcrete walls. Leakage problems were particularly due to service penetrations in the ceiling into the cold roof void and a lack of continuity between the floor slab membrane and the walls. There had been sequencing issues by the builders so that, for instance, the ceilings had been installed after partitions were built. JRHT and the builders are to be congratulated on allowing such a forensic examination of the project, which allows others to learn from this. The standard of construction was of a good quality but it was suggested by the team from LMU that perhaps too much attention had been paid to the hempcrete and not enough to other details.

Plot 6, one of the single-storey bungalows was left empty for a period and this made it possible for LMU to conduct a 'coheating test'. This a relatively new methodology developed at Leeds, where a house is fully and constantly heated for a period of 3–4 weeks, when air temperatures outside are low. This allows the fabric to warm up and the house to be stressed in terms of humidity and response to external thermal shock. Data can be collected over an extended period and be much more reliable than short-term checks, it is claimed.

Coheating is a false situation, as the house is not occupied, although it does have the advantage of eliminating variables of human behaviour. Other co-heating tests are being carried out on other housing projects in the UK but usually for much shorter periods, such as a week. It is not easy to find houses that will be left empty for a month.

At Domary Court the co-heating test will have yielded a wealth of data, which should be available from LMU or JRHT in the future. Relative humidity was monitored but they said that there did not appear to be any significant difference related to the drying out of the hempcrete walls. Also the LMU team claimed that the thermal performance of the walls did not seem to improve as the walls dried out. This could be a reflection of the methods and equipment used, and it is hard to draw any firm conclusions from this one project. LMU claimed that their heat flux sensors indicated that the insulation value of the walls was significantly worse than the claimed design U-value. Apparently Lime Technology had stated a U-value of $0.19\,W/m^2K$ based on tests that they have had carried out previously, but the LMU results indicated a U-value in the region of 0.4. This is a surprising result as it is worse than other in-situ test figures based on independent work carried out by Plymouth University. (Bevan 2008) Possible explanations are that the hempcrete had been over tamped and was thus too dense. Unfortunately, despite visiting the site during construction, LMU had not taken any test cubes, so no checks were made of the density of the walls.

The co-heating test confirmed problems with the ceilings in the cold roof construction. While the fibreglass insulation appeared to be effective where it had been placed correctly, LMU suggested that there were problems at the edge of the loft where there was not sufficient continuity between the loft insulation and the head of the hempcrete walls. It is not known whether Lime Technology's recommended details had been followed but this also calls into question the policy of using a cold roof. Warm roof construction can be much more effective and easier to detail at roof edges.

Table 2.8 Domary Court, York, organisations

Joseph Rowntree Housing Trust: 6 houses

JRHT, The Homestead, 40 Water End, York YO30 6WP

Browne Smith and Baker Architects, 77a Beverley Road, Kingston-upon-Hull HU3 1XR

Mansell Construction, Loversall Court, Tickhill Road, Balby, Doncaster DN4 8QG

Mechanical Engineer: BES Consulting Engineers Ltd, Block 3, St Cuthbert's House, Aycliffe Business Park, Newton Aycliffe DL5 6DN.

DACWood Consulting Engineer, East Ings Farm, Bulmer, York YO60 7ES

Project Manager: Frank Cawkwell, Faithful & Gould, 3200 Century Way, Thorpe Park, Leeds LS15 8ZB.

Figure 2.23 Domary Court: fibreglass insulation used in roof

Figure 2.24 Domary Court: bungalow

Figure 2.25 Domary Court: terrace

Inverness: CLT and fibre insulation

Type	2 two-bedroom semi-detached wide-frontage houses of 78 m2 each
Location	Inverness, Fife
Builder/developer	Morrison Construction, Albyn Housing Association
Material	Cross-laminated timber
Insulation	Natural wood fibre, Crown Frametherm glass wool
Grants	£40,000 (RHP)

Two projects were funded in Scotland through the RHP, one in Inverness, the other in Fife. The project in Inverness was part of the Scottish Housing Expo (Scotland 2011), which consisted of 52 demonstration houses of many different kinds. These houses were built for sale and a few of them were still on the market at the time of writing, ranging in price from £230,000 to £350,000. This case study project, part funded under the RHP, was 'Plot 4.1' and the two houses built here were sold under a scheme called 'LIFT', which is a Scottish equity-sharing scheme to help first-time buyers. Following an FOI request to the Scottish Government, it was confirmed that the Inverness project received £40,000 in grant from the RHP (Scottish Government 2012). Total cost of the two-house project was £257,737.

The Expo was developed by the Highland Housing Alliance in Inverness and the Highland Council. The renewable house plot was developed by Albyn Housing Association, who developed a number of other affordable houses for the Expo.

The project consists of two two-bedroom semi-detached wide-frontage houses of 78 m^2 each. The architect, John Gilbert, worked with Morrison Construction on a design-and-build basis and thus the architects did not have full control of the specification of materials selected. Morrisons (who are part of the Galliford Try Group) decided to use a form of solid timber construction system for the houses based on cross-laminated timber (CLT). The CLT panels came from a Swedish company called Martinsons (Martinsons 2012). Martinsons specialise in a range of engineered timber products including glu-lam beams. CLT is a multi-layered wooden board in which the various layers are laid crosswise. The panels are structurally strong and can be used to construct multi-storey buildings.

Martinsons is based in Northern Sweden, not far from the Arctic Circle, and use slow growth timber from the Västerbotten region. Martinsons have FSC chain of custody certification and from nearby forests that are sustainably managed by local landowners.

From an environmental and visual point of view, the use of solid timber seems very attractive, and in these houses, a solid timber finish is left on the inside, but the architects were concerned about the nature of the glues used. Glues used in composite timber products can be iso-cyanate, phenol, PVA or PUR (polyurethane) but in this case Martinsons were questioned by the architects who said they were told that any formaldehyde in the glue was below a European standard that sets acceptable levels for formaldehyde. However, on a subsequent visit to Martinsons in Sweden they said that they are now using melamine glues. The architects had wanted to use a form of CLT called Brettstapel, which avoids the use of glues, and nails by using pegs (Brettstapel 2011), but CLT had been chosen instead.

Synthetic glues are considered to be relatively stable, once in place, and manufacturers claim a low health risk from emissions as they are bound up within the building structure. Synthetic glues can be more of a risk during manufacture or in case of fire when hydrogen cyanide can be released. Solid wood, however, is particularly safe in terms of fire as wood chars rather then burning.

Solid wood panels provide thermal mass but very little insulation, not sufficient to meet building regulations or reasonable energy efficiency targets, so 200 mm of natural wood fibre insulation was used externally, fixed to the solid wood panels (Figure 2.28) giving a claimed U-value of $0.13\,W/m^2K$. Despite several enquiries, the builder did not provide details of the fibre insulation that had been used. As this had been outside the control of the architects, they were not able to confirm the product. The consensus seemed to be that it was a wood fibre insulation but it appeared to be a hemp insulation product.

The roof cassettes were fitted with Crown Frametherm glass wool, 400 mm thick, a Knauf product and certainly not a renewable material. As with Callowlands and Domary Court, the DECC requirement for the majority of insulation to be renewable was not followed. The Scottish Government explanation of this is discussed in Chapter 3. External cladding consisted of corrugated aluminium sheet and an STO rendered cladding board.

Predicted annual energy performance/running cost for heating based on the SAP rating (heat only energy usage) 54 kWh/m² resulting in a predicted annual running cost for heating of £73 per dwelling.

Formaldehyde is red listed by some organisation in the USA as not safe at any level.

In 1992, formaldehyde was formally listed by the Air Resources Board as a Toxic Air Contaminant in California with no safe level of exposure. Health risks from total daily average formaldehyde exposures in California from all sources are estimated to range from 86 to 231 excess cancer cases per million for adults, and from 23 to 63 excess cancer cases per million for children.

ARB (2007)

Various standards are set around the world (Ecotimber 2012):
World Health Organization: below 0.10 ppm
European E1 Standard: below 0.10 ppm
OSHA Hazard Communication Standard: hazard warning labels on any product that may emit 0.10 ppm or greater
GreenGuard® Environmental Institute Certification: below 0.05 ppm
State of California: below 0.05 ppm

Table 2.9 Inverness Expo organisations

Albyn Housing Society Inverness: 2 houses
House is at IV2 6GA

Albyn Housing Society, 68 MacLennan Crescent, Inverness, IV3 8DN

Highland Housing Alliance, Scotland's Housing Expo c/o Planning & Development The Highland Council, Glenurquhart Road Inverness IV3 5NX

Contractor: Morrison Construction, 37 Harbour Road, Inverness IV1 1UA

John Gilbert Architects, 201 The White Studios, Templeton Business Centre, Glasgow G40 1DA

QS: WSD Scotland Ltd, Fairways Business centre, Castle Heather, Inverness IV2 6AA

Structural Engineer: Fairhurst and Partners, Ashley Guy, Etive House, Beechwood Park, Inverness IV2 3BW

Figure 2.26 Inverness Expo: house south side. Reproduced by permission of John Gilbert, John Gilbert Architects.

Figure 2.27 Inverness Expo: house north side. Reproduced by permission of John Gilbert, John Gilbert Architects.

Figure 2.28 Inverness Expo: insulation and CLT detail. Reproduced by permission of John Gilbert, John Gilbert Architects.

Figure 2.29 Inverness Expo: interior (Gilbert). Reproduced by permission of John Gilbert, John Gilbert Architects.

Long Meadow, Denmark Lane, Diss: Hemcrete and Breathe hemp flax insulation

Type	114 houses (1st phase 29 houses), CSH Level 4
Location	Long Meadow, Denmark Lane, in Diss, Norfolk
Builder/developer	CZero, Flagship Housing Association
Material	Hemcrete cast walls, timber frames
Insulation	Hemp insulation quilt (Breathe)
Grants	£3,000,000

The development at Long Meadow, Denmark Lane, in Diss, Norfolk, was to be the largest of all the schemes in the DECC RHP, with 114 houses, receiving nearly half of the funding for the programme. The Birmingham-based developers, CZero, had been responsible for a one-off demonstration house at the BRE Innovation Park (Renewable House 2011). In the event, due to a range of problems, only 29 houses were actually built in Phase 1, though more may be built in the future in further phases. Fifteen of the units, including a block of flats, were built for Flagship Housing, a local registered social landlord based in Norwich. The rest were to be sold as affordable houses, though 12 of the 114 were earmarked to be sold at open market prices. This was a large greenfield site at the western edge of a small rural town, which was described as the largest 'rural exception' site in the UK. A rural exception site is where housing is permitted on greenfield land at the end of a settlement but outside the normal planning boundary.

When visited in August 2011, most of the affordable houses were occupied or about to be occupied. The residents seemed enthusiastic about the scheme despite reporting a number of small building defects. The housing association units were not occupied until the autumn of 2011.

The houses were constructed of standard hempcrete cast walls, using permanent shuttering on a timber frame to Level 4 of the Code for Sustainable Homes. Hemp insulation quilt insulation (Breathe) was installed in the (cold roof) lofts.

According to Flagship Housing Association, £1,650,000 was spent on the 15 housing association units, with the whole development so far, costing £2,547,835, according to CZero, in a presentation made at a meeting in the Homes and Communities Agency offices in Milton Keynes. Robert Pearson of CZero said that build costs were in the region of £1,116 per m^2. These issues are discussed in more detail in Chapter 3.

The affordable houses were offered for sale at £109,000 for the three-bedroom houses and £95,000 for the two-bedrooms. This is said to be a 30% discount on normal market prices (normally 20% discounts are offered) (Norfolk RCC 2011). The developers faced high costs with their Section 106 agreement for the development and had difficulties with mortgage lenders unwilling to finance the affordable homes; they said that this seriously hampered the development. While the Ecology Building Society and Co-operative Bank were supportive, mainstream lenders were not. Because of these difficulties, development of the rest of the houses has been delayed. While the mainstream lenders may have raised some queries about the construction and materials used for the houses, the problems were more to do with the market and financial arrangements associated with the discounted sale system.

The design insulation U-value for the hempcrete walls was 0.18 W/m²K, with 0.10 claimed for the hemp insulation in the lofts. Air source heat pumps were provided with MVHR ventilation. An airtightness of 2.0–2.5 /(h.m2) @ 50 Pa was required under the contract but it is not clear whether this was achieved. The building contractors were Barnes Construction of Ipswich, and the Limecrete Company cast the hemp lime.

As with some of the other hempcrete schemes, much of the work was done in the worst of the cold winter weather in 2010/11 and this appears to have led to serious problems with the walls drying out. Considerable expense was involved in using heaters and dehumidifiers to try to dry out the walls; the internal Baumit plasters preferred by Lime Technology, who supply the hemp and lime materials, were changed to a Thistle plaster. While there was a little evidence of damp staining on the walls externally, CZero reported problems with paint peeling off some of the internal walls. This has led the developer to have some doubts about the use of on site-cast hemp lime and they were considering alternative methods and materials for the rest of the development. There was no evidence of any moisture problems with the Breathe insulation in the roofs, and the houses are to be monitored under a programme arranged by the National Non-food Crops Centre.

Table 2.10 Diss organisations

Diss Flagship Housing and CZero Norfolk: 104 houses proposed
http://www.longmeadowdiss.co.uk/

Linford C-Zero Limited, The Penthouse, Grosvenor House, 14 Bennetts Hill, Birmingham B2 5RS www.czero.com

Flagship Housing Association, Keswick Hall, Keswick, Norwich NR4 6TJ flagship-housing.co.uk

Barnes Construction, 6 Bermuda Way, Ransomes Europark, Ipswich IP3 9RU

Architect: Khoury Architects, 50–54 St Paul's Square, Birmingham B3 1QS

QS: EC Harris, ECHQ, 34 York Way, London N1 9AB

Figure 2.30 Diss: completed houses

Figure 2.31 Diss: typical rear elevation

Figure 2.32 Diss: brick arches painted onto the render with some signs of deterioration

Figure 2.33 Diss: three-story housing association apartments

Figure 2.34 Diss: long view showing the future development area

LILAC, Leeds: Modcell strawbale

Type	Co-housing scheme, 20 units 1, 2, 3 and 4-bedroom houses, 200 m² common space
Location	Victoria Park area, West Leeds, Yorkshire
Builder/developer	Low Impact Living Affordable Community
Material	Modcell construction system
Insulation	Strawbale
Grants	£420,00 (RHP)

This project is perhaps the most unusual of all the case studies but also the last one to get on site and was unfinished at the time of writing. Work is now proceeding (Figure 2.36 shows members of the group on site).

The project is to build a co-housing scheme for a community of people, and the group who intend to live in the project initiated the proposal. Co-housing was developed in Denmark in the 1980s and the idea has spread around the world. A group of people build individual houses but share a number of common facilities. There are numerous co-housing schemes in the UK and the idea is gaining popularity for 'senior' housing (Co-housing 2012).

LILAC stands for Low Impact Living Affordable Community (LILAC 2012). It is a member-led, not-for-profit cooperative society. Apart from building individual houses, the scheme will include a common house with a range of shared facilities such as a kitchen and dining area, laundry, multipurpose room, guest room and workshop.

A further aim of the scheme was to create affordable houses for people who might not be able to afford to buy a house in the normal way. To achieve this they have adopted an affordability model in the form of a mutual home ownership society (MHOS), which is an equity based leaseholder scheme.

> An MHOS will ensure that the cost of the homes remains permanently affordable and doesn't follow the extremes of the housing market.
>
> (LILAC 2012)

The cost of the project is divided into equity shares owned by members and financed by the payments that members make each month, which is equivalent to 35% of their net household income. After some deductions, members can take their equity with them on leaving. A financial assessment and payment of a deposit is needed to join the society. Paul Chatterton, a lecturer at Leeds University, and one of the founders of the group, is planning to publish a book giving an account of the project, both as a social experiment, and to record its construction.

The site is in the Victoria Park area of Bramley, west Leeds, Yorkshire, on an old school site. The design of the scheme mixes private dwellings and shared facilities based around a car-free zone, communal gardens, green spaces, areas for growing food and ample cycle storage. Limited on-site parking was provided. As it was a brownfield site, it needed quite a lot of work before building could start and there were lengthy delays getting the local authority to sell the site and to obtain planning permission.

White Design Associates were appointed as the architect and landscape architect because the group decided to adopt the Modcell strawbale construction system for the buildings. The LILAC group wanted to use renewable materials and to ensure that the scheme had as low a carbon footprint as possible. The project managers are CoHo Ltd in York. The registered social landlord (RSL) that was responsible for accessing the RHP grant from DECC, Synergy, was a sort of consortium of RSLs in the Leeds area (not to be confused with Synergy Housing in Dorset). Their role appears to have been minimal.

The development of 20 units is a mix of one- and two-bedroom flats, three- and four-bedroom houses. Most will have private gardens, and the upper flats will have balconies. The homes will be self-contained with kitchens, bathrooms and living space:

6×1-bedrooms
6×2-bedrooms
6×3-bedrooms
2×4-bedrooms
plus a 200 m² commonhouse

The Modcell construction method is quite different from the other forms of construction used in the renewable house programme, as it is the only one using straw. The Modcell system uses prefabricated panels made from a timber frame with straw compressed inside the panels. These are usually made in 'flying factories' in a local farm that has straw available, as near as possible to the site. The straw is scratch-coat rendered with a lime-based render and then the panels are craned into position. The LILAC scheme follows a fairly standard Modcell design with flat roofs. While there are an increasing number of Modcell houses, schools and office buildings, this will be the first social housing scheme (Modcell 2012).

While the straw is a different material from other schemes in the programme, Modcell panels have also been made with hempcrete. However, at the time of writing, work had only just started on site. Ground remediation works, carried out by the local authority – the previous owners – had been completed. As LILAC was keen to keep costs down, due the affordable nature of the project, Modcell was an interesting choice, but due to the early stage of the project it was not possible to obtain any cost information. Clearly the £420,00 grant from the RHP was an important contribution to ensure the affordability of the Modcell technology.

Table 2.11 LILAC Leeds organisations

LILAC Co-operative LEEDS

LILAC. 62 Greenwood Mount, Leeds LS6 4LG http://www.lilac.coop/

White Design, The Proving House, 21 Sevier Street, Bristol, BS2 9LB http://white-design.com/

Modcell, The Proving House, 21 Sevier Street, Bristol BS2 9LB

Project managers: CoHo Ltd, 2 Holly Tree House, Northminster Business Park, Harwood Road, York YO26 6QU

Figure 2.35 Modcell strawbale 'flying factory' as will be used on the LILAC project. Reproduced by permission of ModCell.

Figure 2.36 LILAC: future residents and builders gather as work begins in April 2012. Reproduced by permission of Lilac MHOS Ltd.

Tomorrow's Garden City, Letchworth: wood fibre and Hemcrete

Type	60 houses, mixed 1, 2 and 3-bedroom houses
Location	Tomorrow's Garden City, Letchworth
Builder/developer	North Hertfordshire Homes
Material	Hempcrete, wood fibre (Pavatex)
Insulation	Pavaflex insulation
Grants	£920,000

This project began life as a result of an architectural competition to design a new approach to garden city living and to celebrate the centenary of the 'Cheap Cottages Exhibition'. The aim was to reflect the progressive origins of the Letchworth experiment but also to respond to ecological issues of today (Letchworth 2012). Letchworth was founded by Ebenezer Howard, and addressed many of the issues that have become topical today (Howard 1902). The architectural competition was run in 2007 and was won by architects Stride Treglown with another prize going to Higgs Young Architects.

As the site already had planning permission for housing, and the main architects for the project were Cole Thompson Anders (CTA) who obtained the initial planning permission, they have gone on to design most of the houses. They were asked to incorporate the Stride Treglown and Higgs Young designs into the scheme allocating them three and two plots respectively. CTA became the executive architects and managed the construction of the houses designed by the other two architects.

The Tomorrow's Garden City site is off Talbot Way in Letchworth Garden City, Hertfordshire, 50 miles north of London. The project was developed by North Hertfordshire Homes (NHH) in conjunction with Rowan Homes, which is the private development wing of NHH. They lease the site from the Letchworth Heritage Foundation.

Overall there are 60 homes, which comprise:

market sale properties : 5 × 2 - bedroom flats, 9 × 3 - bedroom houses
HomeBuy (shared ownership) : 26 × 2 - bedroom flats, 6 × 1 - bedroom flats
Social rent : 4 × 3 - bedroom flats, 5 × 2 - bedroom flats, 5 × 1 - bedroom flats

The scheme was due for completion in January 2012, with houses to be handed over in February 2012. There were a number of delays in completing the project even though it seemed well under way during a visit to the site in July 2011, but the first residents moved in, in February 2012 (NHH 2012).

The Letchworth scheme is of particular interest as two different technologies were used to construct the houses and flats but with identical designs. This opened the possibility of comparing the performance of similar dwellings to see whether there is any significant difference between the two technologies. This would have been an ideal project for monitoring funded by the government but instead Diss and Swindon were chosen, as discussed in Chapter 3.

The buildings consist of timber frame structures of two, three and four storeys. Many of the units were built using hempcrete from Lime Technology and the rest were built using Pavatex wood fibre materials from Natural Building Technologies. The build-up of the Pavatex buildings consists of a wood fibre system called 'Diffutherm' which is rendered externally using a similar Baumit render to that used on hempcrete walls. Pavatherm Plus rigid wood fibreboards externally are clad with timber cladding. The scheme uses both vertical and horizontal timber cladding (Pavatex 2011). Pavaflex wood fibre insulation batts were used in the build-up. The rendered finish and timber cladding appearance is similar for both the hempcrete houses and the wood fibre buildings. Warm roof designs were used with 340 mm of Pavaflex insulation between the rafters. Sedum roofs were used to the second floor roofs and a (cheaper) single ply membrane to the third floor roofs. They used 3,200 m² of Pavatherm Plus and Diffutherm and 500 m³ of Pavaflex. A total value of £300,000 of Pavatex products were used.

Constructing the houses with hempcrete went very well and was relatively problem free. However, the details had to be changed to suit the design and this meant that local authority building control (LABC) accredited details were not accepted and new approvals had to be sought from the LABC (LABC 2012).

By comparison, the contractors took a little time to master the Diffutherm and Pavatherm construction in order to achieve the weather and airtightness required, due to the number of ancillary products that had to be used. These include Compriband tape and Wemico base rails for the render (Wemico 2012):

> TP600 Compriband 600 is a soft and flexible open cell polyurethane foam tape impregnated with an acrylic based UV stabilised resin. The resin is water repellent and contains a fire retardant.
>
> (Tremco 2012)

Other components were also required, to provide fixing points and to meet the rigorous standards of the Pavatex system. It is likely that the contractors were unfamiliar with this method of building but they were able to complete the work successfully. A minor fire was reported during construction which resulted in some smouldering of the wood fibre but no major damage was caused.

While there are three different design concepts (including the two small competition-winning designs) used at Letchworth, the renewable materials seem to have been incorporated into the different designs without too much difficulty though detailing issues caused some small delays.

Table 2.12 Letchworth Organisations

Tomorrows Garden City Letchworth: 60 Houses

North Hertfordshire Homes Letchworth http://www.nhh.org.uk/

SDC Contractors Bedford http://www.sdc.co.uk/

Airey Miller Partnership LLP (project managers)
Kelsey House, 77 High Street, Beckenham, Kent BR3 1AN
www.aireymiller.co.uk

Architect: Cole Thompson Anders, 52B, St James's Avenue, Hampton Hill, Middlesex TW12 1HN

Stride Treglown Architects, Promenade House, The Promenade, Clifton, Bristol BS8 3NE
Higgs Young Architects, 54 Boston Place, London NW1 6ER

Figure 2.37 Letchworth: work in Progress on site

Figure 2.38 Letchworth: detail of wood fibre construction

Figure 2.39 Letchworth: Pavatex Wood fibre construction of three-storey units

Figure 2.40 Letchworth: the Limecrete Company mixing hempcrete on site. Reproduced by permission of The Limecrete Company Ltd.

Figure 2.41 Letchworth: manual placing of hempcrete on site

Figure 2.42 Letchworth: detail of roof construction with hempcrete. Reproduced by permission of Anthony Nuttall, Architects.

Figure 2.43 Letchworth: hempcrete construction in progress. Reproduced by permission of Anthony Nuttall, Architects.

Figure 2.44 Letchworth: hempcrete being cast with reusable plastic shuttering. Reproduced by permission of The Limecrete Company Ltd.

Figure 2.45 Letchworth: competition-winning house designed by Stride Treglown under construction. Reproduced by permission of Rob Delius, Stride Treglown Ltd.

Figure 2.46 Letchworth: after completion.

Reed Street, South Shields: wood fibre and stone wool

Type	21 houses (9 three-bedroom, 12 two-bedroom apartments), CSH Level 6
Location	Reed Street, South Shields
Builder/developer	Four Housing Group
Material	Pavaflex, Pavatherm Plus/Diffutherm wood fibre
Insulation	Stone wool
Grants	£320,000

This is a development by Four Housing Group in partnership with South Tyneside Council to create 21 homes. In press reports, the scheme has been referred to as the 'Reed Street Carbon Negative Community Village' and the intention was to exceed Level 6 of the Code for Sustainable Homes, going beyond the requirements of the RHP Code 4 target. The scheme design was said to have achieved a score of 93% at Code Level 6 (Code Level 6 requires a minimum of 90%).

The development consists of nine three-bedroom houses and twelve two-bedroom apartments, According to the builders, Galliford Try:

Under the current definition of zero carbon, the Reed Street development will exceed compliance standards by around 25 per cent. However, once the recently amended 2016 definition comes into force, which removes the inclusion of unregulated carbon, compliance is expected to be exceeded by around 75 per cent. This means the homes will, over their lifetime, not only offset their own carbon emissions, but also contribute to off-setting the emissions of existing homes and will require little to no utility bills for its residents. It will not only allow Four Housing Group to significantly reduce its carbon footprint but also that of its existing housing stock, since every five of these houses built will offset enough carbon to make a standard 2010 Part L House Zero Carbon.

(The Construction Index 2011)

Due to constantly changing government subsidies and definitions, it is unlikely that these claims will mean very much, due to the reliance on renewable energy. Interestingly in their publicity material about the project Galliford Try do not mention the main construction materials for the scheme, wood fibre, stating instead:

The Reed Street homes will be constructed using renewable materials, to have a minimal environmental impact in both the construction and supply chain processes, such as cedar shingles and recycled paper insulation.

(Construction Index 2011)

The principal construction method of the scheme is timber frame with Pavatex wood fibre products and not recycled paper. Further environmental features planned included rainwater harvesting, interactive smart metering to record and monitor energy and water usage, and a mechanical heat recovery system in each home. A small community heating plant-room with a biomass boiler is intended to provide all the heating and hot water needs for all of the homes.

It is claimed that the 85 kW 'peak' photovoltaic arrays of solar panels will be capable of generating enough clean electricity for all of the homes and produce a surplus, which will be exported back to the National Grid, generating a hoped-for income of £1100 per year. The viability of the renewable energy may have been affected by government changes to policy on feed-in tariffs and grants for solar energy. Additional funding on top of the renewable house grant was available to support the extensive renewable energy investment (UKTI 2012).

Work on the Reed Street project began in autumn 2011 with completion planned for early summer 2012 but it has been delayed to September 2012 (Four 2012). The timber frame construction used 220 mm Pavaflex between external wall studs, 80 mm Pavatherm Plus or Diffutherm wood fibre boards over the studs with a wall finish of either white Baumit lime render or larch timber cladding; 250 mm Pavaflex in between timber Eco-joist floor cassettes; 2000 m² Pavatherm Plus or Diffutherm with 700 m³ of Pavaflex (value of NBT products around £200,000).

Also, 500 mm of a stone wool product was used in the roofs (cold roof). Here again is a project that did not use renewable insulation products throughout, despite receiving £320,000 to use renewable insulation materials. Though cedar shingles have been used on the roofs (Figure 2.50). The source of the cedar is unknown.

Table 2.13 Reed Street organisations

Reed Street, South Shields: 12 apartments and 9 houses
Four Housing Group, Three Rivers House, Abbeywoods Business Park, Pity Me, County Durham DH1 5TG http://www.4hg.co.uk/
Fitz Architects, The Place, Athenaeum Street, Sunderland, SR1 1QX
QS: Employers Agent – RNJ Consultants, Newcastle
Galliford Try Partnerships, Try Building, North Innovation House, Daten Park, Birchwood, Warrington WA3 6UT
Consultants: NaREC, CK21, Ian Larnach Associates
Eco Timber frame Systems Ltd, North East Foundry, Templetown, South Shields, Tyne and Wear NE33 5SE

Figure 2.47 Reed Street: general view

Figure 2.48 Reed Street: view

Figure 2.49 Reed Street: detail of Pavatex and brick plinth. Reproduced by permission of Clinton Mysleyko, Fitz Architects.

Figure 2.50 Reed Street: cedar shingle roof. Reproduced by permission of Clinton Mysleyko, Fitz Architects.

The Triangle, Swindon: Hemcrete and hemp insulation

Type	42 housing units
Location	Triangle, Swindon
Builder/ developer	Kevin McCloud (HAB OAKUS), GreenSquare and Westlea HA
Material	Timber frame, cast Tradical Hemcrete walls
Insulation	Black Mountain hemp insulation
Grants	£840,000 (RHP)

This project consists of 42 housing units on a triangular backland site in a suburban area of Swindon that was partly funded by the DECC RHP. It was carried out by a partnership between a private development organisation set up by Kevin McCloud (HAB OAKUS) and a Swindon-based housing association group (GreenSquare and Westlea HA). McCloud, who presents a UK television programme called *Grand Designs*, said that he wanted to demonstrate that it was possible to build higher standard affordable sustainable housing with good quality modern design. There is little doubt that he has largely succeeded in this aim, as this is one of the better-designed projects in this series of case studies. The project has been well documented in two television programmes that were shown on UK Channel 4 in the UK just before Christmas 2011. (Channel 4 2012) The programme focused mainly on McCloud's aims, mistakes and frustrations as a housing developer, the design of the scheme and the hopes and experiences of the occupants, but did include a little about the use of renewable materials and hemp.

The Triangle is located off Northern Road, Swindon, a former caravan storage area and plant nursery in Swindon, and comprises:

16 × 2-bedroom houses

13 × 3-bedroom houses

7 × 4-bedroom houses

4 × 1-bedroom apartments

2 × 2-bedroom apartments.

It was intended to sell some of the houses to create a mixed tenure scheme, but with the recession creating problems with the UK housing market, all the houses were rented to people on the housing list or who moved from other houses in Swindon. The development cost £4.2 million in total, with an RHP grant of £840,000.

The project was given planning permission by Swindon Borough Council in October 2009, and work commenced at the beginning of May

2010 and was due for completion in May 2011. When visited at the end of March 2011 it was far from complete. The scheme began to be occupied in July 2011.

The scheme was intended to demonstrate a significant number of sustainable policies including reducing space used for cars (one car per house), emphasis on cycling and shared space for growing food by the residents. It was hoped that a community would be created through a careful selection process and a series of meetings before people moved into the development. Potential occupants were interviewed and had to show an interest in the environmental aims of the project.

Designed by architects Glenn Howells and landscape architects, Studio Engleback, the scheme has already won a Housing Design Award and is likely to win more. Willmott Dixon, the contractor, is a large mainstream company that has promoted itself as a leader in sustainability. The contractor, when interviewed, said the project was a major challenge coping with a tight timetable, innovative construction methods, difficult site and low budget.

The construction consisted of timber frame with permanent shuttering and cast Tradical Hemcrete walls using Lime Technology's standard details. Hemcrete was used throughout the scheme for the walls, with a Baumit rendered finish with self-coloured pastel colours, which were meant to fit in with the local rendered vernacular.

The lofts were insulated with Black Mountain hemp insulation (supplied by Warren Insulation of Colchester) and thus the scheme was consistent in terms of using renewable materials as much as possible, unlike quite a few of the other projects.

The houses have a 'thermal chimney', part of a passive ventilation system, devised by the architects to be a strong architectural feature (Figure 2.52). When the houses get hot in the summer, rising warm air is to be expelled through the roof cowl. In addition to large windows, the design included a secure louvered system to allow in fresh air without opening windows. However, a mechanical heat recovery and ventilation system was also included. Heating is by an air-source heat pump with under floor heating on the ground floor and radiators upstairs. Tenants spoken to in a second visit complained that electricity bills were unacceptably high. While they were happy with the well-insulated hempcrete walls and said the houses were nice and warm, they felt the MVHR and underfloor heating were too expensive, and electricity should not have been used for these. They also said that using cork tiles on the floor was insulating the floors and reducing the impact of the underfloor heating. They had been told that there would be PV panels on the roofs that would offset the electricity costs but no solar panels had been fitted.

An innovative estate intranet system called 'Hab Shimmy' consists of a wall-mounted screen on the ground floor; it is intended to provide residents with information about energy and water use, and also lets them know when the next bus to Swindon is due! (Hab 2012). There was meant to be a car share scheme but it's not clear whether this is yet functioning

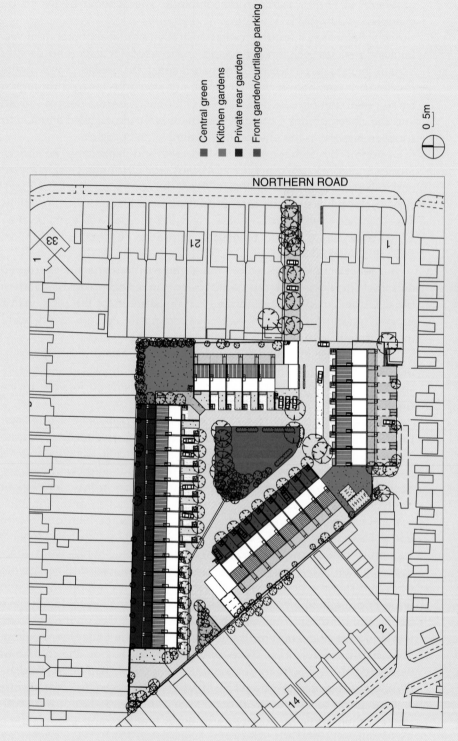

Figure 2.51 Layout of the Triangle in Swindon (based on drawing from Glenn Howells Architects)

Central green
Kitchen gardens
Private rear garden
Front garden/curtilage parking

NORTHERN ROAD

0 5m

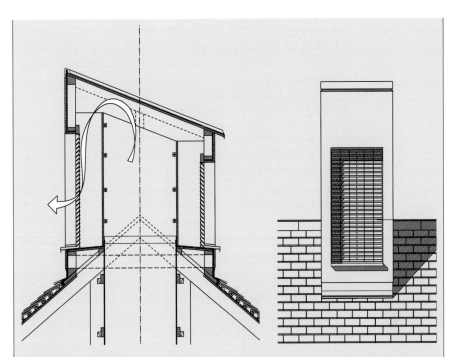

Figure 2.52 Design of the thermal chimney (based on drawings from Glenn Howells Architects)

effectively. Two car club cars could be seen parked on the access road to the scheme during a second visit.

> There are some minor caveats. On talking with residents, it is clear that some find it hard to operate the green systems effectively. And the intranet really is not up and running yet. The one car per household regime is also still a work in progress; only time will tell whether the community can keep the area around the triangle free from fly parking. And the gabions are rather strident as car concealers; the black top seems about to strangle the precious green.
>
> (Kelly 2011)

The architectural quality of the scheme is a result of good design, larger high standard windows and doors and the use of galvanised steel gutters and downpipes (instead of plastic). The scheme avoids the cheapness of some of the other case studies.

Problems with casting the hempcrete were reported, as the work was carried out during the winter, and there were serious problems with drying out during very severe cold weather early in 2011. Plastering and rendering were delayed by this and also by the walls failing to dry out. Some external staining on the walls was evident in March 2011. No problems were reported with the roof insulation. In this project there has been a stronger and more holistic commitment to sustainability, with renewable insulation materials used throughout and care taken to design low energy solutions for heating and ventilation. These measures were adopted as part of the design concept rather than simply as ticking the boxes to achieve a Code assessment though their success is still to be evaluated.

Table 2.14 Swindon Triangle organisations

GreenSquare – Hab Oakus: 42 housing units Northern Road Swindon

Hab: Kevin McCloud, Mulberry House Marketing, Mulberry House, Hunston Road, Chichester, West Sussex PO20 1NP

GreenSquare group incorporating Oakus and Westlea Housing, Barbury House, Stonehill Green, Westlea, Swindon SN5 7HB

Wilmott Dixon Housing Ltd, Hitchin Road Shefford Bedforshire SG17 5JS

Glenn Howells Architects http://www.glennhowells.co.uk/content/home/

Employer's agent: DBK Group

Engineers: Curtins Consulting

M&E Engineers: MaxFordham

Landscape architects: Studio Engleback

Figure 2.53 Swindon: south-facing Terrace

Figure 2.54 Swindon: window shutter detail closed

Figure 2.55 Swindon: window detail showing open louvres

Figure 2.56 Swindon: bike shed. Reproduced by permission of Glenn Howells Architects.

Figure 2.57 Swindon: view of completed houses showing attention to landscape and detail. Reproduced by permission of Glenn Howells Architects.

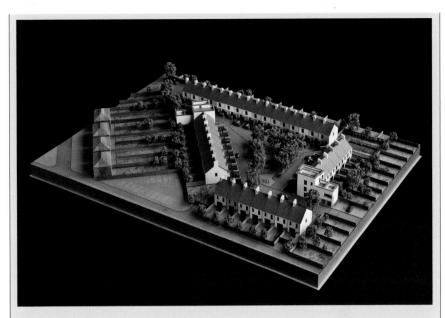

Figure 2.58 Swindon: model of development. Reproduced by permission of Glenn Howells Architects.

Pittenweem: no renewable insulation materials

Type	1 five-person two-storey family house, passivhaus certification
Location	Pittenweem
Builder/developer	Kingdom Housing Association
Material	Timber frame, Supawall system
Insulation	Polyurethane foam insulation
Grants	£35,420

This has been the most difficult case study to record as, apart from timber frame construction, timber windows and a tiny amount of timber cladding, this project did not use renewable materials and certainly no attempt was made to use a substantial amount of renewable insulation materials as was required by the RHP. Thus it appears that it did not comply with the letter of the RHP.

On the other hand it is an interesting project and claims to have achieved an energy efficiency standard better than many of the other projects in the programme as it aimed at the 'passiv haus' standard rather than Code 4. It is a useful project to discuss in terms of comparison with the other case studies as it goes in the completely opposite direction to the intention of the RHP, trialling instead 'modern methods of construction' and passiv haus approaches that were dependent on synthetic petrochemical based materials and products.

Developed by Kingdom Housing Association in Scotland, the project was labelled 'The Kingdom House – A House for the Future'. The dwelling is a five-person two-storey family home on the northern side of Pittenweem, a picturesque East Fife village, at 6 Station Court in a small mixed tenure development. It has a gross floor area of 104 m².

In order to achieve passiv haus certification it has used a timber frame system called the Supawall system made by a company called Scotframe (Scotframe 2012).

Scotframe have offices and factories in Inverurie and Cumbernauld, making the Supawall system under licence. Supawall appears to be based in Preston in Lancashire at a company called Maple Timber Frame.

Extremely low wall and roof U-values of 0.09 W/m²K are claimed for this closed timber frame panel system, comprising 140 mm timber studs sheathed both sides with oriented strand board (OSB) and factory filled with polyurethane foam insulation. In their brochure, Kingdom HA say that the timber frame kit was erected, wind and water tight within one working day. It was possible to see the erection process in a film on YouTube (Scotframe 2012).

A thickness of 140 mm of PUR insulation will not achieve the required low U-values that were the target of this project, so a further 160 mm of external insulation was glued and mechanically fixed to the panels called 'JUB Jubizol S external wall insulation system'. This insulated render system contains a substance called Nanosil which, it is claimed, keeps the facade clean by preventing the build-up of algae and mildew on the surface and is also claimed to be resistant to the effects of ultraviolet light. The insulating material is expanded polystyrene (EPS), though Jub also have a system with mineral fibre.

The nanotechnology self-cleaning surface is a thin silicone and siloxane based waterproof render system and is very different from the lime based render systems used on the other RHP projects. It is claimed to have a high resistance to the effects of modern atmospheric factors. There is no mention of vapour permeability on the Jub literature but they do say that it is breathable in the same way that silicate paints are breathable (Innovate UK 2012). Nanosil can be found in other products because of its antimicrobial properties, and it is marketed as a water repellant additive. It was difficult to get much detail as to its origins but India and USA seem to be the main manufacturing sources. Patents appear to be held with the US military and aerospace industries.

The house has an attractive modern design and the water repellent self-cleaning properties of the insulated render system had not deteriorated when photographed in January 2012 (Figure 2.59 and 2.60). The site is near the sea, so it will be a good test.

Other elements of Kingdom House are Nordan NTech Passive windows, triple glazed, argon filled with an installed U-value of $0.8\,W/m^2K$ with no trickle ventilation. A small projecting bay at first floor level has some timber cladding. The design of the house provides southern orientation for all the habitable rooms. The air permeability was designed to be below 0.6 ach^{-1} @ 50 Pa. A substantial range of renewable energy and mechanical equipment was also installed along with a full MVHR system.

The Kingdom House brochure refers to the 'Renewable Construction Programme' in addition to its Housing Association Grant and 'Cares' Funding (Community and Renewable Energy Scheme) which subsidised the renewable energy equipment.

Details of the full cost of construction were not made available by the Housing Association but the Kingdom House received a grant of £35,420 for renewable materials. The Scottish Government, in response to an FOI request, stated that this was 'only 15% of the cost of the house' which would suggest that the Kingdom house cost £236,130. (Scottish Government 2012). This is over £2,300 per m², which is double the construction costs of some of the other houses in these case studies.

In their brochure, Kingdom Housing Association justify the use of the passiv haus approach as a way of protecting tenants against fuel poverty (Kingdom 2010), but does not discuss whether it is realistic to tackle fuel poverty using solutions with costs that are double those of standard construction. It could be suggested that such a high level of investment is required at an early experimental stage, but passivhaus projects have been built in Germany for 20 years.

It is interesting to note that in Pittenweem, to achieve low energy targets, it was necessary to use an overall thickness of 300 mm of synthetic insulation material, so the walls are much the same thickness as the hempcrete and wood fibre solutions.

When asked why synthetic insulations had been used, rather than the renewable materials required by the grant, the housing association and architects seemed initially confuse. Perhaps the aims and conditions of the DECC scheme had got lost in transmission through the Scottish Government channels. They thought that the polyol material in the polyurethane had come from rapeseed oil, which was a renewable crop based material. It is possible to make polyol for PUR from rapeseed oil but a manufacturer of polyols, interviewed some years ago, as part of another research project, said that the consistency of quality could not be assured with rapeseed oil and so it is not used in normal practice. Brian Woodley of Supawall also confirmed on the telephone that the polyol used in Supawall was synthetic.

When the Scottish Government was asked to explain the process by which approval was given for a grant for renewable materials to be spent on petrochemical insulation, the following somewhat obscure answer was provided.

> The house contains a wide range of sustainability features some of which would not have been eligible for DECC funding, but in these cases we were content for these to be funded from the Scottish Government's housing investment programme. The Scottish Government is satisfied that Kingdom Housing Association spent the DECC funding contribution to the total cost, on appropriate elements of the overall house construction.

The Scottish Government reply did not state what these 'appropriate elements' were. In reply to a further question they then stated that 'the house contains a wide range of renewable materials and sustainability features'. But again they did not clarify what these consist of.

The house had apparently received passiv haus certification from the Scottish Passive House centre (SPHC 2012). Details of the Pittenweem project were available on the SPHC website in 2011 and the certification was discussed with them on the telephone. According to the Scottish Federation of Housing Associations:

> Last year when it was opened, the Scottish Passive House Centre recognised the development as the first affordable rented house in Britain to reach Passivhaus status.
>
> (SFHA 2012)

However, by January 2012 there was no sign of the Kingdom House on the SPHC website.

Table 2.15 Predicted energy data provided by Kingdom Housing Association based on using renewable energy

Space heat demand: 14kWh/m² per annum

Primary Energy Demand 85kW

Air Change ≤ 0.6h-1

Efficient Mechanical Ventilation and Heat Recovery (≥ 75%)

14 kWh/m per annum

Estimated Fuel Costs £91 per annum

Carbon Dioxide Emissions −0.1 tonnes pa

Summary of claimed U-values

Roof (pitched) 0.13 w/m²K

Roof (flat) 0.07 w/m²K

Wall 0.09 w/m²K

Ground Floor 0.12 w/m²K

Windows (installed) 0.8 w/m²K

Door 1.0 w/m²K

Table 2.16 Pittenweem organisations

Pittenweem Kingdom Housing Association: one house

Kingdom Housing Association Ltd, Saltire Centre, Pentland Court, Glenrothes, Fife KY6 2DA www.kingdomhousing.org.uk

Oliver & Robb Architect http://www.oliverandrobb.co.uk/

Surveyors: Hardies

Engineers: Scott Bennett

Main contractor: Campion Homes http://www.campionhomes.com/

Scotframe http://www.scotframetimberengineering.co.uk/

Supawall Ltd, Tarnacre Hall Business Park, Tarnacre Lane, St Michaels, Preston PR3 0SZ

JUB Systems UK Ltd, 4 Copthall House, Station Square, Coventry CV1 2FL http://www.jubrenders.co.uk/

Figure 2.59 Pittenweem: north facing

Figure 2.60 Pittenweem: south facing

References

ARB (December 2007) http://www.arb.ca.gov/toxics/compwood/factsheet.pdf

Bevan R. and Woolley T. *Hemp Lime Construction* BRE Press 2008

Black Mountain (2010) Sheep Wool Insulation Technical Data pdf www. blackmountaininsulation.com/

Brettstapel (2012) http://www.brettstapel.org/Brettstapel/Home.html (viewed 23.2.12)

Channel 4 (2012) http://www.channel4.com/programmes/kevins-grand-design/ articles/suppliers (viewed 7.5.12)

Co-housing (2012) http://www.cohousing.org.uk/ (viewed 8.2.12)

DECC (2012) Final report of the Low Carbon Buildings programme 2006–2011 http://www.decc.gov.uk/en/content/cms/funding/funding_ops/innovation/ historic/buildings_prog/buildings_prog.aspx

Ecotimber http://www.ecotimber.com/guide/indoor-air-quality.html (viewed 16.1.12)

Encon Insulation www.encon.co.uk/products/results/taxonomy:112-sheeps_wool, 123-black_mountain,23-building (viewed 2.3.12)

Four (2012) http://www.4hg.co.uk/Extended_Content.aspx?pg=197 (viewed 10.5.12)

Hab (2012) http://www.haboakus.co.uk/shimmy.htm (viewed 5.5.12)

Hillingdon: Hemp house pioneers green answer to social housing development http://www.hillingdon.gov.uk/index.jsp?articleid=23928 (viewed 31.1.12)

Hills Construction Group http://www.hillsgroup.co.uk/Construction.aspx (viewed 2.3.12)

Howard E. *Garden Cities of Tomorrow 1902*, Faber and Faber edition 1946

Innovate UK (2012) https://connect.innovateuk.org/web/built-nanotech/articles/-/blogs/800584/maximized

Insulation Price http://www.insulationprice.co.uk/ (viewed 22.2.12)

InterNACHI (2012) International Association of Certified Home Inspectors, Inc. Fibreglass Insulation: History, Hazards and Alternatives http://www.nachi.org/fiberglass-insulation-history-hazards-alternatives.htm#ixzz1sOWOZkil (viewed 20.12.11)

JRHT (2010) Annual Review 2009/2010

Kelly (2011) http://www.architectural-review.com/buildings/pursuit-of-happiness/8624083.article (viewed 21.12.11)

Kingdom: Kingdom House Project Overview, 6 Station Court, Pittenweem, www.scotframe.co.uk/nmsruntime/saveasdialog.asp?IID=585&sID… (viewed October 2010, but now deleted)

LABC Local Authority Building Control http://www.labc.uk.com/ (viewed 14.2.12)

LABC Warranty www.labcwarranty.co.uk/ (viewed 14.2.12)

Letchworth Garden City Heritage Foundation www.lgchf.com (17.2.12)

LILAC Low Impact Living Affordable Community http://www.lilac.coop (viewed 2.3.12)

Martinsons (2012) http://www.martinsons.se/home (viewed 16.2.12)

Modcell http://www.modcell.com/ (viewed 2.3.12)

Norfolk Rural Community Council: Rural Affordable Housing Guide http://www.norfolkrcc.org.uk/wiki/index.php/Affordable_Rural_Housing

NHH (2012) http://www.nhh.org.uk/module/page-239/item_id-144/item_action-view_item/item-first-residents-move-into-tomorrows-garden-city-homes/ (viewed 15.2.12)

Pavatex http://www.natural-building.co.uk/pavatex_diffutherm_timber_frame.htm (viewed 13.9.11)

RHP (2011) Renewable House http://www.renewable-house.co.uk/ (viewed 16.9.11)

Rowntree Foundation and charitable Trust www.jrf.org.uk (viewed 2.3.12)

Scotframe Supawall System http://www.scotframe.co.uk/web/site/SF_ContactSearch.asp (viewed 16.1.12) http://www.youtube.com/watch?v=qT_XcXR5daA (viewed 16.1.12)

SFHA Scottish Federation of Housing Associations http://www.sfha.co.uk/hst/archive/fifes-kingdom-house-wins-national-award/menu-id-24.html (viewed 18.1.12)

Scottish Government 2012 Letter from Bill Gillespie, FoI/11/01666 (12.1.12)

Scotland (2011) http://www.scotlandshousingexpo.com (viewed 11.12.11)

Scottish Passiv House Centre http://www.sphc.co.uk/ (viewed 7.5.12)

The Construction Index http://www.theconstructionindex.co.uk/press/view/30-08-2011/galliford-try-partnerships-wins-uks-biggest-carbon-negative-social-housing-scheme (viewed 30.8.11)

Tremco http://www.tremco-illbruck.co.uk/products/00816_index.html (viewed 2.3.12)

UK Trade & Investment http://www.ukti.gov.uk/uktihome/item/142420.html (viewed 2.3.12)

Welsh Government, Letter dated 19.1.12 from the Welsh Government Construction Unit received in response to FOI Enquiry.

Wemico http://www.wemico.com/products/base-profile.html (viewed 2.3.12)

3. The Renewable House Programme: a strange procurement!

The Renewable House Programme (RHP) was established by the UK Department for Energy and Climate Change (DECC) to promote the use of renewable materials in social housing. DECC says that the programme was announced on 15 July 2009 (DECC 2010). Somehow £6 million plus was found at a time when government budgets were being squeezed, and this had to be spent quickly within the 2009/2010 financial year. This was a one-off initiative and did not appear to be part of any wider political policy or ministerial announcement, by the ill-fated Gordon Brown Labour Government, but it did get a mention in a sustainable construction policy document. This funding disappeared as quickly as it appeared and with the advent of a new Government set up by the Conservative Liberal alliance the section of DECC that was responsible for it was disbanded and the policy emphasis shifted to biofuels.

Official interest in renewable construction materials had first appeared through the Department for Food and Rural Affairs (DEFRA). DEFRA had funded the establishment of the National Non-food Crops Centre (NNFCC) in York in 2003. (NNFCC 2012) While this organisation has been largely focused on bio fuels, bio-chemicals and bio-plastics, it also had an interest in crop based construction materials. Through DEFRA support, the NNFCC commissioned Rachel Bevan Architects to write a report on hemp lime construction, which was published in book form by BRE Press as 'Hemp Lime Construction' (Bevan and Woolley 2008). It also supported a number of meetings of a technical working group on renewable materials. This 'Renewable Building Group' had about 12 meetings over 3–4 years and this then led to the establishment of the Alliance for Sustainable Building Products in 2011 (ASBP 2012).

A couple of earlier studies on renewable materials had been carried out by Impetus Consulting (Impetus 2002) and the Construction Industry Research and Information Association CIRIA (CIRIA 2004). These reports had very little impact on public policy and not until the UK Government

Low Impact Building: Housing using Renewable Materials, First Edition. Tom Woolley.
© 2013 John Wiley & Sons, Ltd. Published 2013 by John Wiley & Sons, Ltd.

commissioned a study, which led to the Strategy for Sustainable Construction, in June 2008, did renewable construction materials receive any official recognition (HM Government 2008) This report included a brief commitment to exploring the use of renewable materials. It is hard to track how this came about, as the report was worked on by staff seconded from construction firms, Atkins, Lafarge and Skanska. These companies were better known for support of cement and concrete than for renewable materials but there may have been some lobbying from other government departments. In the subsequent Strategy for Sustainable Construction Progress Report, of September 2009, it was noted that up to £6 million of government funding had been allocated under the LCIF (see below) for '60 or more low carbon affordable homes using innovative highly insulating renewable construction materials.' (BIS 2012)

There are various programmes which appear to be linked to this initiative: The Low Carbon Innovation Fund (LCIF) which was part of a Low Carbon Transition Plan was then referred to as the Low Carbon Investment Fund and also the Low Carbon Industrial Strategy. The funding for renewable housing was referred to as the Renewable Carbon Demonstration Programme and then the Renewable House Programme. This confusion of names is just one indication of how hard it was to pin down the origins of this funding or the direction of policy thinking. The change in names from one government website and policy document to another seemed to happen almost at random and is an indication of the level of policy confusion on how to tackle climate change and reduce carbon emissions among civil servants. This confusion appears to have continued with the change of government, as policy on renewable energy, in particular, has changed almost every month.

Much UK government attention has been focused on the establishment of the Zero Carbon Hub. This organisation was intended to provide advice and policy on how to achieve so-called 'zero carbon targets in housing and building'. The Zero Carbon Hub may have had some success in drawing attention to the need for energy saving but it has provided, at best, only a partial understanding of the issues. It has been run by people seconded from mainstream industry such as David Adams of Knauf, a multinational synthetic insulation manufacturer.

> David Adams divides his time between Head of External Affairs for Knauf Insulation (UK) Ltd and as a Director of the Zero Carbon Hub.
>
> (Zero Carbon Hub 2010)

Over several years there has been no evidence of any interest or support for low impact building solutions or renewable materials, from either the Zero Carbon Hub or other closely linked industry bodies, such as the UK Green Building Council (UKGBC 2012). Zero carbon, for these bodies, is interpreted largely in terms of energy efficiency and not embodied energy or environmental impact. In any case, 'Zero Carbon' had never really meant 'zero' and was redefined when the new Alliance Government took over (as explained in more detail in Chapter 4). Zero carbon targets were defined as between 10 kg and 14 kg of CO_2 emissions per m^2 and not zero!

There was little evidence that Government zero carbon targets were linked in any way to the use of renewable materials and the Renewable House Programme emerged almost from nowhere without obvious policy advice from experts in the field.

DEFRA helped to finance a private developer (Linford CZero Ltd) to build a hemp lime house at the BRE innovation park in Watford (BRE 2012a) in June 2009 (Renewable House 2012). The BRE Innovation Park already had an array of highly innovative projects which had attracted criticism because it was suggested that it demonstrated that achieving the 2016 zero carbon targets were 'too costly' (Vaughan 2007).

A further two houses were added, at the BRE, using low impact construction methods, one of which, sponsored by the Prince's Foundation (BRE 2012b) and was to be built of lightweight hollow clay bricks. The hemp lime house, built by CZero, Lime Technology and Lhoist Ltd, supported by the NNFCC and DEFRA/DECC, was seen as an immediate success as it was built very quickly – in just a few days. It was also completed to a very reasonable budget (unlike many of the other projects in the Innovation Park) suggesting that hemp lime construction could be used for affordable social housing and should be attractive to private developers (Renewable House 2012).

As a result of the success of the Renewable House, it seems that DECC, and the NNFCC, were able to persuade the Treasury to finance a further programme to encourage the use of renewable materials. Plans to provide this finance must have been in place before the Renewable House at the BRE was constructed, if it was launched within weeks of the house being opened as claimed by DECC. However, many experts who were working on renewable materials, were not told that this programme had been launched in July 2009 and did not see the DECC announcement on the website that £6 million was available until many months later.

For instance, as far as can be established, the Renewable Building Group, run by NNFCC, was not told about the July launch. At the 23 September 2009 meeting in York, hosted by the NNFCC, it was not discussed and there is nothing recorded in the minutes. The launch was not mentioned at the fifth meeting, in January 2010, in London, even though it was attended by Iris Anderson, an official from DECC who was one of the main people involved in launching the £6 million programme (Renewable Building Group 2009/10).

The only solid evidence of an announcement is in a document entitled 'The UK Low Carbon Industrial Strategy' which was apparently published in July 2009.

The Government also has a number of initiatives in place to specifically help remove the barriers to the use of innovative low carbon construction materials, including biomass-based products. These range from the publication of technical guides and environmental profiles for a range of crop based construction materials, to funding support for a new material processing plant and the building of a low carbon materials demonstration house at the Building Research Establishment (BRE) in Watford. **The Government is**

investing up to £6 million to construct 60 or more low carbon affordable homes built with innovative, highly insulating renewable materials. The new scheme will demonstrate the viability of these materials, act as a catalyst for the renewable construction materials industry and engage the affordable housing sector in the low carbon agenda. (emphasis added)

(Department for Business, 2009)

By the time some members of the Renewable Building Group found out about the £6 million, in the autumn of 2009 (when the *Strategy for Sustainable Construction Progress Report* was launched), most of the funding had already been allocated to two housing projects, Diss and Swindon, which were committed to using hempcrete materials from Lime Technology. At the launch of the strategy progress report in the House of Commons on 15 September 2009, civil servants who had attended from DECC were questioned about the £6 million mentioned in the report. Their response was to ask if there was a project that could be funded in Northern Ireland from this money. The Department of Social Development in Northern Ireland was only contacted in mid November 2009. In response to a freedom of information request to the Scottish Government, it was stated that the Scottish Office was only contacted by DECC on 21 December 2009 (Scottish Government 2012). It is curious that even though the programme had apparently been launched in July, the regional governments were only contacted in late autumn to put forward proposed schemes.

The Renewable Building Group, supported by the NNFCC, was formed from a wide range of people with interests in many different kinds of renewable materials and there was some concern in the autumn when some members became aware of this DECC initiative. Some members were most annoyed when they discovered that the bulk of the money had already been allocated to two hempcrete schemes. Neil May, Managing Director of Natural Building Technologies (NBT) tackled civil servants at the NNFCC Green Supply Chain conference in York in November 2009 and asked why materials other than hempcrete had not been included in the £6 million programme. Following this, John Williams of the NNFCC and the chair of the Renewable Building Group, Gary Newman, were asked to produce a list of other renewable materials that might be eligible for grant funding. This list is reproduced here as it was issued (Table 3.1) at the end of 2009, some 6 months after the programme had allegedly been announced. A number of other projects were then approved using other materials and some further hempcrete projects were also added, leading to the twelve case study projects discussed in Chapter 2. At this stage it was still a requirement that money had to be spent by April 2010. The time line of this process is summarised in Table 3.2.

It might have been expected that in order to spend £6 million of public money, an open competition would have been held. Such a competition would have required clear criteria as to which materials could be used and there would have been some kind of independent scrutiny of the

Table 3.1 Renewable materials list drawn up by the NNFCC. The information below reproduced as it was issued though two additional columns omitted for clarity

This list has been compiled by members of the Renewable Building thematic working group. The products listed have been approved by the NNFCC as appropriate for consideration for the DECC funded grant scheme to support the construction of 'low carbon affordable homes built with innovative, highly insulating renewable materials'.

For further information please contact: John Williams, NNFCC or Gary Newman – Plant Fibre Technology and Chair of Renewable Building.

Brand	Product description	Manufacturer or supplier(s)	Summary of properties	Country of manufacture	Environmental credentials (incl. bio-based content)
Thermafleece	Sheep's Wool Insulation	Second Nature UK Ltd	Thermal and acoustic insulation 23 kg/m³ λ – 0.038 W/mK	UK	85% w/w bio-based content
Thermafleece PB20	Sheep's Wool & Recycled Polyester Insulation	Second Nature UK Ltd	Thermal and acoustic insulation 20 kg/m³ λ – 0.039 W/mK	UK	60% w/w bio-based content
Tradical® Hemcrete®	Insulating bio-composite for walls in conjunction with a structural frame	Lime Technology Ltd	Insulating, good thermal inertia, fire resistant,	UK	110 kg of hemp shiv per cubic metre. Locks up around 110–130 kg of CO_2/m³
Breathe Insulation	Natural fibre insulation batts based on hemp	Hemp Technology and Lime Technology	Insulation quilt with similar conductivity to mineral fibre	UK from 2010	95% natural fibre
NBT Pavaclad	Pavatherm Plus/ Isolair woodfibre boards	NBT	External wall with ventilated cladding	Switzerland	95–97% waste from sustainable forestry
NBT Diffutherm	Diffutherm board plus Baumit renders	NBT	External wall insulation with render system	Switzerland	98% waste wood from sustainable forestry
NBT Pavaroof	Pavatherm Plus/ Isolair wood fibre boards	NBT	Pitched or flat roofing sarking boards	Switzerland	95–97% waste from sustainable forestry

Product	Description	Supplier	Details	Origin	Composition
Steico	Wood fibre	Ecomerchant brand of Burdens	Natural wood based insulation	Poland	Wood fibre, breathable
Viking	joiner	Ecomerchant brand of Burdens	Wood windows and doors	Estonia	FSC timber, water based paints
Black Mountain Sheep wool insulation	Sheep wool insulation	Black Mountain	Made from 100% virgin wool with up to 15% binder	UK	Min 85% virgin wool
Isonat+	Hemp and wood fibre insulation	Ecomerchant www.ecomerchant.co.uk NBT www.natural-building.co.uk	λ – 0.038 W/mK high density 45 & 55 kg/m^3	France	55% wood fibre 30% hemp fibre 15% polyester binder
ModCell	Pre-Fabricated straw bale panels	ModCell Ltd	FSC/PEFC, pre-fabricated structural timber frame using renewable and sustainable straw bales as its insulating material	UK, Within 3–25 miles of construction site via local 'flying factory' temporary manufacturing units	Straw bales hemp FSC/PEFC timber.

Other Products include

Wood Windows

Wood Window Alliance approved high performance, fully certified wooden windows – see www.woodwindowalliance.com for performance and sustainability standards and a list of suppliers.

Straw bales

Straw bales have been approved for use by Building Control Departments throughout the UK. Straw bales council houses are currently being built by Amazonails (www.amazonails.org.uk). Straw bales are low cost, highly insulating, 100% bio-based and readily available.

Table 3.2 RHP timeline

July 2009 – Renewable house opened at BRE

July 2009 – DECC claim to have launched £6 million programme

July 2009 – 60% of money from the programme allocated to Diss and Swindon projects

Sept 2009 – launch of strategy document which referred to the £6 million

Nov 2009 – NNFCC conference in York

Nov 2009 – Northern Ireland DSD contacted to find eligible project

Dec 2009 – NNFCC asks renewable building group chair to prepare list of approved materials

December 2009 – Scottish Government contacted to find eligible projects

April 2010 – projects were meant to be completed and money spent

Late 2010 – Welsh project complete

2011 – other projects began to be completed

2011 – Reed Street and Callowlands begin on site but not completed until 2012

Early 2012 – final projects in Leeds start on site

process in order to ensure fairness about the selection. It might also have been expected that a list of eligible materials would have been part of the criteria for funding. As the criteria were so loose, quite a few of the projects – as shown in Chapter 2 – did not necessarily use a 'high proportion' of renewable materials as required in the scheme conditions published by DECC.

This process may provide an insight into how the UK Government sometimes works. Despite all sorts of red tape and strict bureaucratic rules about tendering, procurement and fair competition, it is hard to discover what sort of 'due process' was followed to allocate this money. It seems that DECC called upon the English Homes & Communities Agency (HCA) to circulate registered social landlords and ask them if they could identify projects where the money could be spent quickly. A small amount of the money was also offered to regional governments in Wales, Scotland and Northern Ireland, but much later. As a result, two projects in Scotland, one in Wales and one in Northern Ireland were also supported and eight were approved in England.

It was surprising that, having previously spent money on a report about hemp lime construction, DECC had not sought independent advice from the researchers about the programme even though the bulk of projects to be funded were to use this form of construction. The Northern Ireland Department of Social Development did ask for advice but only on a voluntary basis.

It was possible to check the facts about the process outlined above, through responses under the Freedom of Information Act. A student at the Centre for Alternative Technology Graduate School, in Wales, submitted a series of questions to DECC, which were answered by both DECC and the Homes & Communities Agency (DECC 2010; HCA 2010) and he kindly passed this information on.

DECC's reply explained that £6 million was originally available to build 60 homes, but then £6.7 million went towards '283 homes using innovative highly insulation renewable materials'. (While 283 was the intended total, this included 114 in Norfolk where only 29 were built, so in reality only 200 houses were funded by the programme.)

The criteria for the programme were only ever set out in general terms. For instance, it was never clear whether projects had to use a certain proportion of the grant on innovative renewable insulation materials and whether the grant could be used for other things like renewable energy. When officials were questioned about this, they said that the entire grant was meant to go on renewable insulation materials, but as has been seen, this was clearly not the case. Most agencies spending the grant appear to have interpreted it as money that would assist the feasibility of the whole development rather than to pay for renewable materials.

When asked by the CAT student, what criteria were used to evaluate the applications for grant, the replies were very vague, simply stating that DECC and the NNFCC and the relevant delivery bodies, HCA, DSD, Scottish and Welsh Governments followed 'funding and procurement rules', though what rules these were are not stated. When asked why there wasn't a more open and transparent system, timing restrictions are referred to. No list of unsuccessful applications was provided.

In reality what appears to have happened is that DECC and the HCA were so desperate to find any projects on which to spend the money in a short period of time that there was no competition process; any project which appeared to qualify was approved until the money ran out.

However, nearly half of the £6.7 million grant was allocated to just one scheme, the planned 114 houses in Diss, Norfolk. A substantial amount was also committed to the Kevin McCloud scheme in Swindon. This appears to have happened at a very early stage in the process. There appears to have been little consistency in how the money was allocated with substantial amounts going to some and very little to others, unrelated to the size of the project.

CZero (which is a private development company) said on their website that they had received over half of all the funds from the programme, though this statement has now been removed (CZero 2012), but DECC stated that all funds were given to registered social landlords. In the Diss project only 15 houses (apartments) have been built for the local Flagship Housing Association (RSL). The developer CZero built the houses but the grant had to be paid to Flagship HA. The Section 106 agreement as part of the planning approval only required 15 socially rented units, the rest were intended to be affordable for sale (referred to as discounted market sale). The capital cost of the scheme was originally estimated to be £11.5 million, including the Flagship houses, according to Simon Linford (Linford 2011), who said that the grant 'was essential because the scheme was unviable having been negotiated pre crash. We were already going to use renewable materials.' In other words the grant enabled the feasibility of providing low-cost affordable homes, rather than renewable materials. A few houses on the plan for the site were also to be sold at normal market prices. Arrangements for discounted sale of houses has to have local authority approval and also requires the support of mortgage lenders. The scheme at Diss ran into some problems with getting building societies or banks to lend.

At a meeting arranged by the HCA in Milton Keynes on 20 September 2011, Robert Pearson of CZero presented a cost breakdown that stated that 29 houses were built in Phase 1 (presumably including the 15 for Flagship) at a total capital cost of £2,547,835 not including design costs and LABC warranty. Thus not all the £3million grant that had been awarded had been spent. Given difficulties in arranging mortgage finance for the affordable houses for sale, it seems unlikely that any further houses would be built in Phase 2 in the short term, but further phases of the scheme may be constructed in the future which will presumably be funded by the remaining unspent balance of £452,165.

It is not suggested that anything improper occurred here. Flagship and CZero were very open and helpful in response to the research for this book, but it is still hard to understand why the Flagship scheme required such a high subsidy compared with the other projects, which received much less funding, particularly as so few houses were built. All the other projects funded under the scheme were socially rented houses or co-ownership, apart from LILAC, which is a mixed tenure cooperative. Many of the houses were meant to be 'affordable for sale' but due to problems in the housing market, many ended up being rented. It is not uncommon for registered social landlords to have a private development wing, which provides 'low cost' houses for sale. However, at Diss the bulk were for sale.

DECC was asked in the FOI enquiry (Question 26) whether the grant was given for the use of materials that are not renewable. The DECC response stated, 'The grants were awarded for projects willing to maximise/make substantial use of renewable materials' (DECC FOI 2010) and yet grant was given to the project in Fife that used fossil fuel based materials. The Scottish Government confirmed that they had approved this.

As a result of the intervention by members of the Renewable Building Group, and with the provision of the NNFCC approved list of materials, other projects used materials other than hempcrete, mainly wood fibre, sheep's wool and straw, but with much smaller allocations of money compared with Diss and Swindon. Despite this synthetic materials were used in roofs and other elements in some of the projects.

The HCA also stated that one 'eligible' project declined the funding. They state in their FOI reply (HCA 2010) that the money had to be spent by April 2010 and that if not spent could be claimed back. In practice, few of the projects spent the money by April 2010 and thus the money had to be paid out in advance of projects being started on the ground. In order to 'spend' the money, it was paid to the builders or developers or agents in advance of work starting on site, or in one case before even the site or planning permission had been acquired!

At a meeting at the HCA in Milton Keynes in September 2011, to review progress on the projects, it was clear that there had been a great deal of slippage in the programme and that two or three projects had not even started or were only about to start on site (Callowlands, Reed Street and

LILAC). HCA officials stated at the meeting that the programme had been audited (twice) and that no problems had been identified; however, when asked in writing for details of these audits it seems that one audit was simply a general audit of the HCA. No details of the other audit were ever provided. The RHP is simply mentioned in the HCA 2010 annual report (HCA 2010). It has to be assumed that it is acceptable government accounting practice to pay over money for projects that are committed, if not actually built or started, and that this money can be held for over a year or even several years. As all the projects have gone ahead there would have been no need for any money to be paid back, presumably.

Monitoring and evaluation

A key element of the programme, referred to by DECC in the initial statement, was monitoring and evaluation. However, funding for the monitoring was refused in summer 2010, according to the NNFCC. It is not clear why monitoring had not been included in the original £6.7 million as this was meant to be part of the programme. Various bodies interested in carrying out the monitoring were told on 25 May 2010, by John Williams of the NNFCC (Williams 2010), that there was no money, but it then emerged later at the September 2011 Milton Keynes meeting that '£100,000' had been found and that a contract was awarded to Cathie Eberlin of Leading Energy to manage a monitoring programme of two of the projects. While the figure referred to at the meeting was £100,000 for monitoring, it was then confirmed later by John Williams that it was actually £250,000. Both of the projects selected for monitoring were hempcrete schemes, the two initial projects in Diss and Swindon. Other projects appear not to have been given any opportunity to access this funding. According to Williams, money suddenly became available very late in 2010 and 'tight timing' meant that there was very little actual time to determine who would run the projects, but it was tendered to six organisations based on advice from the HCS, Energy Saving Trust and the BRE. It has not been possible to identify who the other five were. The contract was awarded to Leading Energy:

> Due to her monitoring related experience Cathie Eberlin (of Leading Energy) was only appointed to manage the tender winners, translate the data when it came in, and to ensure we had consistency and a reporting back mechanism to NNFCC, DECC and HCA. Total project money available: £250k.
> There are 2 projects: Provision and Installation of equipment – Carnego Systems. Total budget approximately £142k. Data collecting and analysis – Emissions Zero. Total budget approximately £89k. This left approximately £19k to cover all administrative and project management costs going forward.
> (Williams 2011)

This particular process and decision is curious in a number of ways. Firstly, it would have made sense to monitor a scheme where more than one renewable material had been used. For instance, in Letchworth the project had both identical hempcrete and wood fibre insulated houses. Thus a comparison could have been made between the performance of the two technologies. Secondly, it is curious that the monitoring funding was allocated to the projects that had received the bulk of the grant and were the first two to be selected as they were in a better position to fund their own monitoring. By the time the monitoring funding was available there were several of the other projects well under way, but as they received lower levels of grant it might have been better to help them with their monitoring, which was a condition of receiving the RHP grant.

Leading Energy had close personal links to Lime Technology at the time the contract was awarded. Lime Technology supplied the renewable materials and construction system that was to be monitored at Diss and Swindon. While according to the NNFCC, Leading Energy was to manage the process, most of the scientific monitoring work was given to Emission Zero a consultancy firm run by Lubo Jankovic, a lecturer at Birmingham City University School of Architecture, though Birmingham City University was not involved.

Carnego Systems, based in Cornwall, who received £142,000 to supply monitoring equipment for the projects in Diss and Swindon, was also the company that had provided a system called Hab Shimmy to Kevin McCloud's development company for an on-line computer system in each of the Swindon houses. It is understood that the Hab Shimmys were to be useful for the tenants of the houses to monitor their energy usage, though apparently not connected with the energy monitoring of the scheme. However, tenants interviewed at the Triangle, confirmed that there were problems with the Shimmys from the day they moved in.

During second visits to both the projects in Swindon and Diss, it was not possible to observe any monitoring equipment in place such as thermal probes or data loggers. Occupants thought these were in place but were unable to point out where they were and said that they had not seen anyone with thermal imaging cameras and said they had not been involved.

It might have been more sensible for monitoring to be managed by agencies that were completely independent of any of the parties involved in the projects. Some University researchers who had expressed interest in the monitoring process were told, that there was no money available. When £250k did become available for this work they were not invited to tender. Given the innovative nature of this work it may have been assumed that few organisations were properly equipped to carry out such monitoring.

Fortunately some other monitoring and evaluation of the projects is been carried out without funding from DECC or the HCA. The project in York has been assessed by Leeds Metropolitan University through funding from the Technology Strategy Board. Initial results from this work were presented at an open meeting in York on 29 November. Results from the work managed by Leading Energy have not yet been seen though they may have been circulated to others. Analysis will be done by Cardiff Metropolitan University of the Welsh scheme.

The excuse for the unseemly haste in the programme in order to get money spent by April 2010 seems undermined by the lengthy delays in carrying out some of the projects. While some were under way by April 2010 it was not easy for building work to be done so quickly. Such implementation delays are not uncommon in any housing projects, particularly those in the public sector, because there can be many problems due to planning permissions, land purchase, tendering and contracting problems. Design and specification changes would also have been needed as many of the projects selected had already been designed before the RHP grant was awarded.

Perhaps a little more time and care could have been taken to set up the project with a more open and transparent competition process. This would have made it possible for a wider range of approaches and technologies to be selected, using a more considered and scientific approach. In the end more than half of the projects used hempcrete products while other materials such as sheep's wool, wood fibre, hemp insulation batts and straw could have been more strongly represented. For instance, a highly innovative social housing project using straw bale construction in Lincolnshire could have been extended and supported with a grant (Strawbale 2012).

A more scientific protocol for selecting and then monitoring and evaluating the projects could have been established, with help from leading researchers in the field. It would have made sense to set up a small monitoring group with experts in renewable materials from places like Bath, Plymouth, Nottingham, Leeds and Bangor Universities and the NNFCC Renewable Building Group. It would be perfectly normal practice to have such a steering group.

The bureaucratic thoughtlessness has, from the start, potentially undermined the credibility of the programme and thus put at risk how renewable materials could have been perceived. UK government policy for the past few years has been to reduce government funding for research of this kind, and the new Tory/Liberal Alliance Government appears to have withdrawn funding from any innovative demonstration programmes so there is unlikely to be another chance for some time.

It could be argued that this approach was not necessarily the best way to encourage the use of renewable materials. As well as providing significant finance to the 'independent' Zero Carbon Hub, which has acted as a strong advocate for petrochemical based synthetic materials, the Government could have done more to support the Renewable Building Group, which could then have carried out research to explore the benefits of renewable materials. Demonstration projects would also have been a useful tool, but these could have been assisted through a body like the Technology Strategy Board, which has provided finance to a significant number of retrofit demonstration projects (TSB 2012). It seems likely that the Government was poorly advised about these issues and decisions were taken far too quickly.

Due to government changes and financial cuts, there was a risk that the RHP would disappear into the mists of time as there would be no follow-up, and an official report into the programme seems unlikely. The team at the HCA, who were involved, have been dispersed to other roles, and DECC no longer has a brief to support renewable materials. Government politicians have visited the projects at Stanton Harcourt and Swindon but there is no evidence that they were properly briefed about the renewable materials they were looking at!

References

ASBP Alliance for Sustainable Building Products www.asbp.org.uk (viewed 2012)

Bevan R. and Woolley T. *Hemp Lime Construction* BRE Press 2008

BIS (2012) Strategy for sustainable construction ...no longer in force so in Government archives: (7.9.11) http://webarchive.nationalarchives.gov.uk/+/http://www.berr.gov.uk/policies/business-sectors/construction/sustainable-construction/strategy-for-sustainable-construction (viewed 11.5.12)

BIS (2009) Department for Business, Innovation and Skills *The UK Low Carbon Industrial Strategy* URN (July 2009) 09/1058

BRE (2012a) Innovation Park http://www.bre.co.uk/page.jsp?id=634 (viewed 10.2.12)

BRE (2012b) http://www.bre.co.uk/page.jsp?id=2075 (viewed 2.3.12)

CIRIA: *Crops in construction*: Andrew Cripps and Buro Happold, CIRIA RP680, London 2004

CZero http://www.czero.com/ (viewed 28.9.12)

DECC, Department of Energy and Climate Change 10/1507 EIR Request Renewable Construction Demonstration Programme, 30 July 2010

HCA Homes and Communities Agency FOI RFI:2609-10 30 July 2010

HM Government in association with Strategic Forum for Construction: Strategy for Sustainable Construction 2008

Homes and Communities Agency Annual Report and Financial Statements 2009/2010 HC 265, The Stationery Office, London

Impetus Consulting: Market Review of Renewable Insulation Materials: A Summary Report. Impetus Consulting and Pilkington Energy Efficiency Trust March 2002

Linford S. email to the author dated 15 December 2011

NNFCC – the UK's National Centre for Biorenewable Energy, Fuels and Materials http://www.nnfcc.co.uk/about-nnfcc (viewed 28.2.12)

Renewable Building Group (2009/10) Minutes of the 4th and 5th meetings of the Technical Working Group on Renewable Building 23 September 2009 at Ramada Encore Hotel, York, hosted by NNFCC and 27 January 2010 at Davis Langdon in London

Renewable House (2012) http://www.renewable-house.co.uk/news/2/ (viewed 11.5.12)Scottish Government Housing Supply Division FoI/11/01666 (viewed 12.1.12)

Strawbale (2012) http://www.n-kesteven.gov.uk/nk-straw-houses/106433.article (viewed 14.02.12)

Technology Strategy Board (TSB) Retrofit for the Future http://www.innovateuk.org/ourstrategy/innovationplatforms/lowimpactbuilding/retrofit-.ashx (viewed 6.2.12)

UK Green Building Council http://www.ukgbc.org (viewed 5.2.12)

Vaughan R. (2007) Architects Journal 30.08.07 pp.10–11

Williams J. email 25 May 2010

Williams J. email 19 October 2011

Zero Carbon Hub http://www.zerocarbonhub.org/ (viewed 14.10.10)

4. Analysis of issues arising from the case studies

There are a number of general and more specific technical issues arising from the case studies that highlight positive results, but also problems related to the use of natural renewable materials.

Success in using natural renewable materials

In general terms, despite a number of small problems, all of the 12 completed demonstration projects in the Renewable House Programme (RHP) were built and occupied successfully. The use of natural renewable materials in these houses was achieved with few reports of occupant dissatisfaction.

It will be important to do a follow-up study after two or three years and also compare occupant attitudes and energy usage in the RHP houses with some other houses built more conventionally at the same time. If the DECC and the HCA had sought proper academic and professional advice at the start, the importance of funding such a follow-up study could have been included. Only by carrying out such a study can the long-term success, or otherwise, of the programme be properly assessed.

There is anecdotal evidence that many Code 4 type houses built in the UK in recent years – particularly those using modern methods of construction (MMC) – have experienced problems. Occupants complain of higher heating bills than expected, overheating in the summer, noise transmission from adjoining houses and under-performing renewable energy equipment. Other issues such as health problems for indoor pollution are less commonly reported, as awareness of such issues is low in the UK. There are very few published scientific or academic analyses of these problems with most of the reportage being on web sites, blogs and conference reports (building4change 2012; CIBSE (2005); Greenwise 2012).

Low Impact Building: Housing using Renewable Materials, First Edition. Tom Woolley.
© 2013 John Wiley & Sons, Ltd. Published 2013 by John Wiley & Sons, Ltd.

Bodies such as the UK Energy Saving Trust (EST) have a responsibility for evaluation but appear to focus their efforts on promoting low energy design rather than assessing whether it has been achieved (EST 2012). The EST provides general guidance on how post occupancy evaluation should be carried out and they are working with the Good Homes Alliance (GHA) to evaluate some projects.

> Good Homes Alliance monitoring project: We are working in partnership with the Good Homes Alliance (GHA) to support them and their academic partners in an exciting research and development project to monitor and evaluate the performance of a number of high-level sustainable new build homes. Our monitoring protocols are being used across four GHA member developer's sites representing a range of construction types to help understand any gap in design aspiration and as-built performance – monitoring will take place through 2010 and 2011.
>
> The results will allow us to make comparisons between actual performance and design targets such as the Code for Sustainable Homes and SAP, which can be as much as 100% different. They will also better inform us how the homes are actually being used; what the delivered energy use and carbon emissions are in reality; how effective any low and zero carbon technologies are in practice; what the comfort and indoor air quality conditions are like; and how the resident perceives the home.
>
> (EST 2012)

Evaluations of this nature are urgently needed because there is so little data on the performance of low energy housing. The work at Leeds Metropolitan University has shown convincingly that recently built houses rarely achieve design targets in terms of energy efficiency.

> In all of the (LMU) case studies the designer and builder failed to produce low carbon buildings specified ... The industry is attempting to develop low carbon buildings without a real understanding of the construction process and the performance of components used.
>
> (Gorse 2010)

For instance, at the Joseph Rowntree Housing Trust project in York, Elm Tree Mews, dwelling heat loss was 54% higher than designed (JRF 2010). The team carrying out this work at Leeds Metropolitan University emphasised the importance of getting the building fabric right as this will last much longer than the expensive energy systems that are being added into new housing. Through their analysis of a number of projects they are very critical of government policy of encouraging MMC.

> ...the general view, promoted by enthusiasts for MMC, that by adopting new MMC techniques and novel heating technologies the industry will somehow overcome construction process problems and related performance issues is, in our view fatally flawed.
>
> (Wingfield 2012)

The RHP, in promoting the use of renewable materials, can be seen as an attempt to depart from the headlong pursuit of MMC, advocated by both a series of government reports and main stream industry. The construction industry is characterised as backward looking and traditional even though many of these traditional practices have great benefits and might give rise to higher standards. (Callcutt 2007; Ball 2005) Interestingly there is very little technical literature in print on MMC, and promised books on the subject have yet to emerge (Lawson 2010). Goodier and Wei Pan (2012) in their RICS report review the range of views about MMC, and whether it has been a success or not, citing Harty on the resistance to technological change.

> This is partly due to the traditionally slow uptake of technological innovation in house building, and arguably concurs with the view of 'construction as a low tech, low innovating sector'
>
> (Harty 2007)

Despite the assumption that the construction industry is slow to take up innovation, in reality, while new houses may look traditional, with brick outer facing, much of what is done in current house construction is very new and involves a range of materials and techniques that are poorly understood and little tested. Assembling off-site prefabricated panels may appear to be quick and efficient but in an attempt to achieve airtightness and design targets of energy efficiency, buildings are taped and wrapped in various materials and components that may not stand the test of time.

The RHP, in using natural and wet materials like hempcrete, will have looked to the advocates of MMC as a step backwards. Hempcrete is often referred to as a traditional form of construction even though it is in fact highly innovative. Furthermore, companies such as Lime Technology and NBT go much further than many other suppliers, providing training, technical advice to designers and have also adapted their renewable material solutions to meet demands for prefabrication.

Adapting conventional timber frame construction for using natural materials

Two principal methods of construction were used in the RHP case study projects (apart from LILAC Leeds, Pittenweem and Inverness). Both methods were based on simple timber frame panel construction, adapted for hempcrete or with wood fibreboards and natural insulation. On most projects, the softwood timber frame open panels were supplied by specialist subcontractors, and usually consisted of standard 140 mm studs. Further fixing of permanent shuttering boards or other sheathing and such like was done on site. None of the timber frame suppliers appeared to be very much involved in the unusual nature of the projects and any issues to do with the timber frames had to be resolved by the contractor on site. It is normal practice for open timber frame panels to be made off-site and there may be small cost savings compared with making them on site. This did not seem to lead to any particular difficulties. In the case of hempcrete, conventional timber frames were used except that the studs were placed on the inside and permanent shuttering boards fixed to these. Hempcrete was then cast using temporary shuttering installed by specialist subcontractors. The only real problem with this was the severe weather conditions. In the case of the NBT wood fibre Pavatex materials, the contractors and architects reported some problems in complying with the fixing requirements of the Pavatex system though these were all resolved.

None of the suppliers of the renewable materials were in a position to offer a complete construction package when the RHP was set up, though at the LILAC in Leeds, the full panels will be assembled through the Modcell system.

The importance of getting details right and using details appropriate for eco materials

The issue of detailing can be identified as a major question mark for most of the projects. In many cases, existing designs were changed relatively late in the day, to incorporate renewable materials. Significant changes to detailing were not made. In the 'traditional' pitched roof style houses – Abertridwr, Carnlough, York, Diss and Blackditch – no changes appear to have been made to increase overhangs or window and door surrounds. Economy seems to have been the main factor here as extending roof trusses for greater overhangs and using better quality gutters and downpipes would have increased costs.

Conventional eaves boards, tight to the walls, were used in nearly all the projects including Swindon. The Letchworth and Callowlands projects used a more modern flat roof style, again with limited roof overhangs. The LILAC project is based on designs following the standard Modcell 'Balehouse' design with flat roofs and no overhangs at all. At Swindon the design and details took more account of the use of hempcrete and other environmental aims such as natural ventilation. Gutters and downpipes were made of galvanised steel and this gave a higher quality look to the scheme.

It will be interesting to see whether there are any weathering problems due to the lack of roof overhangs and deep window reveals but this may not become clear for some years. With lime based renders and materials such as wood fibre and hempcrete, greater care needs to be taken with detailing and better weather protection. This approach has stood the test of time for many centuries, using traditional materials. However, most of the architects, builders and clients involved in the RHP projects have not necessarily come from a natural or traditional building background and very often the final decisions about detailing were made on site by builders.

The traditional axiom of having a 'good hat and a good pair of boots', often referred to in traditional lime and earth based construction, has therefore not been applied and it will be interesting to see the outcome. On the other hand the proponents of natural and renewable materials are anxious that architects should not be deterred from using such materials because of aesthetic restrictions.

Both Tradical Hemcrete and the NBT wood fibre products have gone though a range of approvals and certification procedures. These approvals are very expensive. For instance, obtaining British Board of Agrément (BBA 2012) certification for just one product may cost £30,000 or more. This is a massive investment for a small company and not all are in a position to obtain such approvals. Hemcrete, for instance began by obtaining LABC system approval (LABC 2012). LABC is a membership organisation representing local authority building control departments and their system of approval indicates that a product will meet building regulation requirements. LABC also promotes a warranty service (LABC Warranty 2012). To obtain LABC warranties, the materials and the construction methods and details have to be approved.

LABC provides registered details on-line so, for instance, Lime Technology have a system called hembuild (an off-site structural panel system) which is registered (14.09.12 – RD 1670911B). It is also possible to access on-line a compliance document, system certificate (LABC 2012) Tradical Hemcrete also has BBA certification. NBT Pavatex systems have BBA approvals and BBA certificates which can be accessed on-line (BBA 2012). For instance, the NBT Diffutherm product certificate is 10/4723.

The construction industry increasingly relies on such certification, and without it many organisations, particularly those in the public sector, will not specify products. There is also a requirement for public sector organisations that building products are covered by warranties, and mortgage lenders for housing also look for these.

While the warranty and certification paper trail is based on genuine, and hopefully rigorous, tests, the performance of products and buildings will depend largely on how well they are installed on the building site. Good design and good construction practice is worth far more than all the certifications and warranties, to be assured that a building will still be standing and performing well in 30, 60 or 100 years' time.

Architects involved in the RHP case study projects said that delays were caused by having to submit a series of revised details if their designs did not comply with the original LABC warranty requirements. As the warranty applies to the material or product, responsibility for getting details approved lies with the materials supplier, but clearly as each project differs, standard details may not be appropriate.

As outlined in Chapter 2, a decision was taken at the Callowlands project to use synthetic foam insulation in some of the wall sections where timber rainscreen cladding was specified. These timber panels, adjacent to some windows and to the entrance porches, were for aesthetic reasons, and the explanation given for using synthetic insulation was that the LABC warranty did not approve the proposed timber cladding over hempcrete. It as also suggested that the LABC warranty would require a membrane behind the cladding to prevent any driving rain reaching the exposed hempcrete. As hempcrete, with a simple lime render, can be used as an external finish, this seems a strange requirement.

At Letchworth, timber cladding over hempcrete was approved, apparently, but there were many other new details to be agreed where designs required parapets, balconies and so on, that may not have been covered by previously approved details. While obtaining warranty approval may have appeared to delay projects, this was probably a result of designs being prepared before the grant became available. Time pressures to get projects on site may have made making detailing changes difficult.

At Callowlands, the implications of changing some of the panels to use synthetic insulation would then have raised the issue of whether junctions between hempcrete and foam insulation would result in good airtightness. Using rainscreen details means that the rainscreen material itself has to be approved. The panels to be used are made from compressed rockwool with thermo-hardening synthetic binding compounds with water based acrylic decorative finish. (Rockpanel 2012) Such panels are claimed to provide a high degree of rain and moisture resistance so the risk of the hempcrete behind getting wet should be minimal. However, at Callowlands, synthetic PIR was used instead of the required renewable insulation because of the warranty approval problem. It is interesting to note that the warranty system appears to have led to the substitution of synthetic products.

These problems indicate the limitations of warranty systems. The warranty companies cannot possibly know every technical aspect of construction materials and systems so they rely on consultants to advise on detailing. Such consultants are likely to be highly risk averse, especially if they are not familiar with the technology being considered. LABC Warranty is completely separate from LABC and is an organisation owned by a company called MD Insurance Services Ltd, based in Birkenhead at the time of writing. LABC and LABC Warranty use the same logo and style on their websites.

Weather issues and hempcrete

Much of the Tradical Hemcrete, used in the RHP projects was cast during the winter of 2010/11, one of the worst UK winters on record, with temperatures falling to −16°C over an extended period. Conservation architects and builders would never allow the use of lime during very cold weather, but the mainstream construction industry, used to working with synthetic materials, carried on even when the weather was bad. This may have led to problems with the hempcrete drying out and could even possibly have affected the setting and carbonation process. At Diss, dehumidifiers were used in an attempt to accelerate drying out as moisture readings showed that they could not proceed with plastering and painting. This was also a problem at Swindon, Blackditch and York though not apparently as severe as in Diss.

The weather and drying out problems did cause some damp staining, though this seemed to be quite limited at Blackditch and York. Problems

Leeds Met (2012) http://www.leedsmet.ac.uk/as/cebe/index.htm

Lime Technology (2012a) http://www.limetechnology.co.uk/projects/project06.htm

Lime Technology (2012b) – Hemclad System http://www.limetechnology.co.uk/hemclad.htm (viewed 2.3.12)

NBT (2012) http://www.natural-building.co.uk/lime_plaster_render_baumit_bayousan.htm

Resistant (2012) Resistant Products Brochure http://www.resistant.co.uk/downloads.php

Rockpanel Rockclad http://www.rockpanel.co.uk/products/rockpanel+rockclad (viewed 2.3.12)

Wingfield, J., Bell M., and Miles-Shenton, D. (2012) *Lessons from Stamford Brook Understanding the Gap between Designed and Real Performance Centre for the Built Environment*, Leeds Metropolitan University

Young, E. (2012) Stepping out of the Mainstream *RIBA Journal* May 2012 pp 34–38

5. Attitudes to renewable materials, energy issues and the policy context

Sustainable development is development that meets the needs of the present without compromising the ability of future generations to meet their own needs
(Brundtland 1987)

Why attitudes and policies affect the use of renewable materials

For those of us who have successfully used renewable, natural and low impact materials in buildings, the benefits seem self-evident. These materials can be easily used, rarely give any problems and provide a better solution to building low energy, healthy buildings. However, this is not how most key actors within the construction industry and government appear to think. Official policies and personal prejudices coincide to make it very difficult for renewable materials to become accepted. In order to understand this, it is necessary to critically review current policy thinking on sustainable construction and energy efficiency.

Climate change and energy efficiency targets

Most governments have committed themselves to reducing fossil fuel energy usage and carbon emissions around the world. Climate change summits come and go and politicians wring their hands but in practice few targets are met and lifestyle demands in both Western developed countries and the emerging economies of Brazil, Russia, India and China (the BRIC countries) demand more and more energy and resources. The Brundtland principle, which remains one of the most elegant and simple statements of what needs to be done, came out of a United National Commission set up in 1983. Thirty years later it seems likely that we will still be compromising the needs of future generations. However, if we were to

Low Impact Building: Housing using Renewable Materials, First Edition. Tom Woolley.
© 2013 John Wiley & Sons, Ltd. Published 2013 by John Wiley & Sons, Ltd.

move towards greater use of renewable materials we would be nearer to achieving the Brundtland aspirations.

One of the biggest obstacles to this is the narrow view taken of the term 'carbon emissions'. The sloppy shorthand of referring to 'saving carbon' means that few people understand what this really means. Burning fossil fuel, or nearly anything else, to create energy leads to carbon dioxide (CO_2) emissions which many believe is a contributory cause of global warming. The debate about whether global warming is really taking place is not central to the Brundtland principle, which is much more focused on resource consumption as a whole. The fossil fuel we use to provide energy is just one of many crucial finite resources that we have to safeguard. As fuel and other natural resources are used up, life becomes more difficult, especially for poorer people, as has been elegantly explained by Heinberg (Heinberg 2007).

Many of the energy intensive processes that we currently depend on to create building materials and insulation, emit CO_2, but they also create many other forms of pollution that further damage natural habitats and resources.

What is carbon?

Talking about 'saving carbon' is almost meaningless because carbon is one of the most prolific elements on the planet. This careless and confusing use of language seems almost deliberate as it distracts people from behaving responsibly. Carbon is an essential part of life; about half the dry weight of all living organisms is carbon. Wood and soils, which hold most of the earth's carbon and mineral resources, such as calcium carbonate, also act as a carbon store. However, the word carbon is incorrectly used interchangeably with carbon dioxide (CO_2 is only about 0.04% of the earth's atmosphere). In the field of sustainable building the term 'low carbon' has become commonplace but it would be better to avoid it as it is misleading. However, it will inevitably creep into discussions in this book because it is so frequently used in the energy debate. 'Low impact' and 'low energy' are probably more useful terms.

The misunderstanding about carbon, low carbon and CO_2 is part of the problem of advocating the use of renewable materials. The argument about using resources more responsibly is still not easily understood by the general public or policymakers. Considerable funding has gone to a wide range of organisations investigating climate change, but much of this work focuses on climate impacts on nature. The climate change industry concentrates on what they call 'adaptation'. They try to predict what will happen to the climate in the future with dire warnings of floods, droughts and changing ecosystems. As governments are scared of the implications of these warnings, plenty of money is pumped into organisations that do little more than 'raise awareness' or enable 'public engagement' or create 'adaptation frameworks' (Adaption Scotland 2012). Real projects that change practice in terms of making buildings cooler (if it is getting hotter) or warmer (if it is getting colder) are thin on the ground in the climate change sector, though a handful of case studies offering superficial guidance about buildings can be found on the UKCIP website (UKCIP 2012).

Similarly, organisations tasked with promoting low energy solutions to future needs seem equally muddled about resource consumption issues. They talk of zero carbon targets even though the concept of zero carbon has little meaning. They are trying to talk about zero energy usage but this is an unrealistic aim. Human activity is always going to involve some energy use. The aim should be to minimise energy use and only to use responsible sources. As our energy comes from the sun, solar power wind and water and possibly geothermal are the most benign sources, but it is often forgotten that a considerable amount of energy is used to build wind turbines or to make solar panels. Ground source heat pumps need electricity to operate. Fossil fuel petrochemicals are stored solar energy resources that are being depleted and that should be saved for those human activities that are vital and cannot be achieved by other means.

Today we put significant levels of energy into keeping our buildings warm or cool and yet with good insulation and building design these could be reduced to very low levels, but it is unrealistic to say it could be zero. By talking of 'zero energy' and 'zero carbon', unrealistic targets act as a disincentive to people to even set out on the road to energy efficiency. However, if we reduced the energy consumption in all buildings to a modest and achievably low level, the savings would be enormous. This can be done in a safer, healthier and much more affordable way than is usually offered by the advocates of extreme solutions that claim to achieve zero energy use. Some of these unrealistic approaches are reviewed in Chapter 7, but the Pittenweem case study in the RHP serves as a useful example of where capital costs are doubled for a relatively small operational energy saving, above that achieved by low impact forms of construction.

Sustainable construction and energy policies

Government policies affecting the way we attempt to reduce energy consumption and make buildings more sustainable, are modified so frequently in the UK that it seems a futile task to attempt to review them all. Some of the work done in the UK also affects thinking in other countries around the world so policy mistakes may be repeated.

In northern temperate or cold climates the main preoccupation is to keep people warm but in large office developments and in warmer countries the need is for cooling or to protect buildings from overheating. Cooling can use even more energy than heating but progressive thinking in hotter countries has learned lessons from traditional and vernacular architecture using passive and natural systems (Roaf 2007).

Unfortunately as developing countries become more prosperous there is a tendency to adopt western building methods with concrete and lots of glass and this leads to greater energy consumption. In the UK, official thinking rarely learns lessons from traditional and vernacular architecture and is instead focused on 'modern methods of construction' (MMC) and legislation with a range of targets, most of which will never be met.

> Through the Climate Change Act, UK Government has committed itself to an ambitious 80% cut in greenhouse gas emissions by 2050 based on 1990 levels; and becomes the first country in the world to adopt a long-term legal framework for reducing emissions through a system of 'five year' carbon budgets, providing a clear pathway towards the 2050 target ...
>
> In relation to new build construction, tighter standards in the form of more stringent Building Regulations and enactments such as the Code for Sustainable Homes are major driving forces pushing the industry towards the goal of low carbon construction.
>
> (HM Government 2009)

It would take another book to explain the many failings of this and similar strategies. The UK Conservative Liberal Alliance Government has continued with many of the policies of the Labour Governments of 1997–2007 and 2007–2010 and political rhetoric always refers to cutting greenhouse gas emissions. One of the main planks in recent policy is the Code for Sustainable Homes, generally known in the business as 'The Code'.

UK Code for Sustainable Homes

The UK Government introduced the Code For Sustainable Homes in 2008, following a previous Eco-Homes rating system (Planning Portal 2012). The code has a range of standards 1–6. Codes 4–6 are very demanding and require expensive and, in the view of some, impractical resource consuming micro-renewable energy installations. Most of the projects in the Renewable House Programme (RHP) aimed for Code Level 4 and in order to achieve this spent considerably more on renewable energy and other mechanical equipment than they did on insulation. Construction materials and fabric insulation represent only a minor proportion of the code requirements and so it is still possible to comply with the Code with only modest insulation standards. The Code has been repeatedly criticised both from the green lobby, for its flaws, and from the mainstream house building industry who thought it was too costly. According to the Royal Academy of Engineering in their criticisms, the Code 'leads to unnecessarily expensive buildings' (RAE 2010).

Another criticism of the Code, from the Good Homes Alliance, is that it is far too prescriptive over fuels and heating systems (May 2008).

> So where developers are obliged to achieve CSH level 4, they are likely to specify electric heating, as the only practical, cost effective solution. ... the consequence of this for building fabric improvement ... means that the building will always be less energy efficient than an equivalent gas heated building, whatever the energy source.
>
> (GHA 2008)

Despite these criticisms, the Code is becoming increasingly adopted as a compulsory planning permission requirement. Initially the Code was only applied to public sector housing but the Welsh Assembly has made it a planning compliance requirement for all new housing, private or social. Northern Ireland, on the other hand, has scrapped it.

The danger of systems like the Code is that there is far too much focus on paper regulation and tick box exercises, and not enough on real changes to building practice and design. While the Code would have ensured that many new houses built in the past 5 years are more energy efficient than they might have been, the checks to see whether the energy efficiency works in practice are very poor. The Code is based on energy use prediction tools such as SAP and SBEM, which have attracted much criticism from professionals and the construction industry. The flaws in these tools are explored in more detail in Chapter 6.

> Senior figures in the house building industry have called for proposed changes to part L of the Building Regulations to be delayed. The Government is aiming to impose stricter carbon emissions targets on homes from October 2013 by changing the building regs. But industry experts have argued that the testing tool for energy performance known as SAP is too unreliable and flawed to proceed.
>
> Speaking at the Zero Carbon Hub annual conference, Home Builders Federation chief Stewart Baseley said: 'Given the demanding standards entailed in the zero carbon policy it is essential that we have a model of SAP that is fully and properly fit for purpose. Without this, builders are in an invidious position in having to design buildings they believe should deliver the necessary performance, but discovering that possibly through no fault of their own, actual performance is not what was predicted.'
>
> (Construction Enquirer 2012)

Institutions such as Leeds Metropolitan University Centre for the Built Environment have argued for some years that houses often fail to achieve in practice the energy efficiency standards that were predicted. A landmark research project at Stamford Brook in Cheshire made these problems very clear. However, the tick box tools of the Code and other measures have failed to take into account the results of this work (Leeds Met 2012).

Professor Chris Gorse and his colleagues at Leeds Metropolitan University say that these problems are largely due to poor construction practice and builders failing to understand the new technologies they have been given.

> In all the case studies the designer and builder failed to produce low carbon buildings specified ... buildings are not meeting their targets. The industry is attempting to develop low carbon buildings without a real understanding of the construction process and the performance of components used. ... the current approach of throwing buildings together and hoping they will work is producing sub-standard buildings.
>
> (Gorse 2010)

This is not entirely fair to builders because very often it is the design and construction system that is at fault, with MMC using synthetic,

along the way, all the better, *but these are second-step choices*' (emphasis added). (McCloud 2011b).

McCloud's view of using low impact materials as a second step choice is a typical view among those who advocate energy efficiency. There is an attitude that *insulation is insulation* what ever harm it does to the environment. Convincing professionals, the construction industry and the general public of the importance of embodied energy is not an easy task. For years many of the leading activists in the sustainable building and energy efficiency world have argued that saving energy through energy efficiency measured over the lifetime of a building is the only game in town. They are adamant that the energy used to make such savings is only a tiny fraction of the energy that can be saved in the long run. Thus they argue that embodied energy is not important and can be largely disregarded. However, the argument advanced in this book is that the most urgent and important task facing humanity is to reduce the energy and resources we use *now*, not in 50 or 60 years' time, and thus the *carbon spike* – the initial carbon expended – is almost more important than the operational energy in buildings. These are far from second step choices.

If, as is currently happening, we install insulation in buildings, using materials based on petrochemicals that are adding to CO_2 emissions, we are actually making the problem worse not better (the carbon spike problem). Other materials such as concrete and plastics also hugely increase embodied energy and CO_2 emissions. Using timber frame instead of masonry is another important way of reducing embodied energy.

Synthetic insulations, made from a range of petrochemical sources or material such as rock, use a lot of energy in manufacture. These materials are also combined with a range of binders and fire retardants, which in themselves are synthesised from fossil fuel resources and may create serious pollution problems across the planet. By ramping up the production of rock-based insulations, synthetic foams, glass fibre and other materials we are making a serious mistake. While these materials may save energy in the long term, they will also cause further damage, as few can be recycled and will end up as toxic landfill.

What is even worse is that there is some evidence that these materials are nothing like as effective and efficient as they are claimed to be. So-called 'high performance' insulations are not as high performing as many seem to think. Such materials can also have a bad effect on health and building durability, and some of them may not perform as well over the life of the building. Such criticisms would be pointless if we did not have much better alternatives, but the alternatives are available from natural, low impact and renewable materials which use much less energy to produce than conventional synthetic materials. Here is some evidence of how this is ignored by many 'experts' on sustainable housing and building.

In a Royal Institute of Chartered Surveyors (RICS) research publication written by Goodier and Wei Pan, in December 2010, setting out 'The Future of UK Housebuilding' the concept of energy efficiency is expounded at great length, but embodied energy is not mentioned at all – *not one single reference*. Interestingly this report also says nothing about natural and renewable materials, indeed the only innovative material mentioned is one using recycled plastic. (Goodier 2010).

Instead Goodier and his colleague Wei Pan are excited about recent high-tech innovations that are completely unrealistic and unproven in terms of cost or practical use in mainstream construction; at the same time, they completely ignore the major advances in achievable renewable low impact materials. '…biomimetics will introduce building materials that mimic and learn from nature, and limits of nanotechnology know no bounds'. (Goodier 2010)

How embodied energy is discounted

The ground rules for ignoring – or at least discounting the importance of – embodied energy were set out in a Sustainable Housing Publication in 1999, quoted at length here as it sets out the fallacy very clearly. (Sustainable Housing gave permission to reproduce two diagrams from this document.)

> As a general rule, the embodied energy of a given building will be overtaken by the energy in use fairly early in the building's life. For example, the Building Research Establishment (BRE) estimated in 1991 that, for a typical 3-bed detached house, *energy in use would overtake embodied energy in a period of 2–5 years*. Assuming the house had a life of 60 years before requiring major refurbishment (which is the minimum stipulated for new build by the Housing Corporation), the energy in use would exceed the embodied energy by 12–30 times.
>
> Diagram 1 (Figure 5.1) illustrates this and shows that, even with the maximum 5-year 'overtaking time' and a life of only 60 years, embodied energy accounts for only about 10% of the lifetime energy use of the building. If the overtaking time were lower and the lifetime of the house a more typical 100 years, then energy in use would be 40–50 times more significant than embodied energy (i.e. embodied energy would account for only 2–2.5% of total energy consumption). (Figure 5.2)
>
> The obvious conclusion from this example is that, *in minimising energy consumption over the lifetime of a building, reducing energy in use is far more effective than minimising embodied energy.* (emphasis added)

The authors of this publication do go on to state that embodied energy in energy efficient houses would be more significant in proportion to lifetime energy costs but that this assumption is based on unpublished 'research' from the Building Research Establishment. This 'unpublished research', like much other work done at the BRE, has not been published in proper refereed scientific journals, so it cannot be challenged or scrutinised. These diagrams entirely ignore the carbon spike problem. In the Finnish research the carbon spike can be seen at the beginning of the graph (Figure 5.3) and this energy use is not compensated for by any savings in operational energy.

Many experts have continued to repeat the energy-in-use mantra that lifetime energy is more significant than embodied energy, and this seems to have received greater strength in recent years through the enthusiasm in the UK and USA for the German passiv haus movement. The UK 'Sustainable

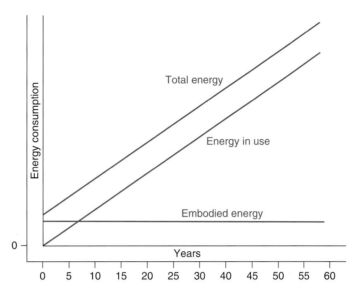

Figure 5.1 Energy consumption for a typical three-bedroom house (Sustainable Homes)

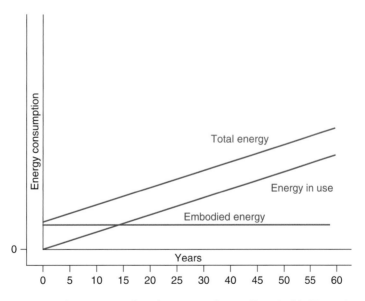

Figure 5.2 Energy Consumption for a low energy house (Sustainable Homes)

Building Association' (AECB), once a champion of low impact construction methods, now seems largely preoccupied with energy in use and has abandoned its holistic roots. The acronym AECB was based on the name of the organisation, the 'Association for Environmentally Conscious Building', but they have now dropped the words environmentally conscious, as much of what they now advocate would be hard to defend as environmentally *conscious or responsible*. Of course it is perfectly possible to build a 'passiv haus' using natural and low impact materials, and examples are shown in Chapter 7.

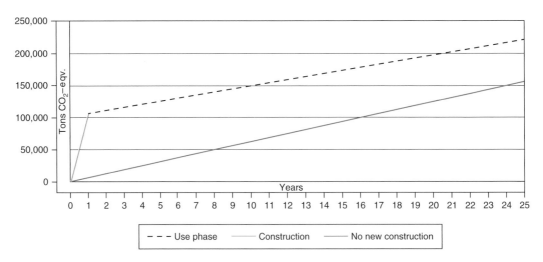

Figure 5.3 Total emissions of the residential area during the 25 year lifecycle showing the carbon spike (from Heinonen et al 2011)

At the 2011 AECB conference, in Nottingham, a draft policy document 'Less is More' was presented by Simmonds and Olivier. Olivier has been an important and highly influential advocate of energy efficiency for many years both in the UK and internationally. However, through his company, Energy Advisory Associates, he has been a critic of the concept of breathing walls (a crucial issue for natural materials discussed later) (Olivier 1999). In the 2011 AECB 'Less is More' presentation (AECB 2012), Olivier and Simmonds entirely ignored the issue of embodied energy; indeed, they barely touched on insulation, building fabric and materials.

Other key figures have a similar view. When giving evidence to the House of Lords in 2005 about *energy efficient buildings*, Oreszczyn and Lowe ignored the issue of materials or embodied energy. The word insulation only appears once in the text as they appear to take the line that energy efficiency is about building services (Oreszczyn 2005).

Another AECB stalwart, Willoughby, in a presentation also titled 'Less is More', given at the 2010 AECB conference, ignores embodied energy and says almost nothing about fabric insulation and materials. Rickaby, who is one of the main advisors on sustainable building to the RIBA, and Willoughby produced Booklet 8 of Climate Change Toolkit for the RIBA. Even though this is titled '*Whole Life* Assessment for Low Carbon Design' (my emphasis) the word insulation only appears twice in its 20 pages. While this document does at least mention the issue of embodied energy talking about embodied CO_2 in the production and transportation of materials, they do not suggest that this could be reduced by using low impact materials. The guidance they give to architects and designers is very confusing on this issue.

Despite uncertainties, the broad distinctions between high- and low-embodied emissions design can be established from available data. An identical design built in different ways in different places will have varying embodied CO_2 emissions, due to factors such as the sourcing of materials and construction methods that are usually seen as outside the designer's control but over which the designer can have significant influence. You should base your decision-making on the best available data about embodied emissions and not give up because of data uncertainties.

(RIBA undated)

Ironically the RIBA Toolkit Booklet 8 uses a picture on its cover of a hemp-crete housing scheme at Elmswell in Suffolk without giving any details of the highly innovative and low impact nature of this project. They admit that 'The affordable housing project combines sustainable strategies for construction, lifetime energy use and landscape' but they do not mention hemp or the use of renewable or low impact materials in the toolkit, leaving the impression that renewable materials are confined to high cost and labour intensive methods such as *thatching*, not something that would realistically be considered for main-stream projects.

For example, elements with large quantities of CO_2-intensive but cheap materials, like cement, have high CO_2 emissions but low cost; whereas elements that are labour-intensive and use renewable materials, like thatching, have low CO_2 emissions but high cost.

(RIBA undated)

The RIBA toolkit refers to available data on embodied emissions. Their source of data on embodied energy is the ICE database published by Bath University as discussed in Chapter 1. The data it contains has not necessarily been independently verified and, in many cases, has been drawn from information published by commercial companies who have a vested interest in promoting their materials (Bath 2012).

David Eisenberg, a well-respected authority on green building in the USA has written

as a long time proponent of the importance of embodied energy here in the US, ... *it was the energy efficiency folks who dismissed the importance of embodied energy* continually until the last few years, not those of us involved in greening the built environment. Their argument was that if you compared operating and embodied energy, you would see that embodied energy was insignificant. My argument was that we were talking about a significant number dwarfed by a huge number, but the size of the embodied energy did not mean that the embodied energy was not important, just that it was made to look insignificant by the size of the operating energy. (emphasis added)

(Eisenberg 2011)

It is hard to understand why campaigners and academics, who discount embodied energy, do not appreciate that in order to reduce emissions we have to do so in all areas of activity, not just how we heat and light our buildings. They seem complacent about the damage being done to the environment by the manufacturers of energy intensive insulation materials and renewable energy equipment even though this will produce CO_2 emissions – and other pollution and damage – much more quickly than in houses that are run using too much gas or oil over the next 60 years. However, the tide is turning, with interest in embodied energy coming from an unexpected quarter, the commercial property development world.

Carbon footprinting

An important study published by the RICS, based on work by Sturgis Associates (RICS 2010) sets out a basis for working out the carbon footprint of buildings and the carbon impact of building works. Sturgis make a strong case for the reuse and conversion of existing buildings in their advice to commercial developers. In the past, developers would tend to demolish old buildings and build anew as they could achieve higher rentals, but Sturgis put forward convincing arguments based on saving money due to the value of reducing the embodied energy and thus CO_2 emissions. They illustrate this with real life case studies based on commercial office development projects and they argue that embodied energy can be as high as the lifetime energy consumption of energy efficient buildings.

> In the case of office buildings, currently some 40–50% of the whole life carbon costs of a typical new development will be due to embodied carbon emissions. This proportion is set to increase due to legislation requiring operational carbon emissions to be reduced to zero by 2019. There is, however, a danger that this pressure will have the unintended consequence of adversely affecting embodied emissions, by requiring the use of increasingly carbon-intensive solutions, the closer we get to zero operational carbon emissions. Understanding the relationship between the underlying embodied and the operational carbon emissions is essential when allocating any resources to reducing emissions overall, as it is crucial to ensure that the physical measures taken to reduce operational carbon usage use less carbon than they save. In addition, from a purely financial point of view, reducing embodied emissions through design can be more effective than reducing operational emissions.
>
> (RICS 2010)

Sturgis provides a 'carbon profiling' service so that clients can make a holistic assessment of their buildings and proposals, taking into account all CO_2 emissions. It is ironic that such a sensible and logical appraisal of the importance of embodied energy should be driven by commercial pressures to save money on large office buildings, whereas 'green' campaigners remain fixated on operational energy issues.

Thus the mainstream world of commercial office development has recognised the importance of embodied energy as it makes good financial sense as well as having environmental benefits. Companies can genuinely claim in their corporate social responsibility statements that they are reducing their carbon footprint by reuse and renovation as well as by using lower impact materials. Carbon footprinting remains in its infancy, however, and there are no agreed methodologies or standards. Data used in the calculations such as about embodied energy from LCAs and EPDS may be flawed, and this can undermine the credibility of the footprint analysis.

However, the inherent holistic nature of carbon footprinting is valuable and should be used more widely. It will lead to an acceptance that embodied energy and the environmental impact of materials used to construct buildings is just as important as operational energy. The failure of advocates of energy efficiency in housing and building is criticised by De Selincourt who describes Embodied Energy as a 'ticking time bomb'. She explains that

> It is cumulative carbon dioxide emissions, over time, that drive climate change. If we can postpone emissions, we reduce the time the CO_2 is in the atmosphere, and therefore reduce the harm done. If, as is widely believed, we are in the last desperate window of opportunity to fend off a climate change 'tipping point' it is especially important to reduce emissions in the present time – which, of course, is where embodied emissions are concentrated.
>
> (De Selincourt 2012)

Passive design approaches

A key issue in this debate is to reclaim the word *passive*. This has been hijacked by the passiv haus industry, even though passive houses require a highly *active* mechanical ventilation and heat recovery system and other mechanical systems. In the early days of eco design, the value of passive solar gain was well understood, but this has been increasingly overlooked. Instead, embodied energy costs are being pushed up in the pursuit of reduced operational energy, through the growing dependence on technological solutions. Commercial pressure on government to subsidise renewable energy equipment, and the growing use of mechanical ventilation measures, is distorting our understanding of how to achieve low impact solutions. The use of passive measures seems to be slipping out of fashion even though these can be much more effective and use far less energy to produce and implement. Indeed, the increasing use of expensive photovoltaic panels on flat roofs and even north facing roofs, and badly placed solar shading, indicates a lack of understanding of even the most basic principles.

At one time, passive design was well understood by eco designers. Using solar gain, with adequate shading and thermal mass together with simple natural ventilation and passive stack solutions has been thrown aside in favour of 'techy' approaches. There are many excellent guides to passive solar heating and cooling (e.g. Chiras 2002) and these measures can be used effectively with natural and low impact materials.

Do natural and renewable materials have lower embodied energy?

If carbon counting, profiling and embodied energy are to become more important, this may give an advantage to natural and renewable materials. It seems self evident that building materials like timber, timber composites, hemp, straw and sheep's wool will use less energy in manufacture as there is far less processing and much lower use of petrochemical resources. Buildings constructed mainly from concrete, steel, synthetic insulations and plastic materials will have higher embodied energy. However, just as there are no zero carbon buildings, hardly any building materials – even natural ones – are zero carbon. Anyone who tells you they have a zero carbon building or product is probably being disingenuous.

Probably the lowest impact is for buildings that use materials harvested on site. A cob house built with mud dug up on the site, thatch and straw from a nearby field, and wood from local forest thinnings uses almost no energy, only the labour of the builders. There are good example of such buildings (Woolley 2006) and this can be a viable and reasonable way to build, though limited to self-builders in the countryside. There are many current advocates and practitioners (mudandwood 2012) using natural materials that can be found locally. However, in British Columbia, local materials are considered as coming from within 100 miles! (Boyer 2012).

Self builders of unconventional houses have run into problems with planning permission, though the Welsh Government has recognised the value of such 'low impact development' (LID) which has made it possible for people who want to live an ecological life style by running self-sufficient small holdings, to get planning permission for developments that would not normally be allowed (Wales 2012). However, there have been more further obstacles with gaining building regulations approval such as at the Lammas Project, (Dale 2011).

Natural and renewable materials that are produced for mainstream construction do use some energy to produce and can rarely be considered as local materials. Hemp requires farm machinery to sow and reap, machines are used to separate the hemp fibre from the shiv. Hemp is transported from farm to processing factory and may even do a second trip for manufacturing into insulation quilt. Wood fibre products may use local timber but it may still be transported some distance. Sheep's wool must travel from the farm to a processing factory and for manufacturing. All materials then involve packaging and transportation to builders' merchants or direct to site. Straw may be sourced locally but not necessarily. It is important to be honest that these materials have some embodied energy from transport in particular.

In order to determine the embodied energy of any product a careful analysis must be done. Energy used from cradle to cradle or cradle to gate (these are known as boundary conditions) can be calculated, and often figures are based on different boundary conditions. In an ideal environmentally responsible world this would be a legal requirement for all products, published on the packaging.

In practice most published figures of embodied energy are 'guestimates', based on assumptions or derived from figures published by manufacturers, which have not been independently verified. You are strongly advised to treat any published figures with a pinch of salt whether for natural or synthetic materials. Generic figures can be highly misleading as flax insulation

Table 5.1 Typical but questionable embodied energy figures

Examples of embodied energy figures Based on Inventory of Carbon and Energy (ICE) 2011		
Materials	Embodied energy MJ/kg	Embodied carbon kgCO$_2$/kg
aggregates	0.083	0.0048
aluminium (general)	155	8.24
Portland cement	5.50	0.93
glasswool	28	1.54
rock wool	16.8	1.05
wool recycled	20.9	NA
flax	33.5	1.7
straw	0.24	0.01
polyurethane foam rigid insulation	101.5	3.48

produced in France may use more energy than that used in Denmark or Holland. An environmental analysis of a product made in Switzerland may have assumed high energy costs as Switzerland mainly uses nuclear power, whereas in reality the energy was supplied from a wood waste CHP plant on site.

In a detailed analysis of the embodied energy of a concrete paving slab, everything was counted including how much petrol was used by their workers driving out at lunchtime to get their sandwiches! (Richardson 2009). It can also be misleading to compare embodied energy in terms of figures published per kilogram, such as in Table 5.1. A lightweight insulation material may appear to have a high embodied energy but when multiplied by the weight used, the total impact is much less than a heavyweight material that might have a lower embodied energy. Yet there is little doubt that professionals often make such simplistic comparisons.

Such figures can also seem baffling when looked at in isolation. The quarry extraction and crushing of aggregates uses far more energy than the harvesting and baling of straw, but if it is assumed that a great deal of synthetic fertiliser had been used, this can push up the figure depending on who is making the calculation. Such figures are really only useful for general comparisons.

The Bath ICE database is exhaustively referenced, so in theory it is possible to trace the sources of information, but it is unlikely that most users of the database will do this. Thus, for example, they are unlikely to see the flaws in the 2004 analysis of flax insulation that gives a distortedly high figure for flax as discussed in Chapter 1 (Schmidt, 2004). A more realistic comparison of figures can be seen in Table 5.2 (Allen 2004). It was worrying to find that some of the references for the source of information in the ICE database are from the Green Building Handbook (Woolley and Kimmins 1997). This should not be regarded as an authoritative source on embodied energy as this information was in itself

Table 5.2 Embodied energy of different building elements derived from various sources

Building element	embodied energy (GJ)*
Walls	
fired brick/block and mineral wool	65.8
straw bale	7.9
hemp/lime	12.6
Insulation	
fibreglass	23.52
mineral wool	14.7
hemp/flax	3.54
wool	3.63
Flooring	
vinyl floor	1.36
linoleum	1.173

*One problem in comparing embodied energy data is a lack of consistency in how figures are expressed. Figures may show MJ/m^3 or per m^2, or in this case gigajoules. Thus such a list is only useful for comparison purposes.
Source: Allen 2004

derived from other secondary sources, and many years ago, when such information was difficult to obtain and to check. On the other hand, some of the other sources used by ICE are original thorough measurements of energy but invariably carried out by consultants on behalf of manufacturers and trade associations. Much care should be taken to ensure that you can access original data and not simply following a circular process where the few experts in the field simply reference each other's papers and books.

We have a long way to go before we can provide firm and independently certified data on embodied energy and this, of course, provides plenty of ammunition for those who are only concerned with operational energy, as they argue that embodied energy information is not reliable. In the meantime, we have to use common sense and accept that natural and renewable materials by and large have a lower environmental carbon impact than synthetic and petrochemical materials.

Carbon sequestration in timber

A further factor to take into account when unravelling the discussion of 'carbon' is that of sequestration. In addition to generally having a lower CO_2 footprint, most natural bio-based materials are also able to lock up CO_2 as they have absorbed CO_2 when growing. Plants and trees absorb CO_2 from the atmosphere and convert it into oxygen, a vital process for the

Table 5.3 Carbon and carbon dioxide equivalent in renewable building materials

Material	Carbon content (%)	Carbon dioxide equivalent (kgCO$_2$e/kg)
hemp	46	1.68
straw	40	1.46
recycled paper	43	1.57
sheep's wool	42	1.53

Source: Murphy 2008

survival of humanity. They then store this CO$_2$ in their fabric and some people argue that this stored carbon can be counted against any embodied energy when making a holistic carbon footprint calculation.

The timber and timber frame industry have long made this claim and there is a small body of scientific and academic literature to back up the sequestration argument. Much less data is available on hemp, straw, flax etc. but these materials may sequester even more than timber. (Table 5.3 – Murphy 2008).

In Canada and the USA considerable research has been done by the international Consortium for Research on Renewable Industrial Materials (CORRIM 2012) to track the life cycle of timber and timber products in construction. They have argued that the use of timber construction can lead to 'carbon negative' structures.

> …the carbon stored in wood products is substantially greater than the emissions from their initial manufacture. That surplus offsets much of the emissions from the nonwood products that are used along with wood in the construction in typical residential structures. Designs that use more wood should be able to offset all the emissions from the nonwood products that may be required, resulting in 'carbon negative' structures.
>
> (Lippke 2010)

Wood transport issues

The embodied energy of timber is also affected by the amount that is imported from North America, Scandinavia and the Baltic countries. There has been a small move towards the use of local timber but there is a prejudice in the UK construction industry that UK and Irish timber is not as good, because much of it was originally planted for paper pulp production. UK government support for biomass heating is also putting at risk all woodland if it is to be chopped down for burning. Some have suggested that to meet UK biomass targets would involve clear felling much UK forest over the next few years, and campaigns against this have become prominent (Stop Burning 2012). Also, for many years illegally logged hardwood has come from tropical rain forests. In 2005, the UK was the worst offender in Europe (Carbon Info 2012).

Carbon sequestration in hemp and hempcrete

According to Pritchett of Lime Technology, supplier of the Tradical Hemcrete products to several of the case study projects, in various conference presentations (Pritchett 2011), hemp absorbs 1.7 times its dry weight of CO_2 and converts it to plant material. He argues that a typical cavity wall using brick and block and mineral wool insulation emits 216 kg per m^2 (of wall) whereas a 300 mm thick Hemcrete wall emits *minus* 31 kg per m^2 (i.e. carbon negative). Thus the ability of hemp to absorb CO_2 offsets the CO_2 emissions from burning the lime and cement that makes up the lime binder and plasters used in Hemcrete walls.

There has been much discussion about the use of 'carbon sinks' as a way of helping to reduce global warming. This usually involves hair-brained, massively expensive ideas such as geo-engineering projects, pumping CO_2 underground, or into microorganisms in the sea. The Inter Governmental Panel on Climate Change (IPCC 2012) has given much consideration to such schemes (Our Climate 2012). However, a much simpler solution would be to build buildings out of bio-based materials. The term carbon negative does not have a very positive ring to it and thus does not provide a useful slogan for promoting renewable materials, but buildings as a carbon sink might be more easily understood. Carfrae and De Wilde argue that 40% of all CO_2 emitted in creating a standard low energy house is tied up in conventional materials but with a strawbale house that is reduced to just 5% (Carfrae 2011). Alcorn and Donn argue that straw and timber can sequester carbon and thus reduce carbon emissions more effectively than renewable energy.

> Strawbale and timber absorptions (1,230 kg) were almost the same as the total emission-reductions from applied energy-minimising technologies (1,277 kg), excluding site-specific wind generation. This is about half of total emissions from a standard house. The CO_2-e reductions from using strawbale and timber represent actual sequestration. The CO_2-e reductions from reduced operating energy, however, only represent avoided emissions from the national grid.
>
> (Alcorn 2010)

Various figures can be found about the sequestration in hemp and hemp concrete. The amount of 'carbon' emitted in hemp production ranges from 2.5 to 3.8 MJ/kg. This figure is high as currently there is a lot of transport involved in shipping hemp around. If it is grown and processed locally this figure will be less. When mixing hemp with lime to make hempcrete, lime binders use between 4.5 MJ/kg and 5.3 MJ/kg in production. Thus a hempcrete wall can be seen as using about 8 MJ/kg of energy. However, hemp also absorbs carbon dioxide in the atmosphere during growth, and can store carbon within the construction element. According to one study (Pervais 2003), 325 kg of CO_2 is stored in one tonne of dried hemp. Lime Technology claims that 110 kg of CO_2 is sequestrated in each cubic metre of hemp lime construction when spray applied, and that shuttered and cast hemp lime sequestrates up to 165 kg of CO_2 per m^3, depending on the level of compaction during construction. This estimate is lower than Pervais as it takes account of the CO_2 emitted when producing lime. Therefore the overall composite is claimed to be carbon negative (Lime Technology 2007).

Further work is required to standardise what has become known as 'carbon counting'. IPCC Guidelines for National Greenhouse Gas Inventories (IPCC 2006) and ISO 14047 are relevant here. Both Robson (2010) and Sadler (2011) have begun the process of producing credible calculations and they have demonstrated that substantial amounts of CO_2 can be sequestered in new house building, simply from timber frame construction (without including other bio-based materials such as hemp). This could represent 50% of the 'carbon' emissions savings as part of UK government targets if all construction used renewable materials.

The Green Deal

Much of the discussion so far has focused on new build construction but it is recognised that the renovation of retrofitting of existing buildings is also crucial to save energy. UK government policy about so-called zero energy housing has been focused on building services and micro-renewable energy generation, but retrofitting existing houses and buildings should create a huge opportunity for renewable and natural insulation materials as they can be much more effective in renovation than many synthetic products. However, this has yet to be recognised and is certainly not reflected in official policies. Many of the current trials and experiments on retrofitting have been based on using synthetic products, which are not likely to be as effective as natural and renewable materials. An experiment in retrofitting buildings at the Building Research Establishment, where a Victorian stable block has been converted using a range of synthetic foam insulation products from BASF ('The Chemical Company') and others, is hardly a model of the best way forward (BASF 2012).

At the time of writing, a much debated proposal to save energy in housing in the UK is the Green Deal (Carrington 2011) through which private financial institutions will be asked to give loans to householders to encourage them to insulate their houses. Companies including British Gas, Carillion, EDF Energy, Goldman Sachs, HSBC, Kingfisher, Lloyds Bank and a number of supermarkets were expected to take part. Several organisations who were expected to back the Green Deal pulled out once details were confirmed (Cuff 2012). The Green Deal has been criticised by organisations such as WWF and the National Insulation Association because the incentives for the scheme are poorly worked out – 'Industry warns of rocky road to Green Deal success' (Business Green 2012). Conservative politicians even mounted a campaign to ditch their own party's policy due to rather bizarre right wing views that climate change policies are unnecessary (Harvey 2012).

The Green Deal is aimed at retrofitting existing houses but the financial and energy organisations tasked with carrying this out do not necessarily have the expertise to ensure that the right insulation is used in the right way. The programme is based on the assumption that fitting insulation to existing buildings is a straightforward task but that is far from being so. Wrongly applied insulation can damage building fabric and lead to dampness, condensation and even building failures. The Green Deal will not provide expert professional advice to householders though efforts are being made to establish training centres.

Natural and renewable materials could have a big part to play in renovation but this does not appear to be on the Green Deal agenda and the only reference available on the DECC Green Deal website to materials says:

> The products actually installed in the property must meet health and safety and performance standards referred to in a Green Deal Code of Practice (to be consulted on). DECC will work with stakeholders to investigate *which new products could be on the horizon* and what processes and innovations are driving up the performance of measures and driving down costs. (emphasis added)
>
> (DECC 2011)

Natural and renewable materials are currently available and in use rather than being 'on the horizon' but the valuable contribution they might make to retrofitting is not referred to in the Green Deal. Instead official policies promote the use of synthetic and petrochemical based products.

Official promotion of synthetic insulations

Many official bodies tend to refer to all insulation materials as though they were the same and do the same job: 'Insulation is insulation'. In fact certain insulations are inappropriate for certain uses and are frequently wrongly applied. Non-breathable polyurethane foam is sprayed onto breathable walls, thus trapping dampness, for instance. Mineral fibre products are used in situations where it can become damp and may not function as effectively.

Official bodies also give the impression that only main brand insulation materials are acceptable for regulation purposes. A leaflet on the website of Wigan Council Building Control that lists 'acceptable insulation materials' is typical of the kind of information provided by official bodies. Wigan Council claimed that this guidance was issued by the UK-wide body Local Authority Building Control (LABC) but LABC denied this when contacted. However, similar guidance can be found on other local authority building control websites (Table 5.4 – Wigan 2012).

It is somewhat surprising that a public sector body like Wigan Council should promote products by their trade name such as *Kingspan, Kooltherm, Celotex GA 3080Z, Jabfloor 70* and *Rocksilk*. They do say in very small letters at the bottom of the leaflet that 'other acceptable products and methods of construction are available', but the vast majority of designers and specifiers and members of the public would assume that they have to use the proprietary products named in the guidance in order to comply easily

require a relatively small proportion of agricultural land to grow the hemp. Hemp Technology argue that if industry were to build 200,000 new houses in the UK it would still only require 250,000 hectares of land on which to grow the hemp. This is about 5% of all arable land (Hemp Technology 2012). In any case only about 28 per cent of the 17.5 million hectares used for agriculture in the UK is allocated to arable crops (nearly 5 million hectares), whereas 67 per cent is grassland (Angus 2009).

Sheep's wool comes from shearing sheep and the meat from the sheep is also a food source, unaffected by using the material in buildings. Most sheep also use rough upland pasture, so do not threaten other agricultural production. Timber for construction has a valuable role to play in producing oxygen from CO_2 and providing important natural habitats. If sustainably managed, forestry for construction is a sustainable activity (FSC 2012). Many timber construction products are also by-products from other forestry activity. Thus bio-based materials do not present a threat to food production in the UK and would be unlikely to do so in many other countries.

Transport and localism

Another criticism of bio-based materials is the distance travelled by the materials from farm to processing factory and manufacture. This is a real problem as it increases the embodied energy of natural and renewable materials. For instance, as there has been only one main processing plant for hemp in the UK, in Halesworth, Suffolk, hemp does travel quite a distance though smaller processing plants are now emerging in Yorkshire and other places.

It does not make a lot of environmental sense for bales of bulky plant material to be shipped around Europe but this is what currently happens. Processing in France, Poland and elsewhere means that materials are moved from one country to another. Lightweight insulation materials are even more bulky and require large containers. Many of the wood and hemp based insulation materials and board products are currently produced in Austria, France, Switzerland or Slovakia. The reason for this is that the market is very small and thus it is hard to attract investment for large or even small processing plants in every region. If the benefits of renewable materials were supported by government policy and the advocates of energy efficiency, and if the manufacturers of synthetic petrochemical materials were forced to pay the true environmental costs, then there would be greater demand, and local production would be more viable and worthwhile.

Most UK sheep's wool has traditionally been processed in the Bradford area but there are also factories in North Wales and Devon. The distributors of natural materials are not always up front about where their materials are actually coming from as everyone wants to think that they are using local materials. The British Wool Marketing Board controls the UK wool market (British Wool 2012) and they operate a central marketing system for wool. Sheepwool Insulation in the English West Midlands and Wicklow in Ireland

(Sheepwool Insulation 2012) have done a good job promoting the use of this product in Ireland and the UK but the product is currently made in Austria. The National Trust in England and Wales has used sheep's wool insulation for farms in North Wales but, instead of using wool insulation sourced and made in Wales, a few miles away they have used a product, imported from Austria! When contacted, the National Trust explained that they had bought Welsh wool insulation in other projects and were not aware that the Irish product came from Austria.

Coleshill is one of a number of National Trust estates to install sheep wool insulation. Other estates include 51 farms and 38 cottages on the National Trust's Ysbyty Ifan Estate near Betws-y-Coed in North Wales and 36 properties at the village of Wallington in Northumberland. In Wales, the properties have been insulated with 3,000 m² of sheep's wool with tenants expecting to see a saving of up to 20 per cent in their energy consumption as a result of the new insulation. The idea has been especially welcomed by the sheep farmers who live on the estate, who see a major benefit in the new market emerging for wool products, and a further 38 farms in south Wales are now to be installed with 1,000 m² of wool.

(Green England 2012)

Cost

There are also many people and organisations that assume that natural and renewable materials must be more expensive and therefore dismiss them out of hand, often without seeking quotations. If synthetic petro-chemical products were to pay the real environmental costs of their production, based on 'full cost accounting', then natural and renewable materials would always win on cost grounds (Bebbington 2011). Sadly natural and renewable construction materials can be seen as part of a niche market and many companies exploit the fact that customers are willing to pay more in much the same way as organic foods are priced more highly. However, if the consumption of natural and renewable materials grows to the volumes of synthetic material, the unit cost will most certainly reduce. Another cost factor is that many natural and renewable materials are more expensive in the UK as they are imported from other countries in mainland Europe and if production increases in the UK this will bring costs down.

A further factor in terms of cost perception is that many specifiers look at alternative materials in terms of direct substitution. Sheep's wool for mineral fibre, hempcrete for polystyrene or wood fibre for polyurethane. This is a false comparison as the natural renewable materials can offer much more in terms of building performance and buildability and even replace other materials which are no longer necessary. These factors may not be considered by estimators. Unfortunately, the RHP may leave some people with the impression that natural renewable materials will only be used if there is a grant or subsidy. In fact, the majority of subsidy in the case study projects, went on renewable energy equipment and the cost of the insulation materials was not substantially greater than if synthetic manmade materials had been used!

References

AECB http://www.aecb.net/conference2011.php (viewed 3.2.12)

Adaption Scotland, http://www.adaptationscotland.org.uk/4/5/0/Projects.aspx (viewed 28.2.12)

Alcorn, A. and Donn, M. 'Life cycle potential of strawbale and timber for carbon sequestration in house construction', Second International Conference on Sustainable Construction Materials (June 2010) Ancona, Italy

Allen, P.K. (2004) 'Home Grown Houses: The potential for large-scale production of renewable construction materials from crops grown in the UK, and possible impacts', The 21st Conference on Passive and Low Energy Architecture. Eindhoven, The Netherlands, 19–22 September 2004

Angus, A., Burgess, P.J., Morris, J. and Lingard ,J. (2009) 'Agriculture and land use: Demand for and supply of agricultural commodities, characteristics of the farming and food industries, and implications for land use in the UK'. *Land Use Policy 26S* 2009 S230–S242

BASF 2012 www.basf.co.uk/.../DBD937_BASF_Victoria_Terrace_HR.pdf (viewed 13.4.12)

Bebbington, J., Gray, R. and Hibbit, C., (2001), *Full Cost Accounting: an Agenda for Action.* Certified Accountants Educational Trust 2001

Boyer, M., http://www.good.is/post/100-mile-houses-expands-the-locavore-movement-from-food-to-architecture/ (viewed 10.2.12)

British Wool Marketing Board, www.britishwool.org.uk (viewed 3.5.12)

Brundtland (1987) *The Report of the Brundtland Commission, Our Common Future,* Oxford University Press

Bullock, S., Childs, M. and Picken, M. (2009) *A Dangerous Distraction: Why Carbon Offsetting is Failing the Climate and People: The Evidence.* Friends of the Earth, London, June 2009

Business Green, http://www.businessgreen.com/bg/news/2118394/industry-warns-rocky-road-green-deal-success (viewed 28.2.12)

Carbon Info (2012) http://www.carbon-info.org/carboninfo_083.htm (viewed 27.3.12)

Carfrae, J. and Dewilde, P. (2011), 'The Leechwell Garden House: a passive solar dwelling built from renewable materials' PLEA Conference, Brussels 2011

Carrington D. (2011) 'Firms unite to make homes energy efficient' *The Guardian* 3.10.11 p. 23

Chiras D.D. (2002) *The Solar House: Passive Heating and Cooling.* Chelsea Green Publishing Vancouver

Construction Enquirer (2012) http://www.constructionenquirer.com/2012/02/03/house-building-industry-calls-for-revised-part-l-delay/ (viewed 7.2.12)

CORRIM (2012) Consortium for Research on Renewable Industrial Materials http://www.corrim.org (viewed 28.2.12)

Cuff, M. (2012) 'M&S and Tesco missing from green deal list' *The Guardian* Thursday 5 April 2012 p. 17

Dale, S. and Saville, J. (2011) 'The compatibility of building regulations with projects under new low impact development and one planet development planning policies: critical and urgent problems and the need for a workable solution' unpublished paper (2011)

DCLG (March 2012) National Planning Policy Framework

Davis, I. and Harvey, V. (2008) 'Zero carbon: what does it mean to homeowners and house builders?' NHBC NF9 (2008)

De Selincourt, K. (2012) 'Embodied Energy – A ticking time bomb?' *Green Building Magazine*, Spring 2012 pp44–48

DECC (2011) What measures does the Green Deal cover? July 2011 www.decc.gov.uk/../decc/../green_deal/1734-what-measures-does-the-green_deal_cover. (viewed 3.8.12)

Eisenberg, D. (2011) private correspondence through the Global Straw Bale Network (GSBN) Development Centre for Appropriate Technology Tucson Arizona http://www.dcat.net/resources/index.php

FSC (2012) http://www.fsc-uk.org/ (viewed 13.1.12)

GHA Position Paper March (2008) http://www.goodhomes.org.uk/library_files/17 (viewed 25.3.12)

Goodier, C. and Wei Pan (2010) 'The future of UK housebuilding' RICS Research Paper, Royal Institute of Chartered Surveyors, London (October 2010)

Gorse, C., Johnston, D. and Miles-Shenton, D. (2010) 'Low Carbon Housing – Failings in Construction practice and attention to Detail'. UCLan Detail Design in Architecture 9 4–5 November 2010

Green England (2012) http://www.green-england.co.uk/site/news?id=Wallace__Gromit_insulation_idea_gives_welcome_at_National_Trust_village_ (viewed 11.5.12)

Harvey, F. (2012) 'Climate of extremes bedevils Tories' green policy' *The Guardian* 16 April 2012

Heinberg, Richard (2007) Peak Everything New Society Publishers

Heinonen, J., Säynäjoki, A. and Junnila, S. (2011) 'A Longitudinal Study on the Carbon Emissions of a New Residential Development'. *Sustainability* 3, 1170–1189 2011

Hemp Technology, www.hemptechnology.co.uk/environment.htm (viewed 7.3.12)

HM Government (2009) in association with Forum for Strategic Construction Strategy. Sustainable Construction Progress Report, September 2009. Crown Copyright./2 K/9/09/NP URN 09/1244

IPCC (2006) http://www.ipcc-nggip.iges.or.jp/public/2006gl/index.html (viewed 13.2.12)

IPPC (2012) http://www.ipcc.ch/ipccreports/tar/wg3/index.php?idp=25 (viewed 13.2.12)

Leeds Metropolitan University http://www.leedsmet.ac.uk/as/cebe/projects/stamford/ (viewed 28.2.12)

Lime Technology (2007) *Tradical Hemcrete Information Pack.* http://www.limetechnology.co.uk/upload/documents/Hemcrete/tradical_hemcrete_info_pack_updated.pdf (viewed 17.1.10)

Lippke,B., Wilson, J. Meil, J. and Taylor, A. (2010) Characterising the Importance of Carbon stored in Wood Products, Wood and Fibre Science (March 2010) V42 Corrim Special Issue

McCloud, K. (2011a) Video promotion of Kevin McCloud's book: 43 Principles of Home: Enjoying Life in the 21st Century http://www.youtube.com/watch?v=Bgl7c0SxgrM (viewed 6 February 2011)

McCloud, K. (2011b) personal email 8 February 2011

May, N., Warm, P. and Grant, N. (2008) *Green Building Magazine*, Autumn 2008, p.33

Monbiot, G. (2011) 'Government redefines zero as it abandons green homes commitment' http://www.guardian.co.uk/environment/georgemonbiot/2010/nov/26/zero-carbon-homes (viewed 29.11.11)

Mud and Wood (2012) http://www.mudandwood.com (viewed 5.5.12)

Murphy, R.J. and Norton, A. (2008) *Life Cycle Assessments of Natural Fibre Insulation Materials.* York: National Non-food Crops Centre

Olivier, D. 'Breathing Walls, Myth or Magic?', *Building for a Future* Vol.9 No.3 November 1999

Oreszczyn, T. and Lowe, R. (2005) Evidence to the House of Lords select committee on science and technology: energy efficient buildings. University College London, The Authority of the House of Lords: London, UK 2005

Our Climate (2012) http://www.ourclimate.net/sequestration.htm (viewed 7.2.12)

Pervais, M. (2003) Carbon storage potential in natural fiber composites, *Resources,Conservation and Recycling*, Vol.39, No.4, pp.325–340

Planning Portal UK http://www.planningportal.gov.uk/buildingregulations/greener buildings/sustainablehomes (viewed 28.2.12)

Pritchett, I. (2011) (Lime Technology) in various conference presentations. http://www.buildinglimesforum.org.uk/2011-conference

RAE 2010: The Royal Academy of Engineering London: Engineering a Low Carbon Built Environment – The discipline of Building Engineering Physics (January 2010)

Richardson, C.M. (2009) 'The embodied carbon labelling of building products', PhD thesis. University of Huddersfield

RICS 2010 Research Report: Redefining Zero. May 2010 RICS with Sturgis Associates

RIBA (undated) Climate Change Toolkit 8, Whole Life Assessment for Low Carbon Design, Royal Institute of British Architects and Energy Saving Trust London

Roaf, S., Fuentes, M. and Thomas, S. (2007) *Ecohouse: A Design Guide* Architectural Press 2007

Robson (2010) 'Carbon stored in harvested wood product materials in the UK' (unpublished paper)

Sadler (2010) 'Biogenic materials for housing as a climate change mitigation strategy for the UK' 2010 unpublished paper

Sativa Bags http://www.sativabags.com/hemp_information/hemp_friend_of_the_earth.cfm (viewed 28.2.12)

Schmidt ,A., Jensen, A. et al. (2004) 'A comparative LCA of building insulation products made of stone wool, paper wool and flax' *International Journal of LCA* Vol.8, No.5, p.317

Sheepwool Insulation (2012) www.sheepwoolinsulation.i.e. (viewed 5.5.12)

Stop burning (2012) http://www.stopburningourtrees.org

UK Green Building Council (2012) http://www.ukgbc.org/content/materials (viewed 5.5.12)

UKCIP, http://www.ukcip.org.uk/case-studies/ (viewed 28.2.12)

University of Bath (viewed.1 http://www.bath.ac.uk/research/features/embodiedenergy.html (viewed 28.2.12)

Wales Government http://wales.gov.uk/consultations/planning/ruralhousing consult/?lang=en (viewed 28.2.12)

Wigan (2012) Building Control Guidance Leaflet 12 Guidance for designers Part L2006.doc http://www.wigan.gov.uk/Services/Planning/BuildingControl/Application Forms.htm (viewed 16.2.12)

Williams, J. (2012) *Zero Carbon Homes: A Road Map* Earthscan 2012

Woolley, T. (2006) *Natural Building* Crowood Press 2006

Woolley, T. and Kimmins, S. (1997) *The Green Building Handbook Volumes 1 and 2* 1997 and 2000 Spon

Zero Carbon Hub http://www.zerocarbonhub.org/news_details.aspx?article=13 (viewed 28.2.12)

6. Building physics, natural materials and policy issues

Few people in the UK built environment field even recognise the importance of building engineering physics, let alone know how to apply the principles in the design of buildings. Building projects are traditionally led by architects, not engineers, but building energy performance hardly features in architectural education. This lack of essential knowledge to inform strategic design decisions has led to the perpetuation of an experimental approach to building performance, rather than an approach based on synthesis, rigorous analysis, testing and measurement of the outcome.

(RAE 2010)

This statement from the Royal Academy of Engineering is an indictment of current built environment education in the UK. However, similar problems can be found throughout the world, in architecture and other built environment disciplines. At the ARC-PEACE international conference in Copenhagen in April 2012, a resolution was adopted on the education of architects and planners:

We urge professional schools to develop curricula and train instructors to teach the architectural and planning skills necessary to create healthy, socially sustainable environments and create buildings and plan cities with smaller carbon footprints that reduce consumption and conserve energy.

(ARC-PEACE 2012)

It seems remarkable that in 2012, a group of architects and eminent professors from all over the world, including Sweden, India, Peru, USA and Canada should find it necessary to call on universities and professional bodies to address socially responsible and ecological issues. Professional bodies such as the Royal Institute of British Architects and the International Union of Architects pay lip service to sustainability, but in practice many architecture schools have become art-house style and fashion centres that worship

Low Impact Building: Housing using Renewable Materials, First Edition. Tom Woolley.
© 2013 John Wiley & Sons, Ltd. Published 2013 by John Wiley & Sons, Ltd.

famous signature architects, few of whom have much concern for sustainability. It is a worrying prospect for the future.

Despite this, there are many, often small, hardworking architecture and engineering practices that are strongly committed to environmentally progressive design, but often they are swimming against the tide. They can be undercut by larger commercial firms whose commitment to sustainability rarely goes beyond greenwash. Those architects and engineers who want to push the boundaries of green and sustainable design are hampered by a lack of technical back-up, particularly in the area of building physics and building science. This is also a major problem for companies developing and selling natural renewable materials because current regulations and building science tools are biased in favour of petrochemical based materials and conventional approaches to building.

There are a number of areas of concern and topics discussed in this chapter including:

- lack of good building physics understanding
- poor systems of assessing energy performance and a lack of attention to thermal mass
- inadequate simulation and prediction tools
- weak government and EU policy directives on materials and buildings
- poor assessment of material environmental impact and performance
- lack of understanding of moisture and durability in buildings, breathability and hygroscopicity
- insufficient attention to health, pollution and indoor air quality issues.

Holistic design

A key principle of ecological building and design should be to adopt a holistic approach. In other words all important issues from energy use to environmental impact should be given *equal* consideration. As has already been discussed in Chapter 5, there are many 'experts' who tend to focus on just one issue, such as operational energy, and downplay the importance of other issues such as embodied energy or indoor air quality. However, to be truly committed to environmental responsibility many more issues other than energy efficiency should be given equal attention.

Also there is a complex interrelationship between external weather, internal humidity, and the nature of materials, ventilation, design and detailing. Unfortunately the agencies and areas of building scientific knowledge in this field are mostly compartmentalised and unrelated, leading to a poor understanding of how buildings actually perform in their totality.

Furthermore the use of natural and renewable materials is disadvantaged because conventional approaches to building physics and related environmental and energy science have been largely based on the performance of masonry construction and petrochemical based lightweight insulations. Regulations and building science methods are constantly evolving as technology changes, particularly as we move away from masonry to timber construction.

When the proponents of natural and renewable materials expound their advantages such as their good environmental performance, health and good indoor air quality, breathability, ability to handle moisture and humidity and an excellent thermal performance, these claims are not always backed up by enough solid data. Conventional wisdom and conventional architectural science is often used to discount these claims. Unless building physics theory and practice changes, the claimed benefits of renewable materials remain vulnerable to challenge by detractors.

It might be reasonable to expect that the principles of building physics would be based on good science and be independent of commercial vested interests but it soon becomes apparent that the discipline of building physics is very weak in the academic sector and often driven by commercial funding. Universities and testing bodies in the UK are largely dependent on funding from industry. The lack of independent and critical science is self-evident when searching the literature.

In addition, over the past few decades, most of the changes in this area have been driven by regulations and compliance requirements that have not always been based on the best of science. For many years it was considered sufficient for thermal performance to be regulated simply by prescribing levels of insulation. Then it was realised that insulation performance was weakened by air leakage and cold bridging. Various calculation methods were introduced and strengthened as efforts were made to make buildings respond to the new agenda to reduce carbon emissions and reduce energy consumption. While these changes have been based on scientific advice, this has rarely been subject to proper independent analysis and has often driven more by pragmatic and political decisions.

'Robust' and then 'accredited' details (Planning Portal 2012) were introduced but these are often inflexible, based on conventional building practice and, in the view of some, unworkable. As discussed in Chapter 5, many of the attempts to achieve energy efficiency fail to work in practice.

More recently it has been understood, that issues such as thermal mass and the performance of materials in terms of moisture also play a big part, though this is barely recognised in many regulations and calculation methods in the UK. Natural, renewable materials have important thermal mass and moisture handling characteristics, so as these become better understood and incorporated into regulatory systems, then natural and renewable materials will be more readily accepted.

Increasingly designers are relying on computer simulation methods to predict the performance of buildings. These simulation tools rely largely on assumptions that are not always backed up with hard data, derived from real-time building performance. Indeed, it can be argued that there exists a parallel universe of experts sitting behind computers designing virtual buildings and energy strategies that have almost nothing to do with real buildings. These tools also have built-in assumptions that favour conventional materials and construction methods, though one or two like WUFI (Fraunhofer 2012) recognise the importance of moisture in buildings.

As regulations and new tools have been overlaid on each other, over the years, fundamental errors of concept and science become reinforced and built into new systems. Assumptions and conventional thinking become accepted wisdom and are rarely tested in practice. Often these assumptions are based on claims and data from industrial companies who are promoting their materials and products. These build commercially biased information into calculation tools. It is not uncommon to hear builders, specifiers and even building science experts, refer to generic materials such as breather membranes and foam insulations by the leading trade names such as Tyvek and Kingspan rather than their generic terms. This is symptomatic of the very pragmatic approach to specification and a ready acceptance of the technical information supplied by such companies. The bulk of continuing professional development (CPD) seminars attended by professionals are organised by commercial companies. This acts to the disadvantage of natural renewable materials and products, as smaller and newer companies do not have the resources to do the promotion, professional training and lobbying that the larger manufacturers of conventional products use.

European standards, trade and professional organisations

Organisations responsible for setting standards, carrying out tests and providing technical guidance are rarely free of commercial pressures. Attempts by the European Union to introduce greater standardisation for materials quality and environmental performance have been balked for years by effective lobbying of European trade organisations. The EU Construction Products Directive was initially approved in 1988 and made clear that pollution issues were important. However, little has been done to enforce this objective:

> *Annex 1 Essential requirements 3. Hygiene Health and the environment*
> The construction work must be designed and built in such a way that it will not be a threat to the health or hygiene of the occupants or neighbours in particular as a result of any of the following:
> * the giving off of toxic gases
> * the presence of dangerous particle or gases in the air
> * the emission of dangerous radiation
> * pollution or poisoning of the water or soil
> * faulty elimination of waste water, smoke, solid or liquid wastes
> * the presence of damp in parts of the works or on surfaces within the works
> (EC 1988)

More recently the Construction Products Regulations have replaced the Directive and make provisions for CE marking of materials. However, they have not made Environmental Product Declarations (EPDs) compulsory and have not specified that they should be third-party EPDs (in other words prepared by an independent assessment body). This is a result of conservative industry pressure to ensure that strong environmental standards were not enforced and remain voluntary:

> When a construction product is covered by a harmonised standard or conforms to a European Technical Assessment, which has been issued for it, the manufacturer shall draw up a declaration of performance when such a product is placed on the market.
>
> *For the assessment of the sustainable use of resources and of the impact of construction works on the environment, Environmental Product Declarations should be used* **when available**. (emphasis added)
>
> (EU 2011)

Environmental lobbying at European level is relatively weak due to the high costs of gaining access in Brussels and Strasbourg, while large commercial companies and trade organisations are able to maintain permanent offices in Brussels. FIEC, the European Construction Industry Federation, for instance, has an office at Avenue Louise in the centre of Brussels, just down the road (also in Avenue Louise) is the European Insulation Manufacturers' Association (EURIMA). The European Cement Association is a couple of streets away. Plastics Europe, part of the Global Plastics Federation is a bit more out of town, as is PU European the Polyurethane manufacturers' association.

EU construction product regulations are managed through national government agencies and they have not pushed very hard for stricter and independently enforced environmental controls. In the 'Zagreb statement' calls were made for greater use of natural resources and recycling.

> We think a requirement promoting the sustainable use of natural resources in construction works should be added into the future CPD. The sustainable use of resources can be enhanced; when an adequate product marking and appropriate design ensure that any hazardous substances in construction works can be easily separated for suitable treatment during demolition. Here European requirements to limit the presence of dangerous substances in construction products would make recycling easier.
>
> (Umweltbundesamt 2012)

However, the final regulations are very vague and weak in terms of resource consumption as there is no mention of non-renewable resources or embodied energy.

> The construction works must be designed, built and demolished in such a way that the use of natural resources is sustainable and in particular ensure the following:
> (a) reuse or recyclability of the construction works, their materials and parts after demolition;
> (b) durability of the construction works
> (c) use of environmentally compatible raw and secondary materials in the construction works
>
> (EU 2011)

Table 6.1 UK Organisations concerned with building and environmental standards

Organisation	Status	Interest in renewable materials
Building Research Establishment (BRE)	Private trust	Set up the Centre for Low Impact Materials in Building (CLIMB), supports research centre at Bath University
British Board of Agrement	Private linked to BRE	Will certify renewable materials through an expensive process
NHBC	Provides warranties for house building	Their guidance on natural materials in 2011 is limited (NHBC 2011)
NHBC Foundation	Private trust linked to BRE, provides research funding	Little evidence of interest in renewable materials and has not supported any research (NHBC Foundation 2012)
LABC	Local authority building control association	Has shown some interest in renewable materials
LABC warranty	Private insurance company	Has provided warranties for natural and renewable materials
British Standards Institute (BSI)	Quango	Little evidence of interest in renewable materials
Construction Industry Research and Information Association (CIRIA)	Private trust	Little evidence of interest in renewable materials
Construction Products Association	Private association	Has shown some interest in renewable materials
BSRIA: consultancy, test, instruments and research organisation mainly on building services	Private member association	Little evidence of interest in renewable materials
Chartered Institute of Building Services Engineers (CIBSE)	Member organisation equivalent to American Society of Heating, Refrigerating and Air Conditioning Engineers (ASHRAE)	Little evidence of interest in renewable materials
Energy Institute	Private members association	Little evidence of interest in renewable materials
TRADA	Industry association	Little evidence of interest in renewable materials
CERAM	Private trust testing body	Can do testing of natural materials
Energy Saving Trust	Quango	Provides some information on renewable materials including hemp, hemp lime, sheep's wool, wood fibre and cellulose (EST 2010)
Carbon Trust	Quango	Little evidence of interest in renewable materials
Zero Carbon Hub	Quango	Little evidence of interest in renewable materials
UK Green Building Council	Industry membership association	Has shown some interest in renewable materials but has nothing on its website under 'materials'

EU regulations have been valuable in pushing the agenda on sustainable construction, even though many regard them as further red tape, but powerful lobby groups have been very successful in limiting the scope of the Construction Product Regulations. This is despite progressive policies set out by the EU in September 2011 about resource efficiency. This advocates better information on the environmental footprints of products, and quote an OECD report which says prices are distorted by environmentally harmful products being subsidised by governments (Section 3.4). In a section headed '5.5. Improving Buildings', the EU states:

> Existing policies for promoting energy efficiency and renewable energy use in buildings therefore need to be strengthened and complemented with policies for *resource efficiency*, which look at a wider range of environmental impacts across the life cycle of buildings and infrastructure. (emphasis added)
>
> (EN 2011)

Without efforts at a European level to keep the environmental agenda alive it is unlikely that much would be done within the UK to push out the boundaries or support the resource efficiencies of natural and renewable materials. Organisations in the UK involved in materials and energy issues are numerous (Table 6.1) and most have their own commercial agenda and vested interests, and these rarely follow a holistic concern with environmental impacts. Few have shown much interest in renewable materials.

Building physics – lack of good research and education

Very few UK universities offer courses or research programmes on building physics. The Chartered Institute of Building Services Engineers (CIBSE) presently accredits only 16 undergraduate degrees as suitable for Chartered Engineer in building services engineering, from 12 institutions, including the Open University.

So serious is this problem that the Royal Academy of Engineering set up a scheme to place leading practitioners from professional consultancies, such as Arup and Buro Happold, into Bath, Bristol, Cambridge and Sheffield Universities as visiting professors, to try to generate interest in building physics. Excellent programmes are available in other parts of the world such as the USA (University of Berkeley) or the Netherlands (Technical University of Delft) and there are institutes in Germany and Denmark, but even at an international level the literature on building physics is very thin.

> Put bluntly, there are not sufficient of the brightest and best entering a career in the design of buildings as a system, and the systems within a building. An underpinning knowledge needed in that area is that of Building Engineering Physics.
>
> (RAE 2010)

The RAE report neatly sums up the current problems of how bad the situation has become as a result of a plethora of new energy regulations and requirements such as from the Code for Sustainable Homes. Many people, currently offering services as energy assessors or code assessors have limited training and expertise. No prior qualifications or experience are needed to become a domestic energy assessor in the UK. It is possible to qualify as a Code for Sustainable Homes assessor, following a four-day course, an exam and membership of the BRE Approved Accreditation Scheme (Sustainable Homes 2012). To become a BREEAM assessor involves even less with either a two or three-day training programme. Prior qualifications and expertise are not required. "There are no pre-qualification requirements to becoming a BREEAM International assessor. The only thing we stipulate is the need to have a very good understanding of written and spoken English." (BREEAM 2012)

> This position has led to a new type of professional, a sustainability consultant or code assessor … *The field has no recognised codes of practice or professional standards and work is often undertaken by consultants from wide ranging backgrounds who may not be conversant with the principles of building engineering physics, or even engineering.* This lack of consistency results in enormous variations in the standard of service provided by practitioners.
>
> *Thus the design of buildings, traditionally disconnected between the disciplines, has become even more fragmented. A design team may often now comprise architect, structural engineer, building services engineer, sustainability consultant and code assessor all vying to be seen as the champion of sustainability. However, these teams often fail to communicate and co-operate to make the key strategic decisions that will reduce demand on mechanical and electrical solutions for comfort and climate control.* (emphasis added)
> (RAE 2010)

Thus the work of current energy practitioners is not underpinned by a consistent and scientifically based set of principles. The UK Government requires buildings to comply with standards such as BREEAM and LEED but "the industry lacks sufficient information, guidance and mechanisms to design and construct buildings to achieve such targets'. (RAE 2010).

The National Audit office says that 80% of houses have failed to achieve environmental performance targets since 2002 and that the same is likely to be true of other buildings. They also point out that poor professional expertise leads to buildings that appear to be more expensive, yet energy-efficient buildings do not need to be more expensive if well designed: "buildings aiming for a high environmental performance are no more or less expensive than conventional buildings" (EEBPP 1999).

Lack of data and good research on sustainable buildings

A further difficulty for research and education in the field of building physics is the lack of good data and feedback from completed projects in the UK. This is due to the disappointing record of the Carbon Trust (Carbon Trust 2012) and the Energy Saving Trust (EST 2010). Type 'best practice' into the Carbon Trust's search engine and you will find 'no results'. The

Carbon Trust seems only concerned with building services and mechanical processes and publishes only one fact sheet on building fabric (Carbon Trust 2007). Only mineral wool, rigid foam and polystyrene are referred to.

The RAE is very critical of the Carbon Trust:

> The Energy Efficiently Best Practice Programme (EEBPP) was the UK Government's *principal energy efficiency information, advice and research programme for organisations in the public and private sectors. ... Since the transfer of the EEBPP to the Carbon Trust in 2002, the wealth of information, amassed over many years has gradually become unavailable and is now largely out of print.*
>
> (RAE op cit)

Bordass and Leaman (2005) have kept alive interest in post-occupancy evaluation of buildings. Their 'Probe' programme was funded by the UK Government from 1995 to 2002, and some 20 case studies were published in the Building Services Journal. Leaman and Bordass established the Usable Buildings Trust, which was then hosted by Arup Associates (Arup 2012), but lack of significant funding has limited what it has been able to do. Without good feedback and careful objective analysis of completed projects little can be done to improve practice in the future. The dearth of good research and data is made worse by government policy that insists that research should be largely funded by industry and that any results must be market ready almost immediately. This means that critical or analytical research is rarely funded at all. As the RAE states in their criticism of the Carbon Trust:

> There is also a need for fundamental research in many areas relating to energy supply and carbon reductions, not just in the area of building engineering physics, which is inadequately supported at present due to the established funding mechanisms. In order to qualify for funding from bodies, such as the Carbon Trust, researchers must be able to demonstrate a route to market, limiting the opportunities for more fundamental research with a broad range of application not linked to one industrial partner. Thus, we are failing to develop potentially beneficial lines of research due to restrictions in the funding criteria. It is important that we find new and more agile means of supporting both.
>
> (RAE 2010)

Similar criticisms can be made of the UK Technology Strategy Board, which has been the main UK Government agency responsible for research in the built environment. It has aims largely focused on the needs of industry:

> Technology Strategy Board – Our Strategy – *Concept to Commercialisation*: The vision of the Technology Strategy Board is for the UK to be a global leader in innovation and a magnet for innovative businesses, where *technology is applied rapidly, effectively* and sustainably to create wealth and enhance quality of life. (emphasis added)
>
> (TSB 2012)

Applying technology to enhance quality of life sounds fine, but unless such work is underpinned by good independent scientific research it may have the opposite effect. The intention is always to promote commercial development, irrespective of whether it benefits society and protects the environment. To date, only a little government-funded independent research has gone in the development of natural and renewable materials.

Energy simulation and calculation tools

Increasingly buildings are designed using computer-based energy simulation and prediction tools in order to predict energy and environmental performance. In the UK, the official tools are the Standard Assessment Procedure (SAP) and the Simplified Building Energy Model (SBEM), and calculations using these tools have to be submitted as part of building regulations compliance. Ever since these tools were introduced, professionals and the construction industry have been grumbling about them, and there is frequently a huge gap between how buildings actually perform in practice and what is submitted in the SAP or SBEM predictions.* However, as long as predictions that appear to comply with the regulations are submitted, everyone is happy, except the building occupant, who finds that they spend more on energy than they had expected! Some effort is made to assess whether buildings comply, once completed, for instance by carrying out blower door tests to check airtightness while, this has become routine and does not do enough to improve design and building quality. Often it is hard to rectify failings once a building is completed, but the cost of carrying out tests during construction means that this is not carried out sufficiently.

In pursuit of targets of 'zero-carbon', energy consumption standards in buildings continue to be tightened, but this will not necessarily lead to better designed, better performing or better insulated buildings because the UK construction industry is complaining, not so much about objectives but

---

*SAP is the UK Government's Standard Assessment Procedure for energy rating of dwellings. SAP is a compulsory part of the UK Building Regulations. Every new house has to have a SAP rating. SAP estimates the energy efficiency performance of dwellings expressed on a scale of 1 to 100. The higher the number, the better the rating. SAP predicts heating and hot water costs based on the insulation and airtightness of the house, and the efficiency and control of the heating system. The calculation uses the BRE's Domestic Energy Model (BREDEM) either by using a SAP worksheet or one of the approved SAP calculation programs approved by the BRE.

Simplified Building Energy Model (SBEM) is a software tool developed by the BRE that provides an analysis of a building's energy consumption. It is used for non-domestic buildings in support of the National Calculation Methodology (NCM) and the Energy Performance of Buildings Directive (EPBD). The tool helps to determine CO_2 emission rates for new buildings in compliance with the UK Building Regulations. It is also used to generate Energy Performance Certificates for non-domestic buildings under construction, for sale or let. SBEM makes use of standard data contained on associated databases and is available with other software. It was originally based on the Dutch methodology NAN2916:1998 (Energy Performance of Non-Residential Buildings) and has since been modified to comply with the CEN Standards.

the inadequacies of tools like SBEM and SAP, claiming that they are unworkable. There is an interesting debate to be had about whether it is the tools that are at fault or the poor standard of building construction. In reality it is probably both. However, there is a disjuncture between computer-based tools and actual building practice. There is little doubt that buildings using natural and renewable materials are at a disadvantage, as SAP and SBEM have built into them assumptions about conventional materials and too great a dependence on U-values that are drawn from commercial brochures. The other problem is a predetermined set of assumptions about the efficiency of heating and other mechanical systems. SAP is preoccupied with heating and heating systems rather than low energy design. There are built-in weightings and assumptions that are open to question. While fabric heat loss is part of the calculation, thermal mass while considered, is rarely given sufficient attention. This is a methodology more concerned with heating systems rather than designing energy-efficient buildings.

A good critical analysis of SAP and SBEM systems is not easy to find because SAP assessors themselves are more concerned about software flaws than the fundamental inadequacies of the system.

> According to this research, the actual CO_2 associated with the operation of new housing could be more than twice as much as that predicted by SAP calculations. There are several reasons for this. The first is that SAP is not an effective modelling tool, and for various reasons does not predict energy demand accurately.

> (Taylor 2008)

Apart from tools which are required as part of the UK Building Regulations, there are many, simulations tools concerned with energy in buildings. The US Department of Energy lists *over 400 building energy software tools throughout the world and even this list has many omissions.* (US EERE 2012).

There are over 30 listed in the UK with a growing number of tools that claim to provide building performance predictions that are much wider than energy performance and can be integrated with CAD design tools. For instance, IES is widely used:

> VE-Pro is a cutting-edge suite of building performance simulation tools. Used by leading sustainable design experts across the globe, it creates understanding of the performance impacts of different low-energy design strategies.

> (IES 2012)

In their downloadable Apache Tables, IES list all the insulation materials in their database with conductivity figures. *No renewable natural materials are included.* (IES 2012).

While such tools can have their use, most fall short of a holistic approach and this limits their applicability to ecological designers. One of the main exceptions to this rule is WUFI, a tool produced by the Fraunhofer Institute in Germany, which considers the importance of moisture in buildings and how this can have a significant effect on thermal performance. WUFI has potential for those using natural and renewable materials as it takes account of the hygroscopic characteristics of materials, a key issue for natural materials.

> The Task Group 'Moisture Calculation' established in 2000 within the European Technical Committee TC89 (Thermal Performance of Buildings and Building Components) is working on similar objectives. Thus the prerequisites for standardized application of hygrothermal simulation methods in civil engineering and architecture are being devised both on a national and on an international level.
>
> (Fraunhofer 2012)

Given the problems and complexities associated with thermal modelling tools, designers tend to rely increasingly on specialist consultants. Architecture students and other building professionals do not necessarily understand how to use these tools, since building science and physics, as has already been shown by the RAE, may not be taught in university courses. Many insulation and materials suppliers offer such prediction calculations as part of an agreement to supply their materials, and designers will therefore be accepting the commercial biases built into these.

For many, the use of such tools, is simply a practical means to an end, to get approval for a building under regulations or codes, and they are unlikely to consider the ethical and ideological assumptions that underpin such tools.

In a brilliant critique of computer simulation tools, Williamson argues that

> claims about simulation can lead to a spurious impression of accuracy and therefore legitimacy. Likewise, inappropriate applications of simulation may result in wrong decisions and an erroneous allocation of resources.
>
> (Williamson 2010)

He explains that most discussion of tools focuses on the accuracy of the maths or algorithms, but that this overlooks the fundamental assumptions behind the use of such tools.

> Built environment simulation is steeped in an empiricist/positivist tradition, which assumes that the world 'out there' is essentially knowable and that the 'true' nature of an external reality is discoverable through the application of the methods of science. The assumption on which building performance simulation is predicated is the notion that it is possible for knowledge produced through the application of simulation to approximate closely an external 'reality'.

He argues that, with the complexity of buildings and the built environment, it is almost impossible to validate simulations with a perfect empirical real building experiment, but the authors and users of such tools choose to ignore the possibility that tools might be giving the wrong answers.

A review of the proceedings of the IBPSA (the International Building Performance Simulation Association) Conference shows almost no authors have addressed issues of the uncertainties inherent in simulation analysis. At the 2009 IBPSA Conference in Glasgow, no papers addressed this important problem. Researchers, practitioners and policy-makers must realize that simulation can never pretend to offer the kind of certainty which experts with their scientific knowledge and with greater or lesser credibility claim to offer.

(Williamson 2010)

It might seem reasonable for governments to set targets and regulations for buildings to reduce energy consumption, but if these targets are rarely, if ever, met and assessment and predictions tools give misleading information, we are left in a situation where no one really knows whether so-called zero carbon targets can be achieved. Instead with a plethora of complex regulations and standards, an army of tick box *envirocrats*, poorly qualified assessors and expensive but questionable computer tools, the result is a cynicism about sustainability and reducing carbon emissions. The construction industry then becomes resistant to even more regulations and requirements. Adopting a holistic approach, which appears to introduce even more environmental regulations, is likely to be resisted, as yet more red tape.

Assessment of material's environmental impact and performance

Perhaps one of the biggest obstacles to the uptake of natural and renewable materials has been the lack of a robust but acceptable method of rating the environmental impact of materials and products. The Code for Sustainable Homes, BREEAM, LEED and many other tools used around the world, are very weak on the issue of materials. BREEAM and The Code use the assessment system promoted by the BRE, the Green Guide to Specification. This document is treated by many within the construction industry as the last word on the rating of materials and yet it has been widely criticised. The 'Green Guide' has failed in the past to give good ratings to some environmentally friendly materials, particularly insulations, instead favouring petrochemical higher embodied energy products. Products and materials that many environmentalists would regard as unacceptable such as uPVC and foam based insulation materials get a much better rating than some low impact materials.

Its possible to access the Green Guide (BRE 2012) ratings online. As you do this, you will notice that almost everything gets an A or A star rating. For instance a building system called insulated concrete formwork (ICF) gets an A star. The ICF demonstration building at the BRE innovation park has been demolished.

Thin coat polymer modified render on ICF consisting of 2 sheets expanded polystyrene grade 200e joined with 100 mm light steel C studs at 300 mm centres, infilled with in situ 65% GGBS C30 concrete with plasterboard and emulsion paint.

(BRE 2012)

heat recovery is meant to offset this, though the effectiveness of this is still a matter for debate. There are also a range of innovative solutions that have been trialled where fresh air intake is warmed through heating systems or even the building fabric. Humidity sensitive mechanical extracts can also be used, that minimise the use of electricity only speeding up the extraction rate when humidity rises from cooking, showers or baths. Where there is a great deal of moisture and humidity in buildings, some kind of mechanical ventilation seems unavoidable and the old system of trickle vents in windows is no longer practicable when high levels of energy efficiency are required. There are those of us who advocate opening windows to let in fresh air (Purging) but this is not usually considered a very energy efficient practice if the windows get left open!

Most building fabric solutions in the UK involve the use of plastic vapour barriers, and these can be both impermeable and permeable. So-called 'breather' membranes were introduced in the 1980s in an effort to reduce the risks of interstitial condensation, but there is concern that as levels of insulation and air tightness increase, breather membranes may not cope as effectively.

Breather membranes are compared to Gortex coats in that they are showerproof but allow body heat and moisture to escape. There is no substantial evidence of failures of breather membranes as yet, but there are examples, especially in cold roof designs of water condensing on the underside of membranes and dripping onto the insulation below.

In view of these risks, more sophisticated (so-called intelligent) membranes have been developed and these are used in conjunction with a great deal of 'sticky tape' to seal all the joints to try to ensure good levels of air-tightness. One of the best known of these membranes is INTELLO Pro Clima:

> The Difference between Conventional Technology and the new INTELLO: To prevent structural damage, the usual approach is to concentrate on reducing moisture stress.
>
> To exclude the likelihood of structural damage and mould growth, it is advisable, apart from considering moisture stress, to concentrate on the drying capacity of a structural system. Systems with a high drying capacity and a simultaneous reduction in moisture stress, as provided by vapour membranes/retarders with a humidity-variable diffusion permeability, like INTELLO® are still very safely and reliably protected against structural damage even if subjected to unanticipated moisture stress."
>
> (Pro Clima 2012)

It is not easy to understand how the 'humidity-variable diffusion permeability' of the INTELLO membranes actually work in practice, but their literature also refers to the drying capacity of structures. Natural renewable materials have such a 'drying capacity' in that, as hygroscopic materials, they can, in theory, absorb and then release moisture. Synthetic fibre and foam insulation materials do not have this capacity and cannot absorb moisture without losing their insulation capacity.

Having stored hemp flax, wood fibre and sheep's wool in an old damp second-hand haulage container, where condensation drips off the translucent plastic roof, it is clear after two or three years that the natural materials do not suffer, and they recover if they do get wet. There is no sign of mould growth either. Thus there should be similar performance in buildings even if there is high humidity and dampness present, providing the materials are able to breathe and dry out. This is because of the hygroscopic nature of natural materials. Hygroscopicity is the ability of a material to absorb moisture and then release it again. Hygroscopicity ratings for materials are not normally given, but information on moisture permeability is sometimes published. Permeability and hygroscopicity are not the same, though they are related.

However, if such materials are sealed up in structures or with finishes that cannot breathe then they can also suffer from rot. The whole fabric structure has to be breathable.

This is a difficult concept for many professionals because they assume that natural materials will rot if they become damp whereas synthetic materials are safer in water. There is no doubt that natural materials, if left soaking in water for a long period, due to a flood or badly detailed building, will suffer, but this would apply to most building materials.

Very little information on these issues can be found in the standard textbooks and technical guides on building physics or building science. One of the best and most comprehensive building science textbooks (Pohl 2011) gives an excellent introduction to thermal issues in buildings and also the basic concepts of sustainability, but amazingly it doesn't mention moisture permeability, breathability, hygroscopic materials or thermal mass, though there is a brief section on condensation. Pohl draws attention to the lack of research in this area.

In fact, there is a growing body of research into moisture impacts on the performance of materials. Hens (2007), one of the leading figures in the field, does not deal with natural or renewable materials but he does point out that synthetic materials do not cope well with water.

> Foams sometimes experience an irreversible deformation as a result of the combined actions of temperature and vapour pressure fluctuations in the pores. Water which enters the pores by interstitial condensation is responsible for the latter.
>
> (Hens 2007)

However, Hens' highly technical book, containing hundreds of building physics equations, that provide the basis for calculations and computer simulations, is not helpful for architects and others wishing to access simple applications for building design. More useful is Szokolay's *Introduction to Architectural Science* (Szokolay 2007) This classic book should be studied by all those who wish to understand how thermal and other related properties of building actually function. The picture is much more complex than that used as the basis for SAP or SBEM calculations.

Unfortunately even Szokolay does not deal with the performance of hygroscopic materials in terms of moisture but it is extremely helpful in understanding the dynamic thermal performance of insulations and building fabrics, which are discussed below. A more accessible summary of moisture

Table 6.3 Vapour resistance

Vapour resistance for some typical materials: R-factor	
Synthetic top coat plaster	1500
Clay plaster	40
Polyurethane foam with foil	10,000
Woodfibre insulation boards	25
Mineral wool, flax, sheep's wool insulations	6

Source: adapted from May, N. 16/04/2005: *Breathability Matters: The Key to Building Performance* (http://www.natural-building.co.uk/PDF/Case%20Studies/Breathability_in_buildings.pdf). Accessed 5.5.12.

and breathability issues can be found in several papers by Neil May of Natural Building Technologies (NBT), published on the Internet. While May is in the business of selling natural materials for NBT, he is also a student of building science and much can be learned from his papers (May 2009).

Vapour permeability is a key issue in understanding how materials perform in buildings. Water molecules can pass through both insulations and solid materials, depending on the permeability of such materials. While most moisture will pass out of a building through ventilations systems, it is also important to understand the vapour permeability of the building fabric. Vapour permeability is measured in terms of the resistance to moisture (R-factor). The bigger the R-figure, the less permeable the material. Synthetic plasters and plastic (acrylic) paints are highly resistant, as are synthetic dense foams like polyurethane (see Table 6.3).

Hygroscopicity is the ability of materials to absorb and release water vapour (which is a gas) as relative humidity changes in the surrounding air. Some materials which have high pore sizes (and are thus vapour permeable) lack the ability to retain water vapour. Porosity and hygroscopic behaviour of materials varies a great deal. The way bricks absorb moisture is very different from timber for instance. The speed of water vapour absorption also varies significantly. Some materials, such as sheep's wool insulation, can absorb moisture vapour quite quickly but there is a limit to how much can be retained. However, its capacity is normally fine for most conditions. Hempcrete can also cope with moisture, and hemp has particular characteristics in this regard, discussed below. The capacity of materials to retain moisture in this way means that they can help to manage humidity and this if often referred to as *buffering*. Buffering humidity in buildings can be very useful in terms of maintaining good indoor health and reducing risks from mould growth. A further factor to consider is capillarity, which defines how the material handles liquid water.

Materials that are hygroscopic and also have thermal mass can absorb more moisture than says a lightweight insulation material. This has been long understood for earth buildings and is one reason why the advocates of 'cob' (handmade from earth and straw) construction claim that it has health benefits even though the thermal insulation is theoretically poor. If humidity is in the ideal range of 40–60% in a building, comfort will improve.

Buildings constructed from largely synthetic materials with plastic membranes and finishes, as is the case in many new buildings, cannot buffer humidity, and unless ventilation is very effective at extracting moist air, condensation and hence mould growth can build up more easily.

The ideal materials to use are those, which are 'vapour open' and thus moisture permeable, but also have good hygroscopic abilities to buffer humidity. Thus mineral wool insulation materials are as vapour open as sheep's wool, but have low hygroscopic abilities and cannot buffer moisture.

Construction industry regulations have been mainly concerned to ensure that materials are not able to absorb moisture or allow water to penetrate into a building, as they may be used in high-risk areas where they can get wet. Thus synthetic materials are marketed on the basis of their water resistance and in some high risk locations this may be valuable. This has lead designers to think in terms of keeping moisture out rather than dealing with it effectively inside buildings.

Moisture Resistance Tests by the British Board of Agrément confirm that Supafil Cavity Wall Insulation will not transmit water to the inner leaf. Nor will they transmit moisture by capillary action across the cavity or from below DPC level. This has been confirmed by independent research conducted for the Energy Saving Trust, which shows that cavity wall insulation does not add to the risk of water penetration.

(Knauf Insulation 2012)

Breathability

Breathability is a much misunderstood term and makes little sense unless measured carefully in terms of moisture permeability and hygroscopicity. It has been loosely bandied around in discussion of ecological building in the past but really needs to be underpinned by a careful understanding of building science and physics. Materials such as lime plasters and renders, which are assumed to be breathable, may vary significantly depending on what lime is used and how. Breathable and hygroscopic materials have to be used carefully in construction build-ups where moisture is absorbed is then able to escape. Tightly sealed forms of construction, even where vapour open materials are used, can end up with interstitial condensation problems.

Synthetic acrylic paints are sometimes referred to as breathable, but when asked, the majority of companies selling paints, plasters and other materials can rarely tell you whether their product is vapour permeable, or or give you a rating. On the other hand some modern finishes and paints such as clay paints or silicate external coatings, will come with details of the permeability/vapour open characteristics.

Problems are likely to be found where traditional masonry cavities are fully filled with insulation, as any moisture built up cannot escape. Retrofitting of buildings such as injecting insulation into existing cavities may be also a risky activity. Where non breathable plastic air tight membranes are used with natural materials they may be a risk of condensation. There have been circumstances where sheep's wool insulation has become damp and this is regarded as a failure of the sheep's wool, whereas it's more likely faulty detailing and an inability of the whole construction to breathe properly.

This is a complex and complicated aspect of natural building and yet building regulations and technical guidance provide very little help on these issues. Dampness and moisture problems in buildings are likely to become more serious as buildings become more airtight and energy efficient. The mainstream construction and materials industry has much to learn about these issues.

A good example is an attempt by Kingspan insulation to deny the importance of breathability, based on research which they commissioned from Cambridge Architectural Research (CAR) (Brown 2008). Heath, writing in *Green Building Magazine*, cited this study stating that

> Breathability *should not* be a key factor in choosing insulation materials. Instead looking at the longevity of the thermal performance of different insulation materials is the key. (emphasis added)
>
> (Heath 2009)

This has led others to deny the significance of breathability and support the argument that higher embodied energy synthetic materials are preferable to natural renewable materials, as discussed elsewhere in this book. However, Kingspan have commented on breathability by using an image in a document they produced showing a red herring! Kingspan provided data to CAR, which was then used to prove that the vast majority of moist air in buildings is removed by ventilation and air leakage, and that vapour open walls provide only a small contribution to this. The CAR paper remains inconclusive about the contribution of breathable materials and is a useful discussion of the issues, though it completely fails to mention hygroscopicity. The issue of mould growth is discussed by the Cambridge researchers in general terms but they come to no conclusions as to its relationship with breathability. However, Kingspan say

> Breathable constructions and the breathability of insulation products are therefore at best a side show, in reality they are a complete red herring in the avoidance of surface condensation, mould growth and exacerbated dust mite populations.
>
> (Kingspan 2009)

An interesting example of questionable 'information' about polyurethane insulation can be found on a PU Europe website (PU Europe 2012) even claiming that it leads to 'healthier buildings'.

There is a great deal of misunderstanding about breathability, for instance Kevin McCloud of Grand Designs, when asked about his support for the idea that energy in use was more important, (see Chapter 5) said that urethane insulation is 'marginally breathable'

I am not dogmatically 'pro' or against natural materials just as I am not dog-matically 'pro' or against synthetic materials. Breathability matters in many cases in construction but so does durability. Urethane foam is not something I relish having in my house but it is marginally breathable and serves a pur-pose in tight spaces.

(McCloud 2011)

McCloud explained in an email that his company HAB had commissioned a study by Dr Caroline Rye looking at the role of breathable materials in ret-rofitting old buildings. This study is important because of pressures to increase insulation in old and historic buildings.

Thermal mass and energy performance in buildings

A key factor in the ability of materials to handle moisture is their mass as well as their hygroscopic characteristics. Natural materials seem to perform better than synthetic products.

…natural fibre insulations … will actively absorb up to 10% of their mass volume as water in changing humidities. This compares with only 1% with mineral wool insulation, and none with plastic insulations of any sort.

(May undated)

Mass and moisture levels are important in understanding the thermal per-formance of insulation and building fabric. There is some evidence that wall and roof constructions using natural renewable materials perform better than similar constructions using synthetic materials because of their ability to deal with moisture.

Recent experiments in a climate chamber at the Centre for Alternative Technology being carried out by Tucker and Eshrar (Tucker 2012) show some very interesting results where thermal performance has been corre-lated with relative humidity. When natural insulation materials were com-pared with manmade fibres, (MMMF) in conditions of high humidity, water condensation was observed in the climate chamber with the MMMF, but hemp and sheep's wool were able to handle the extra moisture. Thermal insulation performance appears to deteriorate when MMMFs become wet, but this is not the case with some natural materials; indeed, the thermal performance may even improve slightly when additional moisture is pre-sent. This may be because water is a good medium to store heat and so the insulation materials, if they can handle moisture, can also appear to hold heat for longer.

This, like so many aspects of natural and renewable materials, is counter-intuitive, because we have been taught that water is bad for building mate-rials. Thermal conductivity is measured in hotbox tests in a completely dry situation. This is why R- and U-values can be highly misleading because they are based on tests in unrealistic conditions that do not reflect how the materials will perform in real buildings. Hotbox tests can be constructed to simulate real walls but even then humidity, dampness, cold bridging etc. are not part of the standard test protocols.

The British Board of Agrément warns of this when carrying out guarded hot box tests to BS EN ISO 6946: 2007, Annex B

> it is important to ensure that any test samples used are constructed in a form representative of actual use of the product on site, otherwise apparent performance could exceed that which will actually be obtained in the building.
>
> (BBA 2012)

However, hotbox tests are not able to simulate real conditions in buildings and should only be treated as an indication of how a material might perform. Tests can be carried out on real buildings in an effort to assess actual thermal performance but these can also be unreliable. Various sensors and probes are used in walls, linked to data loggers, and over time measurements can give an indication of what is really happening. Probes can be very unreliable giving false readings if they are not fully in contact with the material they are assessing. (Pilkington et al. 2010)

> Heat losses from the probe's open end and the material adjacent to it were shown to currently prevent reliable values being obtained for building insulation materials.
>
> (Pilkington 2008)

It may seem heretical to say so, but it could be suggested that figures for thermal conductivity provide nothing more than a rough guide to how materials might perform. Those architects and specifiers who base their choice of insulation materials and wall build-ups on U-values supplied by manufacturers are deluding themselves. This is one reason why, as confirmed in the work at Leeds Metropolitan University, so few buildings actually meet the predicted targets in practice.

The only way to assess how effective a building is thermally is to measure the performance of a completed building over a period of time such as in a coheating test with fewer variables in empty buildings. The best way to compare performance would be to build a series of identical houses or buildings (all with the same aspect and weather conditions) using different materials and compare them over time.

A crucial factor that affects the performance of insulation and wall build-ups in real buildings is thermal mass. Most insulation materials, especially synthetic ones, are lightweight and have very little thermal mass or the ability to increase their mass by absorbing water vapour. Many natural insulation products are also lightweight though they are mostly hygroscopic. Wood fibre insulation boards have some thermal mass and hemp lime, as used in many of the case studies, has significant thermal mass.

Thermal mass is important because building fabric has the possibility of storing heat and letting it back into the building slowly, helping to retain warmth and thermal comfort. This issue became apparent when lightweight timber frame construction became popular and it was realised that houses cooled down very quickly when people were out during the day and no heating was on. Extra energy was needed to warm up the house later. If the insulation had been working well then surely the warmth should have been retained but this is rarely the case in buildings with lightweight synthetic insulation materials. This is a worry for the timber frame industry, which has recognised this as an issue, but they seem to remain confused to how to address the problems (UKTFA 2012).

In order to understand this it is necessary to realise that heat is actually lost through insulation and it is the speed at which this takes place that is crucial in understanding its performance. Thermal conductivity is a factor of time as well as insulating properties.

Morton carried out an important experiment in Perthshire, Scotland, where he had designed a timber clad house with cellulose insulation. In order to slow down the loss of heat and provide thermal mass unfired clay bricks, made locally, were included in the timber frame internally with a clay plaster finish. Not only did the thermal mass of the earth improve the thermal performance but it was also successful as a moisture buffer. The walls performed 30% better than the predicted U-value. They were not able to make definitive conclusions on how much this was due to the thermal mass but observed that the overall performance of the house was weakened by insufficient thermal mass in the roof. Logging temperature and humidity over a year provided a great deal of data on thermal lag but also moisture performance. Weather, ventilation and occupant behaviour were also recorded. There was a complete absence of condensation in the house despite high levels of relative humidity, and the researchers concluded that:

> the difference in internal relative humidity from what could be expected in conventional domestic construction under these conditions indicates a moderating influence that could be attributed to the ability of the large surface areas of unfired clays to absorb and release moisture in response to changing conditions.
>
> (Morton 2005)

Thermal mass is not only important in terms of retaining heat but also in terms of keeping buildings cool. Thermal mass can be added to a building by using unfired earth (Morton 2008), but this can also be achieved using renewable materials such as hemp, hempcrete and wood fibre which also provide insulation.

Thermal mass is often linked to solar gain. At one time it was seen to be an advantage to use a lot of south-facing glazing (even though this will lose heat in the winter) so that the house can capture solar gain which can then be stored within any thermal mass in the building. This sounds good in theory but only really works when systems are in place to regulate the amount of solar gain.

The cement and concrete industry got very excited a few years ago about thermal mass being a good selling point for their products, and many architects have since tried to use heavy concrete structures to store heat or cool buildings at night by evening out temperature fluctuations but this proved to be a questionable concept.

The assumption was based on an influential report by Arup (2004) from which the industry claimed significant energy savings for concrete buildings, but most of the figures published (ASBL 2007) were based on computer simulations rather than assessment of buildings in practice. It took a while to realise that the thermal lag associated with heavy masonry structures has too slow a response time to fit with the 24 hour cycle of weather and occupancy. Concrete may not be sufficiently responsive to provide the right thermal conditions when required. Thus thermal mass can be a blunt instrument and hard to manage unless you have a material such as hempcrete that is more responsive. Perhaps one of the most curious recent examples of the use of concrete for thermal mass is at the Woodland Trust HQ building. Given that the building was constructed from timber, it seems somewhat perverse to bolt precast concrete to the ceilings, meaning that the timber structure had to be even stronger to cope with the weight of the concrete. (This is concrete 2012) It is not known whether the architects considered earth or hempcrete as an alternative way of including thermal mass.

This BREEAM 'Excellent' rated building designed by Feilden Clegg Bradley Studios combines timber and concrete to provide a solution that is architecturally interesting and performs both structurally and thermally.

Precast concrete panels were bolted onto the ceiling, covering 50% and acting as thermal radiators and are a novel solution to providing thermal mass to a timber-frame building. During the daytime the exposed concrete panels absorb heat and provide radiant cooling effect. At night, air is introduced through high-level windows to cool the concrete ready for the next day. (emphasis added)

http://www.thisisconcrete.co.uk/case_studies/
woodland_trust_hq.aspx

Students of vernacular and traditional buildings, especially those in warm countries will know that heavy masonry structures, particularly made from earth, can keep buildings cool, though when it is very hot cool air movement from natural ventilation is also necessary. Heavy masonry traditional buildings made from earth or stone can also stay warm in the winter but generally need a steady heat input. Once thermal mass cools down it can then radiate 'coolth' and more heat is required (Minke 2006).

It is generally understood that to renovate masonry buildings by placing the insulation on the outside – so that the thermal mass can retain heat – is the more efficient way to insulate buildings. However, this is often not possible if the external appearance has to be retained. The solution is to use insulation and wall build-ups that include both insulation and thermal mass. This is where hemp lime/hempcrete has significant benefits as it has the ability in one form of construction to provide both insulation and thermal mass. Crude U-values for hemp lime would suggest that it is not such a good insulator and yet hemp lime buildings appear to function more effectively than might be expected just as the Perthshire earth brick house did. This is partly because of the thermal mass effect.

Hemp lime masonry is able to retain heat as well as preventing it escaping. Tests carried out by Lime Technology and others have shown that its response time fits with a 24-hour cycle and thus temperatures (with minimal heating) remain the same internally despite significant temperature fluctuations outside. Thus in a house it takes very little additional energy to lift and maintain the internal temperature at a comfortable level.

The building physics of this is well explained by Szokolay (2007) even though he would not have come across hempcrete. He explains the dynamic response of buildings in terms of 'capacitive insulation', how the thermal capacity of materials has the effect of a delaying action on heat flow. He explains the importance of periodic heat flow analysis and says that while 10 mm of polystyrene and a 220 mm brick wall have identical U-values their thermal behaviour is quite different. The brick wall has a density of 375 kg/m^2 whereas the polystyrene only 5 kg/m^2

> in the brick wall each small layer of the material will absorb some heat before it can transmit any heat to the next layer. The stored heat would then be emitted with a considerable time delay.
>
> (Szokolay 2007)

He explains that stored heat in the brick can flow back into the building whereas this cannot happen with the polystyrene.

This concept of the time lag or 'decrement delay' is crucial to understanding the thermal performance of buildings. Information on materials and construction build-ups should always give the decrement factor as well as the thermal conductivity or U-value. However, most lightweight insulations have a poor decrement factor and do little to even out temperature fluctuations. This is ignored in most building physics and technical guidance.

As hemp lime construction has been used in France for 20 years, there has been a significant amount of research carried out by university research institutes, mainly in France but also in the UK and Germany. Much of this has addressed some of the issues referred to above in areas of building physics and science.

While hemp lime structures have some limitations as a wet system and with drying out, they also provide many advantages. Apart from being non-toxic, fire resistant, strong and durable they can also provide both thermal mass and reasonable insulation. The solid composite walls (and it is also used in floors and roofs) are breathable and hygroscopic. Very few materials or composite solutions can do this in such a simple way. It is possible to combine lightweight insulations with heavy thermal mass materials but this is not as effective as combining the two into one material. Where energy efficient constructions do not perform as effectively as expected this can be explained by the complication of too many layers and components and buildability issues. This is a problem that should not occur with hemp lime if it is built properly.

There is plenty of practical and anecdotal knowledge of how hemp lime is effective as a building solution and understanding of this, in terms of building physics and science, is growing. Research at Bath University in the UK, in Lyons and Rennes in France and in Louvain in Belgium has begun to piece together the unique performance and characteristics of this remarkable composite. Some interesting work has also been carried out by a succession of Masters and PhD students at the Centre for Alternative Technology Graduate School in Wales and at Trinity College, Dublin.

Some work is still based on simulations using WUFI, but there are also empirical results based on data from real buildings. The main commercial developers of hemp lime in the UK, Lime Technology and Lhoist (Lime Technology 2012) (LHOIST 2012), have also invested in certification through LABC and BBA and other institutions, and this has required significant rigorous testing. Fire tests have demonstrated that hemp lime walls have an excellent fire resistance. Bath University has assessed some structural issues, and in Belgium and France, the importance of the hemp shiv size and content, moisture, structure and acoustic issues have been analysed.

France has a hemp construction association, Construire-en-chanvre (Chanvre 2012). Its website includes a 100-entry bibliography on hemp construction and information on other technical research. Some of this research was presented at a conference in Darmstadt in November 2011 (Bath 2012). A comprehensive bibliography in English is also available in a major study of the prospects for hemp lime in Ireland commissioned by the Irish Environmental Protection Association. This report includes a detailed discussion of the relationship between building regulation requirements and hemp lime standards (Daly 2012). Hemp lime construction is now well established in the USA. Canada, Australia and many other countries. An Irish based international hemp building 'association' has organised conferences and workshops in Ireland and Spain (IHBA 2012).

The importance of this work is that scientific results and technical information are now available to an extent only rivalled by strawbale construction. With the establishment of the Alliance for Sustainable Building Products (ASBP 2012), more scientific and technical information on other natural and renewable products should become more readily available.

The exploration of the relationship between thermal resistance, moisture content and permeability issues is beginning to yield results in terms of understanding the thermal performance of natural materials. Hemp is particularly interesting as it seems able to absorb a great deal of moisture without significant risk of decay, provided that it can dry out again. Water absorption is part of the curing process, because the lime binder content has to gain strength through carbonation, but the water content also plays a part in the thermal capacity and mass of the material. Air pockets within the composite, inside the hemp contribute to the insulation properties, but research is needed to fully understand how the thermal properties vary as these air pockets become saturated.

Hemp lime is an inherently porous material because of the microscopic porosity of both hemp shives and binder mix and the macroscopic porosity resulting from the arrangement of particles. Measures of total porosity out-lined ranged between $71.1\%_{vol}$ and $73\%_{vol}$. Hemp lime materials can absorb moisture and allow water vapour to move through the building fabric. Measures of reported dry vapour resistance in range between 4.50 and 7.68 with typical values of 4.80. Water absorption coefficient of hemp lime values range between $0.075\,kg/(m^2\sqrt{s})$ and $0.15\,kg/(m^2\sqrt{s})$.

(Daly 2012)

Work at the University of Rennes (Collet 2011) has compared the perfor-mance of sprayed and cast (or moulded) hemp lime and found that, with spraying, the composite may be a little more porous but results so far are inconclusive. Research on the difference in performance between different lime formulations has also been carried out in Rennes and Lyons. Hemp lime walls with greater density and with aggregates added can achieve quite high strengths but this is at the expense of thermal performance (Hirst et al. 2010). Variation in size and shape of hemp shiv have also been analysed (Picandet 2011).

There are a significant number of variables in the performance of hemp concrete as it is referred to in France:

* particle size of the hemp shiv
* fibre and dust content mixed in with the shiv
* whether the shiv is dry or wet when it goes into the mixer
* the formulation of the lime binder used – some use a pre-formulated binder from commercial manufacturers, while others produce their own mix on site
* the proportions of hemp to lime binder and whether other aggregates like sand are added
* how the mix is prepared before placing ...what sort of mixer is used
* how the hemp is placed, into temporary shuttering, using permanent shuttering, whether it is sprayed
* tamping or compaction of the composite in the shuttering
* the amount of water that is used
* how long the wall is allowed to dry out before finishes are applied

While other materials such as wood fibre, hemp fibre and sheep's wool have hygroscopic properties the solid hemp lime composite has much greater thermal mass and much greater self-strength. However, hemp lime materials and mixes can vary considerably, depending on what is used. These and other variables are significant but it should not be assumed that this makes hemp lime masonry too complicated. As scientific research clarifies the best approach to each of the above, the specifier and builder can get the best advice as to the correct mix, materials and processes to use.

Some experiments carried out by architects and builders, who have tried to avoid using the certified Tradical materials from Lime Technology, have run into problems, particularly in Ireland where standards for hempcrete have not been in place. For instance, some have used hemp containing too much fibre, because the shiv and fibre have not been separated. This tends to absorb and hold much more water and can therefore take significantly longer to dry out. Scientific work in France has confirmed this to be the case.

Saving money through sourcing locally processed hemp is attractive but smaller-scale machinery may be less effective at separating shiv and fibres ('decortication'). In some cases in Ireland the hemp has also been mixed with cheap hydrated lime and inappropriate renders have been used, leading to walls remaining damp and not drying out. There is some benefit in some fibre being included in the mix for hemp lime plasters but not for solid insulating walls.

Others argue that the hemp should be soaked before being mixed with lime. This may also slow down the drying out if too much water is used.

Some research has been done on the use of hemp lime blocks but this is not the most effective use of the material as the wall is not as strong, with the need to use mortar between the blocks. Casting a solid wall is much simpler. However, bocks can be used in some circumstance for infill (Lanos and Collet 2011).

Research has demonstrated excellent acoustic properties in hemp lime walls, in terms of sound absorption and transmission. On-site acoustic testing has shown sound reduction of 57–58 dB for separation walls of hemp lime mix. Reported sound absorption values range between 0.3 and 1 αW with an average value of 0.7 αW. (Daly 2012).

There is still much work to be done to assess and understand thermal properties of hemp lime. Reviewing the available literature in the Irish EPA study, what has been reported so far is listed:

> Thermal conductivity values for hemp lime wall infill range between 0.05 and 0.12 W/(mK) depending on the density and composition of the mix. Low density mixes of about 220–275 kg/m^3 correspond to 0.05–0.06 W/(mK), medium density mixes of about 300–350 kg/m^3 correspond to 0.07 W/(mK), and higher density mixes of 450–550 kg/m^3 correspond to 0.11–0.12 W/(mK).
>
> (Daly 2012)

However, crude R- or U-values in themselves do not explain how hemp lime will perform. Research in Belgium using WUFI simulation software has measured the relationship between thermal changes and moisture (Evrard 2005 and 2006).

Such analyses of 'dynamic' thermal performance can begin to explain how an unusual material composite like hemp lime can be completely different from predictions based on steady state U-value figures. The thermal mass of the material evens out the heating up and cooling down of the building fabric to such a successful extent that temperatures inside hemp lime buildings remain largely constant despite significant temperature fluctuations outside. Because of this hemp lime is being widely used for buildings in which food and wine are stored. A steady temperature of 14 °C can be maintained without any heating or cooling input thus saving significantly on energy bills (Arnaud 2009).

Indoor air quality

Another key issue for natural and renewable materials is that of indoor air quality (IAQ) and building health issues. For reasons that are still unclear, the relationship between buildings and health has never been high on the agenda in the UK and concern for healthy buildings varies throughout the world. Air quality is also given little attention in mainstream building science and physics. It has been important in Germany, and much pioneering work has been done there, particularly by the Bau-Biologie movement (Baubiologie 2012). While it is on the agenda it does not seem to have been as significant in the Nordic countries. In the USA, there seems to be a much greater awareness of the issues, and much important work has been done there by the Healthy Buildings Network, (Healthy Building 2012), the Pharos project (Pharos 2012) and Environmental Building News (EBN 2012).

Interest in healthy buildings receives little attention through organisations like the World Green Building Council (WGBC) movement. Search the WGBC website for 'healthy buildings' or 'indoor air quality' and you will get 'no results found'. Even the International Council for Research and Innovation in Building and Construction (CIB) has only recently established a working group on Health and the Built Environment (TG77) in 2009 (CIB 2009).

WHO work has tended to focus narrowly on dampness and mould growth, ignoring wider issues of IAQ. A recent World Health Organisation publication (WHO 2009) and a 223-page WHO report on housing and disease (Braubach 2011) concentrates almost entirely on dampness and moisture, and only gives the briefest mention of the dangers of emissions from toxic materials, citing a 1999 study which in itself was largely to do with dampness.

> In addition to bioaerosols, indoor dampness may result in elevated concentrations of microbial volatile organic chemicals as well as increased chemical emissions of building materials, such as phthalates
>
> (Braubach 2011)

The ability of natural materials to buffer humidity and help to create healthier buildings by reducing the risk of mould growth and dampness is important, but the WHO reports fail to address this issue. They do highlight the very disturbing growth of asthma and respiratory illnesses but relate this largely to poor housing conditions and fuel poverty. There is no doubt that this is a worrying problem, but dampness in poor housing has been around since the industrial revolution and what has really changed has been the higher exposure to dangerous chemicals emitted by synthetic building materials and other household products. Unfortunately there have been very few medical epidemiological studies that have addressed this issue and thus little data is available.

The WHO do at least identify the problem of formaldehyde but say nothing about how it gets into houses, schools and other buildings. Instead they call for more research to find the sources:

There is the need for a better characterization of indoor sources and concentrations for formaldehyde in European countries. The evidence available to date suggests that indoor exposure to formaldehyde is a significant risk factor for lower respiratory symptoms such as wheezing.

(Braubach 2011)

Surprisingly the WHO report fails to mention that formaldehyde has been classified as a carcinogen in some countries including the USA

Formaldehyde has been classified as a known human carcinogen (cancer-causing substance) by the International Agency for Research on Cancer and as a probable human carcinogen by the U.S. Environmental Protection Agency

(National Cancer Institute 2012 – also see EPA 2011)

Many synthetic insulation products and timber glues still include formaldehyde, and while industry is moving away from these, some still admit to lower concentrations remaining in their products. Other synthetic products contain a range of toxic chemicals, polyurethane composites being some of the most worrying. In particular there are serious concerns about the use of sprayed polyurethane, particularly in the USA. Some foams contain about 20% soya and are marketed as though they were *natural products*. There has been at least one reported death related to a spray foam applicator in the USA (Pharos 2012).

There are three main risks from such dangerous chemicals being incorporated in buildings: direct or indirect emissions into indoor air; dangers

Table 6.4 Typical hazardous chemicals found in sprayed polyurethane foams according to the Pharos Project

Hazards of common sprayed polyurethane foam (SPF) insulation ingredients

Possible constituents	Health and environment risks
Methyl bisphenol diisocynate	Asthmagen; suspected carcinogen; Chlorine and formaldehyde used in MDI manufacture
Lead naphthenate (catalyst)	Avoid exposure to (pregnant) women. 'It is strongly advised that this substance does not enter the environment' National Institute for Occupational Safety and Health (NIOSH)
HFC-245a (blowing agent)	Very high global warming potential
HFC-141b (blowing agent)	Class II ozone depletion substance; high global warming potential; harmful to aquatic organisms
Tris (beta-chloropropyl) phosphate (fyrol)	Chlorinated flame retardant; some flame retardants are persistent, bioaccumulative and toxic

Source: adapted from *Pharos description of current EPA Chemicals of Concern*, Pharos Project 2012 (http://www.pharosproject.net/index/blog/mode/detail/record/95/epa-targets-polyurethane-chemistry). Accessed 6.2.12.

to the workers who manufacture and apply these products; and the highly toxic chemicals released in fires. It is important to remember that the fire retardants used with these materials are also toxic. Such chemicals also cause very significant damage to the wider environment, particularly during manufacturing, spillages and when disposed of as landfill.

The manufacturers and distributors of synthetic insulation materials will argue that indoor air emissions are insignificant because insulation materials are encapsulated in building structures. While this may be true in some building types often there is only a thin layer of plasterboard and plaster separating such materials from the occupant. As more and more agencies start to use synthetic insulation inside buildings, such as through dry lining for retrofit, these risks can increase significantly.

In an important study published by WWF (2003), supported by the Women's Institute and the Co-operative Bank, blood samples were taken from 155 volunteers in 13 UK locations. Worrying levels of chemicals that created risks to human health were found. A WWF advert "Who cares where toxic chemicals end up" in 2002 drew attention to contamination from over 300 manmade chemicals but the advert was banned by the Advertising Standards Authority *following complaints from the chemical industry*.

> The ASA found WWF's scientific research *to be above reproach* on all fronts and rejected every technical complaint. But despite being ruled factually accurate and being in the public interest, the advertisement was nevertheless banned on the grounds that it was 'unduly alarming'.
>
> *In the study, Lancaster University analysed the samples for 78 chemicals, 12 organochlorine pesticides (including DDT and lindane), 45 PCB congeners and 21 polybrominated diphenyl ethers (PBDE) flame retardants, including those found in the commercially traded penta-, octa- and deca-BDEs.* (emphasis added)
>
> (WWF 2003)

PBDEs were widely used as flame retardants in carpets, curtains, furnishings, plastic and synthetic insulation materials, though, due to health concerns, they are not so prevalent today. Synthetic insulation material manufacturers, on the other hand, are not very forthcoming when asked what flame retardants are used, and details are not always given in BBA and COSHH (Control of Substances Hazardous to Health) certificates.

Worryingly high levels of other dangerous chemicals, many associated with plastics, were also found by WWF, so it is surprising that the ASA thought the findings were *unduly alarming*. It says a lot about the kind of society that we live in that a responsible semi-government agency feels it has an obligation to protect the chemical industry from public alarm!

Manmade chemicals such as fire retardants have been blamed for hormone disruption affecting Inuit people in Northern regions, Greenland and Russia, as toxic spillages find their way to Polar regions and are absorbed in high concentrations by polar bears and seals.

Twice as many girls as boys are being born in some Arctic villages because of high levels of man-made chemicals in the blood of pregnant women, according to scientists from the Arctic Monitoring and Assessment Programme.

(Brown 2007)

There is much still to be done in terms of building physics and building science to understand how chemicals are released into buildings and how effectively they are dispersed by ventilation. Highly sensitive meters are now available to check emission levels (PPM 2012). However, designers and specifiers are not necessarily aware of the damage caused by synthetic products to the wider environment.

In the UK, measures to safeguard health and limit the use of dangerous and toxic materials has received little attention. The UK building regulations do not set standards for indoor air quality. References to health in the UK building regulations are largely restricted to ensuring freedom from damp and providing adequate ventilation. As a result, over recent decades, respiratory illnesses related to housing conditions have got significantly worse, despite improvements in ventilation standards.

Building regulations in Nordic countries have included IAQ standards for some years, but this does not seem to have reduced the use of synthetic insulation materials (Sundell 1982). Instead of regulating or reducing the source of emissions, regulations require higher levels of mechanical ventilation. As highly energy efficient and passiv haus buildings introduce mechanical heat recovery ventilation systems, the role of filters used in such systems becomes critical. Ideally the MVHR system should remove contaminants and bring in fresh air but there are worries that filters can become clogged if they are not changed regularly. However, internal polluted air should be expelled in MVHR systems if they are working properly. Many pollutants that accumulate in fabrics inside the home originate from external pollution.

If these systems are not appropriately maintained, ventilation air filters can become saturated leading to potential microbial growth and odour concerns.

(CDC 2012)

At a European level, legislation was introduced in 2007 to control dangerous chemicals. However, the REACH directive (Registration, Evaluation, Authorisation and Restriction of Chemicals) has not had that big an impact on construction materials, and the overlap between REACH and the Construction Product Regulations is not clear. Further work is still to be done on reviewing hazardous substances in construction products but it is very slow.

...under Article 67 the European Commission will review the need for information on the content of hazardous substances in construction products by 25 April 2014 and may extend the obligation to provide information to other substances, specifically with a focus on health and safety and recycling.

(eubusiness 2012)

In the UK, the Health and Safety Executive (HSE) has a responsibility to control chemicals and it has a WATCH group 'Working Group on Action to Control Chemicals'. The HSE also has an advisory Committee on Toxic Substances (ACTS). The WATCH committee does publish its minutes and, according to its website (HSE 2012), it holds open meetings but it has not held one for some years. The WATCH website says "Please watch this space for notification of the date of the next open meeting of WATCH" (HSE 2012).

The HSE official who is the secretary to WATCH, also works for the Advisory Committee on Pesticides, and has roles within the Chemicals Regulation Directorate and wider in HSE. This is an indication of how thinly spread staff with such regulatory functions have become.

While, as a member of the public, it is not possible to attend WATCH meetings, it is clear from their minutes that access for manufacturers of synthetic insulation products is not a problem. The exchange between the mineral fibre industry and the WATCH committee is reproduced at length here, as an example of the relationship between the synthetics industry and the regulators. Here are notes of a meeting on 17 June 2008 in Bootle Town Hall:

> The Chairman opened the item by informing WATCH that two representatives from the mineral wool manufacturers association, Eurisol UK, were attending the meeting to provide members with an overview of key issues relating to insulation mineral wool, and to present a proposal for commissioning a new risk assessment. The Chairman welcomed: Carol Houghton (CJHconsult Associates) and Steve Williams (Knauf Insulation Ltd), attending on behalf of Eurisol UK. He invited Carol Houghton to give a presentation on insulation mineral wool and asked WATCH members to give consideration to a proposal by Eurisol UK for further work on this theme.
>
> Carol Houghton informed WATCH that the classification in the EU of mineral wool as a "dangerous substance" and ongoing activity in relation to EU occupational exposure limits imply that exposure to mineral wools could pose a significant threat to health. She argued that this has led to negative perceptions about the use of mineral wool and creates market concerns; companies are tending to adopt a very cautious approach, fearful of litigation and there have been greater demands for exposure monitoring and the use of a high level of personal protective equipment at sites where mineral wools are used. Eurisol considers that mineral wool is a sustainable material that has numerous potentially beneficial uses and is therefore looking to address the current market concerns.
>
> (HSE 2008)

Eurisol argued that the level of risk posed by present-day exposure to mineral wool is very low, existing controls are more than adequate and that mineral wool was no more dangerous than many other 'dusts'. Eurisol's aim seemed to be to reassure the committee that everything was all right to counter what is being considered by the EU in terms of classifying mineral wool as hazardous. The argument reported in these minutes is very revealing because instead of refuting the suggestion that mineral fibre insulation is dangerous they simply argued that it has beneficial uses! The WATCH committee appeared to be reassured by these flimsy arguments.

> The Chairman thanked members for their comments. He confirmed with WATCH that the committee was interested in the proposed study on mineral wool to be commissioned by Eurisol UK … WATCH agreed that it would be appropriate to consider at a future meeting the outcomes from the proposed study, together with supporting information, in a comprehensive package of papers that would enable the committee to conduct a fuller evaluation of all of the available evidence.
>
> (HSE 2008)

Several years later, having checked with the HSE officials, it was confirmed that no such report from Eurisol (now known as MIMA the Mineral Wool Manufacturers Association), has emerged and thus it does not appear that anything has been done by the HSE to consider the safety of mineral fibre products. The committee has more recently been preoccupied with concerns about asbestos and mesothelioma (HSE 2008). But as long ago as 1988 a report about manmade mineral fibre (MMMF) for the HSE stated

> MMMF can in some circumstances cause irritation of the skin and eyes and upper respiratory tract. Some recent studies have reported an association between mineral wool production and lung cancer, but the exact cause and significance of this are controversial.
>
> (HSE 1998)

Controls of those products and materials that contain potentially harmful substances are currently insufficient. Industry lobbying has been successful at keeping tighter regulation at bay, both in the UK and at European level. There is little chance of dealing with the health issues that are associated with conventional building methods and synthetic materials when regulations are so weak. Thus the healthy alternatives offered by natural and renewable materials seem to be largely ignored by those in official bodies. Companies such as Black Mountain Insulation have published a carefully referenced guide to indoor air quality, in which they argue that sheep's wool insulation can be used to absorb and lock up formaldehyde and toluene emissions as a 'passive absorber'. In a situation where many timber products used in low energy buildings still contain carcinogenic formaldehyde, this can be seen as a useful interim mitigation of the problem (Black Mountain 2012), but it would be better if dangerous and toxic substances did not get into building materials in the first place.

References

ARC-PEACE 2012 Statement on Education of Architects and Planners adopted by the ARC-PEACE meeting in Copenhagen 12 April 2012 http://arcpeace.org/web/ (viewed 5.5.12)

Arnaud L. 2009 Comparative study of hygro thermal performances of building materials. Proceedings of the 11th International Conference on Non-conventional Materials and Technologies 6–9 September 2009, Bath, UK

ARUP 2004 *UK Housing and Climate Change – Heavyweight versus lightweight construction*, Arup Research + Development, Bill Dunster Architects, UK

Arup Associates 2012 http://www.usablebuildings.co.uk/ (viewed 16.2.12)

ASBL 2007 Concrete for energy-efficient buildings: The benefits of thermal mass European Concrete Platform ASBL, April 2007 www.efca.info/../Concrete_for%20 Energy_Efficient_Buildings.pdf (viewed 13.1.12)

ASBP 2012 www.asbp.org.uk (viewed 27.2.12)

Bath 2012 http://www.bath.ac.uk/ace/biomaterials-binders-for-construction-2/ (viewed 6.3.12)

Bau-biologie 2012 http://www.baubiologie.de/site/english.php (viewed 10.12.12)

BBA 2012 Information Bulletin No.5 http://www.bbacerts.co.uk/technical_guid ance.aspx (viewed 13.11.12)

Black Mountain 2012 http://blackmountaininsulation.com/images/pdf/pdf_pas sive_ solutions.pdf (viewed 6.5.12)

Bordass B. and Leaman A. 2005 Special Issue: Building performance evaluation making feedback and post-occupancy evaluation routine 1: A portfolio of feedback techniques Building Research & Information Volume 33, Issue 4, 2005

Braubach M. Jacobs D.E. and Ormandy D. Eds. 2011 Environmental burden of disease associated with inadequate housing: A method guide to the quantification of health effects of selected housing risks in the WHO European Region

BRE Green Guide 2012 http://www.bre.co.uk/greenguide http://www.bre.co.uk/ greenguide/page.jsp?id=2072 (viewed 20.2.12)

BREEAM http://www.breeam.org/page.jsp?id=358 (viewed 5.3.12)

Brown P. 2007 Guardian 12.9.2007 http://www.guardian.co.uk/world/2007/sep/12/ gender.sciencenews

Brown A 2008: Vapour Diffusion Calculations For Breathability and the Building Envelope Mulligan A. and Brown A, Oct 2008 Cambridge Architectural Research Prepared for Kingspan Insulation Ltd.

Carbon Trust 2012: www.carbontrust.co.uk/ (viewed 15.3.12)

Carbon Trust 2007 *CTV 014* Carbon Trust (viewed 15.3.12)

CDC 2012 http://www.cdc.gov/niosh/topics/indoorenv/buildingventilation.html

CIB http://www.cibworld.nl/site/news/newsletter.html?year=2009&number=8 (viewed 8.12.12)

Collet, F., Pretot, S. Chamoin, J. Lanos C. 2011 Hydric characterisation of sprayed hempcrete. European University of Brittany, LGCGM, Rennes, France, 2011

Chanvre Construire-en-chanvre http://www.construction-chanvre.asso.fr/ (viewed 15.2.12)

Daly, P., Ronchetti, P. Woolley, T. 2012 Hemp Lime Bio-composite as a Building Material in Irish Construction, Irish Environmental Protection Agency STRIVE Report 2012 http://erc.epa.ie/safer/iso19115/displayISO19115.jsp?isoID=202

EEBPP,1999 A Quantity Surveyor's Guide to the Cost-Effectiveness of Energy-Efficient Offices, GPG274. Energy Efficiency Best Practice Programme

EBN Environmental Building News 2012 http://www.buildinggreen.com/ (viewed 21.3.12)

EPA 2011 An introduction to Indoor Air Quality http:/www.epa.gov/aiq/formalde/ html (viewed 14.2.12)

EC 1988 Official Journal of the European Community L40/12 21 (December 1988) 89/106/EEC

EN 2011 Roadmap to a Resource Efficient Europe EN 20.9.11 COM 571 Brussels

EST 2010 Insulation Materials Chart CE71 EST 2004 Revised 2010

EU 2011 Regulation (EU) No 305/2011 of the European Parliament and of the Council 9 March 2011 (laying down harmonised conditions for the marketing of construction products and repealing Council Directive 89/106/EEC Official Journal of the European Union L 88/5 4.4.2011)

EU business 2012 http://www.eubusiness.com/topics/single-market/cpr/ (viewed 7.1.12)

Evrard A & De Herde A, 2005, *Bioclimatic envelopes made of lime and hemp concrete, Architecture et Climat – Université catholique de Louvain*, Louvain-la-Neuve, Belgium

Evrard, A., De Herde, A., Minet, J., 2006, *Dynamical interactions between heat and mass flows in Lime-Hemp Concrete*, Proceeding of the third International Building Physics Conference, Concordia University, Canada and International Association of Building Physics

Evrard, A., 2006, *Sorption behaviour of Lime-Hemp Concrete and its relation to indoor comfort and energy demand*, Proceedings of the 23rd Conference on Passive and Low Energy Architecture, Geneva, Switzerland

Fraunhofer Institute, Germany http://www.wufi.de/index_e.html www.wufi-wiki.com/mediawiki/index.php5/Details:Physics (viewed 5.3.12)

HBN Healthy Building Network 2012 (viewed 14.2.12) www.healthybuilding.net/housing/habitat_house.html

HSE 1998 hse.gov.uk/pubns/mdhs/pdfs/mdhs59.pdf (viewed 4.4.12)

HSE 2008 Watch Committee Minutes June 17 2008 (viewed 4.4.12) http://www.hse.gov.uk/aboutus/meetings/iacs/acts/watch/agendas.htm

HSE 2012 Health and Safety Executive http://www.hse.gov.uk/aboutus/meetings/iacs/acts/watch/ (viewed 4.4.12)

Heath P. 2009 *Green Building Magazine* Autumn 2009

Hens H. 2007 *Building Physics Heat, Air and Moisture* Ernst and Sohn 2007

Hirst, E., Walker, P., Paine, K. and Yates, T. 2010 Characterisation of Low Density Hemp-Lime Composite Building Materials under Compression Loading. Second international conference on sustainable construction materials and technologies, June 2010, Ancona Italy

IES Integrated Environmental Solutions http://www.iesve.com/software/ve-pro www.iesve.com/content/downloadasset_2000 (viewed 5.3.12)

IHBA 2012 http://www.internationalhempbuilding.org

Knauf Insulation http://www.knaufinsulation.co.uk/products/supafil_cavity_wall_insulation.aspx (viewed 5.3.12)

Kingspan 2009: Breathability – A White Paper: a study into the impact of breathability on condensation, mould growth, and dust mite populations and health, Second issue, November 2009

Lanos, C. and Collet, F. 2011 Mechanical properties of hempcrete UEB – LGCGM, Equipe Matériaux Thermo-Rhéologie INSA-IUT, Rennes, France

LHOIST 2012 http://www.lhoist.co.uk/tradical/ (viewed 7.3.12)

Lime Technology 2012 http://www.limetechnology.co.uk/ (viewed 7.3.12)

May, N. 2009 Environmental Assessment of Building Materials and the Green Guide: where do we go from here? Good Homes Alliance goodhomes.org.uk/../GHA%20Green%20Guide%20critique%.. (viewed 21.3.12)

May, N. undated: Breathability Matters: The key to Building Performance http://www.natural-building.co.uk/how_to_build_sustainably.htm (viewed 5.5.12)

Minke, G. 2006 Building with Earth: Design and Technology of a Sustainable Architecture Birkhauser

Morton, T., Stevenson, F. Taylor, B. and Charlton Smith, N. 2005 Arc Architects: Low Cost Earth Brick Construction Monitoring & Evaluation http://www.arc-architects.com/research/Earth-Masonry.htm)

Morton, T. 2008 Earth Masonry Design & Construction Guidelines, BRE Publications 2008

McCloud, K. 2011 personal email (9.2.11)

National Cancer Institute 2012 http://www.cancer.gov/cancertopics/factsheet/Risk/formaldehyde (viewed 13.2.13)

Pearce, I. and Parsons, T. 2012 Habitat for Humanity (personal email 24.1.12)

Pharos Project 2012 http://www.pharosproject.net/index/blog/mode/detail/record/95/epa-targets-polyurethane-chemistry (viewed 6.2.12)

Picandet, V., Tronet, P., Lecompte, T. and Baley, C. 2011 Hemp shiv characterisation: Particle size distribution, Water adsorption and Bulk compressibility, Darmstadt Conference 22 November 2011

Pilkington, B. 2008 In situ measurements of building materials using a thermal probe PhD thesis Plymouth University

Pilkington, B., Griffiths, R., Goodhew, S. and de Wilde P. 2010 In situ thermal conductivity measurements of building materials with a thermal probe, ASTM Journal of Testing and Evaluation, v.38 (3)

Planning Portal 2012 http://www.planningportal.gov.uk/buildingregulations/approveddocuments/partl/bcassociateddocuments9/acd (viewed 22.4.12)

Pohl, J. 2011 *Building Science: Concepts and Applications*, Wiley Blackwell

PPM 2012 http://www.ppm-technology.com/ (viewed 3.4.12)

PU Europe 2012 http://www.excellence-in-insulation.eu/site/index.php?id=73 (viewed 16.4.12)

Pro Clima 2012 http://www.proclima.com/co/INT/en/intello.html (viewed 15.4.12)

RAE 2010: The Royal Academy of Engineering London: Engineering a Low Carbon Built Environment – The Discipline of Building Engineering Physics (January 2010)

SETAC Europe 2003 Kotaji, S., Schuurmans, A. and Edwards, S. Life-Cycle Assessment in Building and Construction 2003

Sustainable homes http://www.sustainablehomes.co.uk/assessortraining.aspx (viewed 5.3.12)

Sundell, J. 1982 Guidelines for Nordic building regulations regarding indoor air quality *Environment International* Volume 8, Issues 1–6, 1982, pp. 17–20, Elsevier

Szokolay, S.V. 2007 Introduction to Architectural Science, the basis of sustainable design Elsevier, first published 2004 revised 2007

Taylor, M. 2008 "Building New Houses, are we moving towards zero carbon" in Sinn, C. and Perry, J. Housing the Environment and Our Changing Climate Chartered Institute of Housing 2008

TSB Technology Strategy Board http://www.innovateuk.org/ourstrategy.ashx (viewed 5.3.12)

This is concrete 2012 http://www.thisisconcrete.co.uk/case_studies/woodland_trust_hq.aspx (viewed 7.5.12)

Thornton, J. 2002, PhD. Environmental Impacts of Polyvinyl Chloride Building Materials, Healthy Building Network, Washington, DC 2002

Tucker, S. and Latif, E. 2012 Energy Efficient Bio-based Natural Insulation Technology, Strategy Board Project 2012 unpublished http://uktfa.com/thermal-mass-in-housing/ (viewed 7.5.12)

Umweltbundesamt Promoting Eco-efficient Innovation in the Construction Sector A Contribution from the Network of Heads of European Environment Protection Agencies to the revision of the Construction Products Directive (89/106/EEC) Zagreb, 24 September 2007 http://www.umweltbundesamt.de/produkte-e/bauprodukte/promoting.htm (viewed 5.3.12)

US Department of Energy http://apps1.eere.energy.gov/buildings/tools_directory (viewed 5.3.12)

WHO 2009 Guidelines for Indoor Air Quality Dampness and Mould 2009 Copenhagen ISBN 978 92 890 4168 3

Williamson, T.J. 2010 Building Research & Information Predicting building performance: the ethics of computer simulation 38(4), 401–410

WWF 2003 Contamination – The Results of Biomonitoring Survey WWF Godalming www.wwf.org.uk/filelibrary/pdf/biomonitoringresults.pdf (viewed 15.3.12)

7. Other solutions for low energy housing

Since 2005 there has been a rapid growth of experimental housing projects in the UK. The Renewable House Programme (RHP) is only one of a number of initiatives that provide evidence that many people are keen to try to reduce energy consumption and improve environmental performance. However, many of these attempts are misguided and have used technologies that are unlikely to stand the test of time. The mainstream industry approach to 'zero carbon' housing is the least successful from an environmental point of view because of the narrow focus on operational energy as discussed previously. Many of the timber frame modern methods of construction (MMC) solutions have been poorly thought through and rely on a hotchpotch of plastic and synthetic components that may fail to achieve the intended low energy results. Sooner or later the serious problems inherent in these solutions will become apparent. Misleading zero carbon claims could and should be challenged through the Advertising Standards Authority. On the other hand there are some examples that are well intentioned and even well crafted, but fail to adopt a holistic approach, ignoring the importance of health, pollution and embodied energy.

There are also many examples of projects using low impact, natural and renewable materials that were not part of the RHP. Much can be learned from these projects though it is not possible to go into a great deal of detail here. A small number of other projects from outside the UK are included here as they have some links with the RHP objectives.

Hemp lime houses

A hemp lime single-family house in Nordhoek, near Cape Town, South Africa, was built by Tony Budden of Hemporium (Hemporium 2012) and completed in 2010, drawing for technical advice and inspiration on hempcrete projects in the UK. The Nordhoek house uses a timber frame and

Low Impact Building: Housing using Renewable Materials, First Edition. Tom Woolley.
© 2013 John Wiley & Sons, Ltd. Published 2013 by John Wiley & Sons, Ltd.

Figure 7.1 Hemp house in Nordhoek, South Africa (front). Reproduced by permission of Hemporium, South Africa.

Figure 7.2 Hemp house in Nordhoek South Africa (side). Reproduced by permission of Hemporium, South Africa.

some hempcrete walls but also some hemp fibre insulation and local timber. Experimentation with hemp lime plaster was also a key part of the project. Nordhoek is in quite an exposed position with nothing between it and the South Atlantic, so it will be a good test of wind and weather on hempcrete walls. Research into growing of hemp, by the South Africa Department of Agriculture, has been going on for some years, but so far industrial hemp is not grown commercially, even though conditions are good. As illegal narcotic cannabis is grown in many parts of Africa there is the potential for hemp to be developed there, as an alternative, and for it to be used in low cost housing.

Hemp houses in Ireland

There are quite a number of hemp lime houses in Ireland, and some experimentation with hemp lime renovation. The Irish Government has shown interest in hemp through agricultural trials by TEAGASC at Oak Park (TEAGASC 2012), though it was mistakenly assumed that hemp was only suitable for fibreboard and biomass. A study into the potential for hemp lime in Ireland, commissioned by the Irish Environmental Protection Agency, carried out in 2009/10 is referred to in Chapter 6 (Daly 2012).

There have been problems with some of the hemp lime projects in Ireland, as some businesses have tried to find alternative sources of hemp and to make up their own lime binder mixes to avoid importing materials from Lime Technology in England. Most of the alternative sources of hemp shiv that have been used include a significant amount of hemp fibre and this seems to have led to much slower drying out periods, with the hemp fibre holding more moisture than shiv. There have also been failures of external render where, to save money, cheap hydrated lime has been used. Unfortunately, there remains a great deal of ignorance about lime and the differences between lime putty, hydraulic lime and hydrated lime. Experience to date suggests that for the best results, a careful blend of lime as in the Tradical pre-formulated binder is necessary for the best results. A poor quality render, especially if it is applied to a hemp lime wall that has not dried out sufficiently can lead to failures, especially if exposed to the heavy and driving rain in Ireland. Hemp lime external renders have also been used with poorly detailed strawbale buildings, leading to serious problems.

On the other hand, Ireland has a number of successful projects that have used Tradical lime binder and hemp imported from England, including several hemp lime projects at an 'eco village' in Cloughjordan. Cloughjordan also features other forms of low energy construction. One project designed by architect Niall Leahy for Brenda and Nicole Power of Acorn Energy in Cloughjordan has been very well finished. Temporary plastic shuttering was used as well as permanent shuttering, and thus the build is very similar to that used in the RHP in England. (Self-build 2011).

The eco village at Cloughjordan (eco village 2012) also includes a hemp lime terrace and various projects that have used forms of construction

Figure 7.3 Cloughjordan hempcrete house designed by Niall Leahy. Reproduced by permission of Brendan Power, Acorn Energy.

(involving hemp) that have never been tried anywhere before. These seem to involve a high degree of risk, particularly using loose hemp, untamped hemp lime and clay hemp plasters. One project (Site 84) is said to have used 'the whole of the hemp plant'. The village website includes some 'case studies' though these do not provide much technical detail (eco village 2012).

One product used for quite a few of the eco village houses is Durisol blocks and this has been used with hemp lime plaster at Cloughjordan (Durisol 2012). Durisol is a hollow block made from 'recycled wood' possibly mixed with cement, but details of the mix were not clear from the Durisol website nor on their BBA certificate. Stating that Durisol provides sustainable green construction, they recommend filling the cavity in the block with concrete to give it structural strength but also claim extremely good U-values when mineral wool or phenolic foam is included in the block. Some Durisol projects have also used hemp and lime either as infill or as a plaster, including some projects at the Cloughjordan eco village. Despite this, Durisol has criticised hempcrete on their website stating

> Durisol is made from waste materials that will not rot or burn and provide excellent U vales for Eco Friendly Building. What's more, the Durisol system can be built in all weather and quickly dries. Hemcrete needs to be constructed under controlled conditions and can take many months to dry out. The photograph below shows a home built with Hemcrete, six months after the building was complete and the occupiers had moved in.
>
> (Durisol 2012)

Having made enquiries with Durisol and Lime Technology, as to the location of the houses featured on the Durisol website, which appear to show some damp staining, Durisol removed this page and the above comments from their website!

Another Irish Hempcrete house, in County Longford, designed by Winkens Architecture, (Winkens 2012) was designed to achieve passiv haus certification. The house owner, James Byrne, who is a mechanical engineer, installed the Tradical hemp lime mix himself. (Construct Ireland 2012). Construct Ireland say that it cost €400,000 and is a two-storey house said to be 335 m². If the cost figures are accurate then this has to be one of the most

Table 7.1 Cloughjordan eco village list of projects

Complete and occupied houses
- Certified passive house timber frame
- Durisol block, lime hemp render
- Low-energy Austrian house
- 32-bed Eco-hostel
- Low-energy timber frame, timber cladding
- Terrace of three houses, timber frame and lime and hemp internal and external
- Low-energy timber frame
- All cedar house, recycled newspaper insulation
- Timber frame and loose hemp insulation semidetached, clay hemp plaster
- Durisol and lime hemp house, bakery attached
- Hempcrete house, eco-slate, local timber finishings
- Low-energy timber frame
- Hempcrete house
- Low-energy timber frame
- Scandinavian passive house
- Timber frame, corrugated roof, lime & hemp render semidetached
- Hempcrete house

Almost complete
- All cedar house
- Durisol A rated semidetached, eco-slate, lime and hemp render
- Timber frame, lime and hemp plaster, Irish cedar cladding
- Timber frame, cedar cladding, cellulose insulation, cob, sedum roof
- Durisol external wall, clay and hemp internal walls, lime and hemp render, eco-slate
- I-beam, recycled glass and lime plaster house
- Rammed earth and lime hemp house
- Timber frame with micro reed bed grey water run-off

Under construction
- Curved cob house using hand applied and non-mechanical clay/straw mix, eco-slate
- Hempcrete house with lime and hemp render, clay hemp internal plaster
- Timber frame, sheep's wool insulation, cedar clad house and work unit
- Timber frame, corrugated roof, cedar clad semidetached
- Rammed earth and lime hemp house
- Hempcrete semidetached
- Timber frame, sheep's wool, lime and hemp external, clay and hemp internal, zinc dome
- Curved cob house
- Low-energy double frame timber house
- Eco-Enterprise Centre

Figure 7.4 Longford hemp house designed by Winkens. Reproduced by permission of Winkens Architecture.

affordable passiv haus projects completed so far. It has won one of the Irish Green Awards in 2012.

Local sheep's wool in Scotland

A house in Cairn Valley, south-west Scotland, designed by Mark Waghorn architects, received a great deal of publicity because it was said that it was using 'wool sheared from sheep of the surrounding farms' (Waghorn 2012). A number of people had assumed that this meant that the sheep fleeces were to go straight into the roof! However, when contacted, the owner of the house, explained that the wool had gone to Bradford to be processed in the normal way, so the insulation is much the same as that sold by Thermafleece or Black Mountain.

Claimed both as carbon neutral and carbon negative, the house uses some local timber and is being constructed with a steel frame.

Strawbale houses in West Grove, Martin, North Kesteven, Lincolnshire

Even though there have been many individual self-built strawbale houses in the UK and many thousands around the world, strawbale construction has not been readily adopted for social housing or by mainstream house build-ers in the UK. Thus a small project in Lincolnshire, built with bales, is of

Figure 7.5 North Kesteven strawbale house with tenant. Reproduced by permission of Sleaford Standard.

considerable interest. Designed as a pair of semidetached council owned houses to look very similar to ordinary houses in the area, these two-storey, three-bedroomed houses of an internal gross area of 85.75 m², with strawbale walls of 450 mm with 30 mm lime on both sides. A particularly innovative feature is the party wall between the houses, which is also of load-bearing straw, plastered both sides with lime. (Sodagar et al. 2011).

Using 450 bales for each house, the overall cost was £1210/m². The mainstream builder, Carter Homes, has gone on to construct a community centre in Neatishead, Norfolk, that also includes strawbale walls. Strawbale construction is often promoted as cheaper than other ways of building because the bales can cost £2 each or less, but, due to the labour involved and other aspects of construction there are no significant savings unless there is a significant element of self-build.

There were reports that the Council had difficulty finding tenants to live in the houses, but one tenant, interviewed by the local newspaper, seemed very happy (Sleaford Standard 2012).

Research carried out by a team at Lincoln University calculated the carbon footprint of the strawbale houses. This claims that the materials emissions rate for constructing one of the houses is 151 kg CO_2/m² of gross internal floor area, much less than the average 475 kg CO_2/m² for conventionally constructed new-build homes in the UK, but they also claim that the houses would sequester 82.5 kg CO_2 during the lifetime of the building. It is not clear whether this is a total figure or is per square metre. (Sodagar 2012).

Figure 7.6 Ongar strawbale design by Parsons and Whittley. Reproduced by permission of Parsons and Whittley Ltd Architects.

Another social housing landlord, Hastoe Housing Association, is building four strawbale houses in High Ongar in Essex, designed by Norfolk architects, Parsons and Whittley.

> The construction uses a structural timber frame with straw infill, lime-rendered externally and with a pantiled roof. The original concept of utilising oak shingles on the roofs was abandoned in view of the potential risk of damage by local woodpeckers!
>
> (Parsons and Whittley 2012)

Timber experiments

Conventional timber frame construction does not always use timber in the most effective way from an environmental point of view. Much of the timber used in mainstream construction is imported because home grown timber in the UK is seen as unsuitable. However, attempts have been made to find ways of using local timber.

Innovative work in Wales to develop alternative forms of timber construction has led to the *Ty Unnos* (the house of one night) project (Ty Unnos 2012), a modular form of construction using a timber structure made from local timber (Elements Europe 2012). Developed with the help of Wood Knowledge Wales and Bangor University, the system is designed to use poorer quality Sitka spruce by making box sections which are structural. Initially cellulose (recycled newspaper) insulation has been used with the system but other natural insulations would work just as well. Despite the excellent potential of this system, adoption and use by house builders has been limited. However, a single house project in Ebbw Vale and a small development of four social houses in Dolwyddelan in North Wales have been completed (Dolwyddelan 2012).

Figure 7.7 Dolwyddelan Ty Unnos House. Reproduced by permission of Helen McAteer, Menter Siabod Ltd.

The Housing Expo in Ebbw Vale in South Wales, much smaller than the one in Inverness, with only three homes, includes a timber clad passiv haus developed by United Welsh Housing Association with timber windows to passiv haus standards from a local Welsh joinery firm (The Works 2012). A visitor centre house using the Ty Unnos construction method was also constructed. A third house, three-bedroom house, known as the Dragonboard home, was developed by a Welsh company. Constructed with a steel frame system, its walls are made from a board that is intended to replace oriented strand board and plasterboard, and uses a sprayed foam insulation known as "Icynene." Dragonboard appears to be an American product but possibly manufactured in China, using a mixture of wood waste dust and magnesium oxide, but whether that makes it as green as claimed is open to question.

> In waste management terms, Dragonboard must be one of the 'greenest' boards on the planet
>
> (Dragonboard 2012)

While strong claims are also made about the health and environmental advantages of Dragonboard, the Icynene insulation is a petrochemical based polyurethane product and would be regarded by some as hazardous (see Chapter 6).

Figure 7.8 Ebbw Vale passiv haus

Figure 7.9 Dragonboard house

Scottish Housing Expo

In addition to the Scottish Housing Expo RHP case study houses, a range of other interesting demonstration projects, mainly using timber, were constructed in Inverness. They include the Flower House, which uses CLT timber and wood fibre insulation; the White House with CLT covered with a resin based external coating; the Stealth Terrace, four family homes wrapped in a skin of 'black rubber' and black stained larch cladding and ivy on the facade; the Shed House, which is a fairly conventional timber frame with timber cladding; the Stone House, clad in Caithness Stone; and houses of dense blockwork among others (Scotland's Housing Expo 2010). As far as can be seen, no detailed evaluation has been published of the Housing Expo, from an energy or environmental perspective, but there has been some discussion of the issues around its implementation, and the operational issues of the project. Some might take the view that the Expo was more an opportunity for architects to indulge various design experiments than a serious effort to address sustainability issues.

> The Scottish Government is currently conducting a review of the Expo to evaluate the success of the project and to learn from the ideas and experiences of those who took part in its creation and who visited the event in August 2010.
>
> (Scotland Government 2011)

Using local materials?

The Ty Unnos project is an interesting attempt to use local Welsh timber, and other organisations have also addressed this issue. The 'LoCaL' project, by Accord Housing Association, in the English Midlands, is an interesting attempt to develop local supply systems, where they have set up their own factory to produce timber frame housing panels and modules. This aims to create local employment and cuts out some of the middlemen in the normal industry supply chains. Previously the Housing Association was importing closed timber panels from Norway, but by manufacturing them locally they have created 30 jobs. Projects in Walsall, Darlaston, West Bromwich, Dudley, Wolverhampton and Redditch using the system are planned. The Accord LoCaL initiative is an interesting one, but it was hard to understand why such a simple and basic form of construction, available from dozens of companies throughout the UK, should have had to be sourced in Norway. Accord says that the panels have a U-value of 0.18, using 200 mm of Earthwool insulation (Accord 2012). However, despite the name LoCaL, they are not using local timber or locally made low impact renewable insulation materials that could have been obtained from nearby Black Mountain in North Wales, or even Rockwool in South Wales. Instead they have chosen Knauf Earthwool insulation that is imported from southern Germany. UK renewable materials manufacturers have some way to go to convince such organisations to use their products.

Figure 7.10 LoCaL factory, Accord Housing Association. Reproduced by permission of The Accord Group.

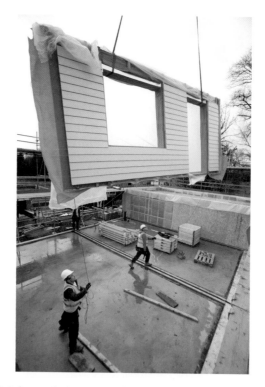

Figure 7.11 LoCaL house being erected on site. Reproduced by permission of The Accord Group.

Greenwash projects?

There are a growing number of projects that claim to achieve zero carbon solutions but the green claims about many of these projects are not always credible. Some environmental organisations have formed partnerships with larger commercial bodies to promote sustainable solutions in the mainstream. BioRegional, that was involved in the construction of the famous BEDZED project (BEDZED 2011), formed a joint venture with a mainstream construction firm, Quintain. BioRegional Quintain built a large multi-storey housing scheme in Brighton, One Brighton, with developers Crest Nicholson and had planned another in Middlesbrough. However, Quintain became a victim of the recession and closed down, leaving the Middlesbrough scheme only partially realised (Guardian 2011a). Known as One Brighton and Middlehaven One, these projects may not be as environmentally sound as is sometimes claimed. However, the One Brighton project used some wood fibre renewable and other materials from NBT.

The Brighton and Middlesbrough schemes are said to comply with the BioRegional 'one planet principles' (One Planet 2012), and quite a number of commercial businesses have signed up to this aim, such as Lafarge, the multinational cement and concrete business, who say that they plan to carry out several one-planet living developments* (Lafarge 2012). The one-planet living principles on the face of it seem very good, but there seems not to be any rigorous way of measuring whether they have been achieved by projects or companies who have signed up. Maybe they are just 'moving towards' the standards!

While there were some innovative features to the 'One Brighton' scheme, designed by architects Feilden Clegg Bradley, it is hard to understand how a scheme using so much concrete and steel could ever be regarded as a model of how to live within one-planet constraints. The concept of one planet is best understood through the global footprinting methodology that attempts to make overall assessments of environmental impact (Footprint 2012).

Most european countries are considered to use about three or more planets share of resources and thus to reduce this activity to one planet impact, by living in equilibrium with planetary resources, would involve very significant changes in lifestyle and resource consumption. Indeed a rigorous analysis of this might suggest that in a wealthy country, like the UK, with a large surplus of empty buildings, we should not be consuming any resources at all to create new buildings. The embodied energy of a large project like One Brighton would be significant and thus its environmental impact could be considered damaging in terms of resource consumption and embodied energy emissions. When asked to justify these claims, Pooran Desai of BioRegional stated

---

*Lafarge claims in their sustainability report from 2009 that cement only emits 0.075 per gramme of cement whereas potato crisps emit 2.2! They say that their ambition is to reduce CO_2 emissions by 10% by 2012. Cement manufacture globally produces about 5% of all CO_2 emissions, so it is a major contributor to global warming. The units for cement and crisps are not made clear. (Lafarge 2012)

I think the issue is whether in urban areas, investment in embodied carbon for high-rise in order to reduce transport (with Brighton at 12 storey's used concrete albeit 50% GGBS, 100% secondary aggregate and post-tensioned to reduce volume of concrete, facilitating a private car free design) is a valid approach.

(Desai 2012)

Table 7.2 BioRegional one planet principles

BioRegional one planet principles (Extract)
- Making buildings more energy efficient and delivering all energy with renewable technologies
- Reducing waste, reusing where possible, and ultimately sending zero waste to landfill
- Encouraging low carbon modes of transport to reduce emissions, reducing the need to travel
- Using sustainable healthy products, with low embodied energy, sourced locally, made from renewable or waste resources
- Choosing low impact, local, seasonal and organic diets and reducing food waste
- Using water more efficiently in buildings and in the products we buy, tackling local flooding and watercourse pollution
- Protecting and restoring biodiversity and natural habitats through appropriate land use and integration into the built environment
- Reviving local identity and wisdom; supporting and participating in the arts
- Creating bioregional economies that support fair employment, inclusive communities and international fair trade
- Encouraging active, sociable, meaningful lives to promote good health and well-being

---

Source: extract from *The 10 One Planet Principles* (One Planet 2012)

Desai, who is a highly respected authority and pioneer of sustainability policies, also confirmed that there had not been any independent analysis of the One Brighton claims, apart from the BREEAM post-construction report.

There are dangers in badging schemes like this as 'green' or 'one planet' as this may give the impression to the residents that they are somehow saving the planet while only making minor changes in lifestyle, other than possibly cutting down on car ownership. They can cut down their personal footprint by catching the train from the nearby station and using less energy to heat their houses, but one-planet principles do not appear to require major reductions in resource consumption to build the houses in the first place.

The ambitious Middlesbrough scheme has only resulted in one completed project, the 80-unit nine-storey Community in a Cube (CIAC), 'Riverside One', designed by *FAT* architects. The rest of the masterplan by Will Alsop and designs by Nick Grimshaw has been left unrealised.

One … resounding fact about CIAC is that simply by living here, in one of the most environmentally responsible developments in the UK, you'll be contributing to the well being of our planet. What could be better than that?

Figure 7.12 Middlehaven 1

Riverside One is designed to be very energy efficient as well as zero carbon. The buildings will be highly insulated to stay warm in winter, with argon filled double glazing and energy efficient lighting and appliances. *The concrete frame construction will enable the building to stay cool in summer by absorbing heat.*

Riverside One has been designed to make full use of local, healthy, natural, reclaimed and recycled materials. *Some of the construction materials are the most advanced and sustainable in the UK, providing the possibility of long-term heath benefits to residents. The energy used to extract, process, refine and transport materials (embodied energy) as well as pollution and waste generated, will be reduced. Locally sourced materials will be used to reduce transport impacts and to support the local economy.* (emphasis added)

(Riverside One 2012)

A charitable view of such projects is that they are trying to make some small environmental changes within mainstream construction, using concrete and steel, though a concrete frame within the building envelope is unlikely to contribute much to keeping a building cool. The idea that local materials have been used should be taken with a pinch of salt. The builder was asked what insulation materials had been used at Riverside One, making 'full use of local healthy and natural materials' but the response from GB-Building was that 'the client does not want to disclose this information' (GB-Building 2012). Fortunately as we live in a relatively open and democratic society it did not take too much effort to find out what insulation had been specified, though this might have been changed by the builder on site. The specification included 80 mm Pavatherm wood fibre boards, so there has been some attempt to use a natural renewable (though not local) product. However, this was only for part of the building. Most of the insulation included various rockwool products, fibreglass and some 60 mm Kingspan boards. Here we have another example of where

Figure 7.13 Middlehaven 2

those involved appear not to discriminate between synthetic and natural insulation, and it is hard to see how such materials could achieve the long-term health benefits claimed.

So-called 'carbon neutral' developments

As explained in Chapter 5, the terms zero carbon and carbon neutral can have little meaning, but that does not stop housing developers claiming that they are building carbon neutral developments. There are numerous schemes being promoted as zero carbon or carbon neutral, though few get near to justifying such claims.

One example of a bold attempt to achieve carbon neutral, is a project, claimed to be the UK's largest zero carbon housing development, which began in 2007. Linden Homes and Affinity Sutton are developing an 85-acre site at Graylingwell Park, an old hospital near Chichester, West Sussex, to build 800 homes.

> The plan is to reduce on-site carbon emissions by 60% and to offset the remaining 40% by building a 1.5 MW wind turbine located off site
>
> (Evans 2012)

It was difficult to find out too much about the wind turbine or even whether it is in West Sussex or Scotland, if it has been built at all! The developers didn't seem too keen on any critical comment on the scheme, saying in an email that they would 'veto any unfavourable use' (in this book) of the information they sent! The claims of being carbon neutral are dependent on a gas-fired CHP district-heating scheme with two 500 kW engines and four 1.1 MW gas boilers and massive thermal storage. For such a large development this seems to make some sense, providing the houses are well insulated. There are potential efficiencies in district heating compared with the Code for Sustainable Homes preoccupation with micro renewable in each house (Graylingwell Park 2012).

The houses include a range of Kingspan, Knauf and Celotex synthetic insulations* (Evans Powerpoint 2011). What is striking about their approach is the complexity of the roof and wall build-ups with so many layers and materials used. This is fairly typical of attempts in mainstream construction to achieve low energy 'zero carbon' results using synthetic petrochemical based materials. It is to be hoped that there will be independent monitoring of the performance of these buildings to see whether the energy efficiency standards have been achieved.

Earth sheltered building

The use of underground or semi-underground house buildings is sometimes presented as a solution to low energy housing, but from an environmental point of view it raises many difficult problems. Firstly earth 'berming' or sheltering can take up a lot of space and is generally only useful in rural locations. It requires single aspect buildings with a lack of cross ventilation, so there is a dependence on mechanical ventilation. The Hockerton Housing project (Hockerton 2012) in Nottinghamshire is a particularly well known and successful scheme and is frequently held up as an example of zero carbon housing. Built since 1998, Hockerton makes good use of passive solar gain with a massive conservatory linking a terrace of houses and a big earth bank on the north side and has inspired many people to attempt eco building through its excellent education and information programme. Yvette Cooper, the UK Labour Government Housing Minister, visited the project in 2007. Hockerton has recently retrofitted two of the houses to a higher energy standard.

To live under an earth bank requires concrete and synthetic waterproofing materials, thus making such projects higher in terms of embodied energy. There is little published evidence on how much solid earth used in this way contributes to thermal efficiency, that might offset the embodied energy of the other materials.

---

*The insulation breakdown at Graylingwell Park – A 350 mm insulation quilt (of unspecified materials) in the *cold roof* with a Tyvek SD2 vapour barrier to ceiling joist, 25 mm Kingspan Kooltherm K7 insulation board and 15 mm Knauf Wallboard in an effort to achieve a U value 0.12 W/m²K. For their *warm roof* either 140 mm Kingspan Thermapitch TP10 between rafters with 25 mm Kingspan Thermapitch TP10 beneath, or 75 mm Kingspan Thermapitch TP10 between rafters with 65 mm Kingspan Thermapitch TP10 beneath. For the walls a closed panel factory insulated timber frame with masonry (cladding?), a 50 mm cavity TF 200 mm 'thermo' membrane 9 mm OSB, 140 mm stud with 130 mm Celotex XR4130, VC foil/25 mm batten to achieve a U-value of 0.17 W/m²K (Evans 2011).

Another earth sheltered scheme in Honingham in Norfolk built by the Flagship group (involved in Diss in the RHP) is a smaller version of Hockerton, designed by architect Jeremy Harrall who wrote his PhD on earth sheltered housing at the University of Lincoln (Harrall 2007). Harrall, in his projects, uses petrochemical based synthetic insulation materials including urethane foam and Dow Styrofoam. Dow promotes one of his projects, the CaNeBuZo development in Lincolnshire, prominently on their website (Dow 2012). Like so many other so-called carbon neutral projects, the embodied energy and environmental impacts of the synthetic insulation are not given much prominence but neither are ethical questions about the role of Dow, in relation to the Union Carbide scandal. Barry Gardiner MP, chair of Labour Friends of India, has been protesting, along with many others about the use of Dow materials at the London Olympics stadium.

> Labour Friends of India and a cross-party coalition of MPs are urging the London Organising Committee of the Olympic Games (LOCOG) to review its decision to award Dow Chemical Company the contract to build the decorative wrapping on the Olympic Stadium. Dow's appalling human rights record in regards to the victims of the 1984 Bhopal gas disaster puts the Olympic legacy at risk.
>
> (Gardiner 2012)

Dow has also been a major sponsor of the Olympics and Dow Styrofoam was used substantially in the construction of the Olympic Village where ethical concerns about Bhopal have led to a campaign by some architects to boycott Dow products.

BRE Innovation Park

The Renewable House at the BRE Innovation Park near Watford. (BRE 2011) was one of a number of demonstration projects as part of the BRE Innovation Park. Many influential visitors and politicians were able to see the renewable house built from natural materials without taking fright and compare it with other demonstration projects that cost considerably more than normal (Vaughan 2007). Not all of the houses that were built on the site still remain, as they were only seen as semipermanent, and people cannot live in them. One or two houses are already being renovated. One apartment building to be built out of ICF (insulated concrete formwork) by a company called CREO Prokoncept, was never completed and was demolished (or 'deconstructed' to use BRE terminology!). ICF is still being promoted as a form of low energy construction (ICF 2012). It involves constructing formwork out of a petrochemical based insulation such as polystyrene, held together with metal ties and then pouring concrete inside the insulation. This was promoted for some time by the Cement and Concrete Association as an ideal form of construction due to its thermal mass, until it was pointed out that the thermal mass was ineffective, as it

Table 7.3 BRE Innovation Park projects

- The Hanson EcoHouse
- The Renewable House
- Osborne's Affordable House
- Willmott Dixon Healthcare Campus
- The Barratt Green House
- The Victorian Terrace
- The Visitors Centre
- The Sigma Home
- The Prince's House
- Innovations in landscape architecture
- The Cub House
- Energy use
- Podpassiv

was enclosed within the insulation. This form of construction has no breathability at all, so requires full mechanical ventilation.

It was not possible to find any significant independent review of the BRE Innovation Park projects (BRE Innovation Park 2011) and it is disappointing that it is not easy to learn lessons from any problems with the buildings. Gaze gives a superficial analysis (Gaze 2009). There has been quite a lot of media criticism such as the claim that the BRE had 'turned its back on evidence-based research in favour of a narrow focus on commercial growth and unproven gimmicks', according to Kevin McGeough of English Partnerships (Olcayto 2008).

One of the projects at the Innovation Park, listed by the BRE as 'The Prince's House' and also called 'The Natural House', was the only other project constructed using natural materials (from Natural Building Technologies). The house was slow to build, but this may not have been due to the materials or design but other issues such as funding and management. Hollow clay block with thin mortar bed solid walls, Pavatex wood fibre and sheep's wool insulation were used.

> Built by The Prince's Foundation for Building Community, the Prince's House is a highly energy efficient structure that nonetheless reflects people's preference for traditionally designed buildings. It is constructed from natural materials including aerated clay block, lime based renders and plasters, and insulation using compressed wood fibre and sheep's wool. The thermally coherent shell delivers energy efficiency and good indoor air quality, is simple and quick to build and is designed to appeal to an increasingly eco-aware homebuyer.
>
> (BRE 2011)

Masonry construction for low energy houses

Despite the general shift towards timber frame construction and the advantages in terms of speedier construction and carbon sequestration, some low energy projects are still being constructed with masonry.

Lancaster cohousing

One example is a new 'cohousing' development in Lancaster at Halton Bank. Cohousing projects consist of individual house units, with a cooperative ideal and perhaps mixed tenure, and schemes usually include a common house as is planned for the LILAC RHP project in Leeds. There are some 30–40 cohousing groups in the UK in existence or planning developments, quite a few planning houses for older residents. (Cohousing 2012).

One of the first pioneering cohousing schemes at Springhill in Stroud, designed by Architype Architects, was constructed in 2002/3, consisting of 34 houses. It was an example of environmental best practice at the time, using timber frame, timber cladding and cellulose insulation. However, the Lancaster project has opted for concrete block cavity walls and synthetic insulation.

The Lancaster co-housing project states on the cohousing website says that it will 'be built on ecological values in partnership with our architects, Ecoarc'. In a Guardian article, they say that cohousing offers a *healthier way* to live and a more sustainable business model (Guardian 2011b).

Planned on a spectacular riverside site, the scheme was designed to meet Code Level 6 and has been well documented in *Green Building Magazine* including a very useful critical account of the failings of The Code (Parks 2012). The houses are being built predominantly with concrete block cavity wall construction though some timber panels are also being used. It was difficult to find out what insulation was being used in the cavity walls, but there are pictures of polystyrene on the cohousing website. It is not clear whether the Lancaster scheme hopes to achieve passiv haus status, but other advocates of passiv haus in the AECB extol the virtues of masonry construction.

> Love it or loathe it (and some people really loathe it …) … cavity wall construction is still very much an intrinsic part of UK Housebuilding, comprising 75% of new housing in 2010. To meet climate change targets, buildings in the future will need to have wall U values of 0.15 to 0.1 W/m^{2}K, with airtightness 10 times better than current building regulations, minimal thermal bridging and thermal bypass (air movement around insulation). How do we as a nation get from where we are to this low energy nirvana? Do we jettison the cavity and embrace timber frame and solid masonry with rendered external insulation? Or do we work with what we have in the short to medium term, while maybe moving towards alternative methods?
>
> (Butcher 2011)

According to Butcher, the decision to go with cavity masonry at Halton Bank was taken as a result of an exercise, by the Lancashire builder Whittle Construction, in which they were asked to rate different construction methods. This resulted in the conclusion that timber frame would be much quicker but would cost £80,000 more. Whittle preferred cavity walls as they were used to them and could use their own labour. It is not clear whether environmental impact issues were part of the discussion, despite the ecological aims of the group.

Bill Butcher of Green Building Store Ltd was a key figure in the development of what is frequently billed as UK's 'first' passiv haus. The Denby Dale project was also constructed with masonry cavity walls. The enormously wide cavities at Denby Dale are well illustrated on Knauf Insulation's website, as the insulation used was glass wool (Knauf 2012). Bill Butcher is an advocate of the idea that operational energy is much more important than embodied energy even though his company, Green Building Store, used to be a pioneer of ecological building methods and materials. His move away from environmentally friendly materials to synthetic petrochemical based products has led many to accept that such products are acceptable in low energy housing.

It is possible to construct passiv haus buildings using natural renewable and breathable materials, but few in the UK have so far chosen to do this. Advocates of passiv haus rarely refer to materials or embodied energy and do not promote sustainable materials. Siddall, of Devereux Architects says, 'Passiv haus is arguably THE low energy, low carbon design standard' without any mention of embodied energy (Siddall 2012). In a presentation by Wolfgang Feist, at the UK Passiv Haus Conference in 2010, the only insulation material shown is an Isover product. (Feist 2009). Isover, part of the St Gobain group, are the leading manufacturers of fibreglass.

However, it is possible to find passiv haus projects using ecological materials in Austria, and there are some in Germany. For instance, a three-storey timber frame office building for the Catholic Church used natural insulation, mainly hemp and some cellulose, though some rockwool was also used for fire safety reasons giving a U-value of 0.11 (Christophorous Haus 2012).

Most Passiv haus practitioners seem to have no problem with using and certifying uPVC windows made by companies like Schuco and Sheerframe, despite the many environmental objections to uPVC. The claimed energy efficiency performance of uPVC windows are taken ahead of the negative environmental impact (EAS 2012).

Hafod Housing Association with Holbrook Construction have built two passiv haus certified houses in South Wales that use uPVC windows but claim that their uPVC windows are free of lead, using an 'organic stabiliser' (Litchfield 2012).

The term 'passiv haus' is a curious one, as the passiv haus concept requires the use of active mechanical heat recovery systems for ventilation and is far from passive in its operation. The benign concept of passive solar design has been taken over, though many passiv haus designs do include southerly orientation to use solar gain. This is not without its problems as super-airtight houses can then overheat if there is not adequate shading!

More recently, an alternative to passiv haus has emerged using the term Active House, and there is now an Active House Alliance, with an office in Rotterdam.

Active House is a vision of buildings that create healthier and more comfortable lives for their residents without impacting negatively on the climate and environment – thus moving us towards a cleaner, healthier and safer world.

(Eriksen 2010)

The Active House group appears to advocate a more holistic and flexible approach, but it is underwritten by a wide range of industrial companies and a few universities and architects; these include the Velux Corporation and SPU Insulation (who manufacture polyurethane insulation). They seemed to have secured the endorsement of Connie Hedegaard – the European Commissioner for Climate Action. In *Showhouse Magazine* R. Hunt claims to compare the virtues of passiv and active houses in a recent article without really explaining how the two differ. He even mentions the Triangle RHP project in Swindon and its ventilation system, but it is isn't clear whether this is meant to be an active house (Hunt 2012). An example of an active house appears to be the Velux Corporation Carbon Light houses in Kettering, UK. Distinguished by a very large number of velux rooflights on the roof this promotes the active house concept of health being enhanced by having maximum daylight. This is managed by a WindowMaster building management system that monitors the heat, CO_2 and light levels within the dwellings. It will automatically adjust the window and blind positions to suit the optimum indoor comfort levels required, according to the promotional literature. Active house does not offer an expensive assessment and approval system. (Velux 2012).

Plastic house Affresol

A curious attempt to produce a low energy house, claimed to achieve Code Level 5, is a modular house system developed in Swansea in South Wales with the help of the Carbon Trust Entrepreneurs Fast Track scheme. This is a non-timber-frame form of construction made of TPR.

> The TPR panels are bolted together to form the load bearing frame of the house which can be externally clad with brick, block or stone, with the interior insulated and plastered as any other house. The roof is tiled from recycled materials.
>
> (BBC News 2010)

Photographs of the house, with walls apparently made out of TPR plastic waste, appeared in various newspapers in 2010 (Andrews 2010).

TPR is Thermo Poly Rock in which plastic waste, that might have gone to landfill, is mixed with a polyunsaturated polyester resin and was apparently used to create cast walls. This idea was promoted as a housing solution by Goodier and Wei Pan in their RICS report on the future of housing (Goodier and Wei Pan 2012). Affresol is now promoting TPR as a structural frame material rather than to make solid walls. In a second prototype house, other materials will be used for walls and insulation with the plastic composite being used for the frame.

Hunt R. 'Wars of the houses' *Showhouse Magazine* March 2012 pp 41–44

ICF 2010 Insulating Concrete Formwork Association UK http://www.icfinfo.org.uk/ (viewed 26.3.12)

Janda, Kathryn B. 'Buildings don't use energy, people do' *Architectural Science Review*, Volume 54, No. 1, 2011, pp. 15–22(8)

Knauf Insulation http://www.knaufinsulation.co.uk/case_studies/denby_dale_passivhaus.aspx (viewed 26.3.12)

Lafarge www.sustainablelafarge.co.uk/legacy.asp (viewed 26.3.12)

Litchfield Group http://www.litchfield-group.co.uk/group-news/sheerframe/?story=224.Sheerframe (viewed 26.3.12)

Markus, T. and Nelson, I. 1985 An Investigation of Condensation Dampness and development of Survey Methods for Condensation Dampness, Investigation Department of Architecture and Building Science, University of Strathclyde, January 1985

Olcayto, Rory 'Experts Blast BRE's unproven gimmicks' *Building Design* 27 June 2008

One Planet 2012 http://www.oneplanetcommunities.org/about-2/approach/the-10-principles/ (viewed 30.4.12)

Owens, S., and Driffill, L. 2008 'How to Change Attitudes and Behaviours in the Context of Energy' *Energy Policy* 36:4412–4418

Parks, E., Sear, J. and Yeats, A. *Green Building* Spring 2012 Vol. 21 No. 4

Parsons and Whittley 2012 (viewed 19.4.12) www.parsonswhittley.co.uk/forthcomingproje.html

Pearson, C. and Delatte, N. 2005 Ronan Point Apartment Tower Collapse and its Effect on Building Codes *J. Perform. Constr. Facil.* 19, 172

Riverside One http://www.riverside-one.com/vision (viewed 26.3.12) http://www.gazettelive.co.uk/news/teesside-news/2011/11/15/developer-pulls-out-of-middlehaven-scheme-84229–29779108/

Scotland Government 2011 http://www.scotland.gov.uk/Publications/2011/03/25110122/37

Scotland's Housing Expo 2010 http://www.scotlandshousingexpo.com/houses.php (viewed 7.1.12)

Shipworth D & Shipworth M 2009 Energy Institute University College London ESRC/TSB Public policy seminar on 'How people use and misuse buildings' www.esrc.ac.uk/_images/Shipworth_26_Jan_09_tcm8–2390.pdf

Siddall M. 2012 (Devereux Architects) http://www.greenspec.co.uk/passivhaus-in-the-uk.php (viewed 12.5.12)

Sleaford standard http://www.sleafordstandard.co.uk/community/community-news/three_little_pigs_thrilled_to_be_moving_into_straw_house_1_2763357 (viewed 26.3.12)

Sodagar, B., Rai, D., Jones, B., Wihan, J. and Fieldson, R. (2011) 'The carbon reduction potential of straw-bale housing', *Building Research & Information*, 39:1, 51–65

TEAGASC 2012 http://www.teagasc.ie/publications/view_publication.aspx?PublicationID=395 (viewed 21.4.12)

The Works 2012 Ebbw Vale in Wales, Social Houses http://www.theworksebbwvale.co.uk (viewed 23.4.12)

Ty Unnos 2012 www.elements-europe.com www.wfbp.co.uk/woodknowledge-wales/files/Ty_Unnos_Leaflet.pdf (viewed 24.1.12)

UK Economic and Social Research Council 2009 http://www.esrc.ac.uk/funding-and-guidance/collaboration/seminars/archive/buildings.aspx (viewed 16.4.12)

Vaughan R. *The Architects Journal* (30.8.07)

Velux http://www.velux.co.uk/aboutvelux/modelhome2020 (viewed 26.3.12)

Waghorn, Mark Architects (House in Cairn Valley) http://www.markwaghorn.co.uk/#!__cairn-valley http://inhabitat.com/carbon-neutral-home-breaks-ground-in-cairn-valley-scotland/ (viewed 26.3.12)

Winkens Architecture www.winkens.ie/hemp.htm (viewed 26.3.12)

8. A future for renewable materials?

There are many different current approaches to energy efficient house construction in the UK. Some of these were illustrated in Chapters 3 & 7, ranging from low cost solutions by commercial developers and social landlords to highly expensive passiv haus projects for one-off clients. A wide range of materials and construction methods can also be seen, from traditional masonry adapted to low energy standards to timber frame, structural insulated panels, solid timber and even solid plastic! There is a danger that the Renewable House Programme (RHP) projects will be forgotten in the confusion caused by so many different approaches.

Many architects and the construction industry in general, remain very confused about how to proceed with low energy houses, and official guidance, standards and regulations only add to the confusion. Research and academic work is either used to validate the use of petrochemical based materials for large suppliers or is critical of current construction methods. Very little good work is being done to simplify and select the most effective and affordable approaches. Furthermore, the policy focus has shifted away from new build to renovating the existing stock of buildings. This has distracted attention from learning the lessons of recent new build experiments. Many thousands of new build houses are still required in the UK and across the world and it is important that these are built well, to decent standards of space, design and construction.

The focus on retrofit may be correct, as there are far more existing buildings than those that will be newly built, and much energy is wasted from the current stock of houses and other buildings that were built to much lower standards. As with new build there are many attempts to use synthetic petrochemical based insulation and other materials in retrofit and renovation. Many of these materials are unsuitable for use with old buildings and are likely to lead to serious damage and decay. The thermal performance is unlikely to be as good as claimed. Natural and renewable materials, on the

Low Impact Building: Housing using Renewable Materials, First Edition. Tom Woolley.
© 2013 John Wiley & Sons, Ltd. Published 2013 by John Wiley & Sons, Ltd.

other hand, can be used much more effectively in old and existing buildings. This, however, will have to be the subject of another book!

Despite the recognition in some quarters that improving the fabric of buildings is the most important and effective way to save energy, UK Government policies have instead put much more emphasis and subsidies on houses as micro generators of renewable energy and other technical and mechanical measures. However, as soon as renewable energy increased in popularity, governments throughout Europe began to realise that this was a costly approach and have reduced or withdrawn subsidies, leaving the renewable energy industry feeling badly let down.

> At the end of last year, with little warning, the nascent solar industry was plunged into chaos when ministers decided to slash support for clean energy.
>
> (Guardian 2012a)

> The German government has said it has been forced to cut subsidies for solar panels, because demand was so high it could no longer afford to support the green technology.
>
> (Guardian 2012b)

Despite undertakings to reduce carbon emissions, green policies are being downplayed and instead the increasing tendency has been to leave energy measures to market forces. It is likely that many novel solutions for both low energy house building methods, renewable energy and other technological solutions will fall by the wayside as they fail to have commercial success in a very competitive market. Due to this market free-for-all there has been very little official guidance as to standards and specifications that would be approved, other than the normal requirements of the building regulations.

Natural and renewable materials and building fabric solutions on the other hand have not been subject to much government grant and subsidy in the UK, apart from the RHP. It is to be hoped that, as a result, they will be in a better position to withstand the recession, the absence of government support and be an industry that is able to stand on its own feet. There is some evidence that this may be the case.

As the level of grant varied so widely in the RHP it should be clear that the subsidy had much less to do with using the materials and more to do with the feasibility of particular projects. While natural and renewable materials may remain a little more costly than synthetic products, it is important not to draw the conclusion from this book that such materials will only be used if they are subsidised.

The use of renewable and natural materials should not be seen as just another short-lived experiment in a chaotic marketplace. So far, surprisingly, most companies manufacturing or selling natural and renewable materials have managed to survive, despite the recession and falling funding and orders for materials. If ecological solutions can survive in a difficult market without significant subsidy then this should ensure a longer-term survival.

Unfortunately the current economic downturn may mean that there has been insufficient investment in innovation and it has been difficult for companies to increase production and thus reduce costs. Despite this, new products are appearing all the time and customers are still willing to pay a little more for the quality and performance offered by natural and renewable materials.

Middlemen

One of the most significant threats to survival can be seen in the problem of supply chains. The construction materials industry is full of middlemen – organisations that distribute materials or organise group purchasing schemes. Rather than saving money, middlemen take a cut and are thus involved in pushing prices up and the profits of the producers down.

Often the middle men do not hold any stocks of materials or even run their own transport; they simply act as agents, taking a slice while doing very little, other than processing the orders. The materials may go straight from the manufacturers to the building site, but the paperwork has a much more complicated route, passing through several hands. Manufacturers are forced to sign agreements with such middlemen to try to ensure a wide distribution network, and it is often impossible to source materials directly from the factory as agreements with distributors prohibit this.

There are eco distributors who are also middlemen and some do a good job providing education and information to clients. Builders merchants have played an important role in the construction industry. However, as many large-scale merchants do not stock certain natural and renewable products, contractors will try to substitute inferior or synthetic materials.

The bigger and more powerful multinational producers of materials such as Kingspan, St Gobain and Knauf, have a much stronger control of the market and ensure greater volumes of sales. They rely heavily on the ignorance of specifiers and customers who are unable to discriminate between the genuine and the slick marketing of environmental claims. As illustrated in Chapter 5, trade names are interchangeable with generic descriptions in day-to-day practice. Resisting this and choosing less well known and harder to source materials requires extra effort and a commitment to environmental principles on the part of designers and their clients.

The majority of ecological, natural and renewable products are manufactured by smaller companies but most follow conventional capitalist modes of business and commerce, though many have higher ethical and certainly environmental standards. There are few examples of alternative business models such as cooperatives, even though these might be particularly useful in dealing with the middleman problem. The majority of businesses working in the ecological field are fighting for survival and rarely have the luxury of exploring other ways of doing business. They have to operate within the market that exists.

Despite this there has been much cooperation, even between competitors, and the establishment of the Alliance for Sustainable Building Products

CDS Co-operative Development Services www.cds.coop

CHP Combined heat and power

CIAC Community in a cube, housing project in Middlesbrough, UK

CIBSE Chartered Institution of Building Services Engineers www. cibse.org/

CIRIA Construction Industry Research and Information Association www. ciria.org/

CLT Cross laminated timber, solid timber panels made with strips of wood glued together

Cohousing A form of collectively owned housing with shared facilities www.cohousing.org.uk/

CSH Code for Sustainable Homes, A UK system of awarding points for environmental and energy performance for housing

CPD Continuing professional development.

CPD-EU The European Union Construction Products Directive

CZERO Private development company based in Birmingham called Linford CZERO Ltd. www.czero.com

DECC UK Government Department of Energy and Climate Change www. decc.gov.uk/

DEFRA UK Department of Environment, Food and Rural Affairs www. defra.gov.uk/

DSD Northern Ireland Department for Social Development www.dsdni. gov.uk/

Embodied energy A measure of the energy (and CO_2 emissions) used to manufacture and deliver a material or product, sometimes referred to as embedded energy which is a misleading term as the energy has been consumed, and is not embedded in the product

Emission Zero A consultancy in Birmingham, which was awarded a contract to monitor the RHP www.emission-zero.com/index.htm

EPA Ireland Environmental Protection Agency Ireland www.epa.ie

EPD Environmental Product Declaration

EST UK Energy Saving Trust www.energysavingtrust.org.uk/

EURIMA European Insulation Manufacturers Association www.eurima.org/

FIEC European Construction Industry Federation. www.fiec.org

Footprinting A wide range of organisations provide methods for measuring carbon used by an individual or organisation

Formaldehyde Chemical found in a wide range of products and adhesives, classified as a carcinogen (cancer causing) and irritant. It is associated with allergies and dermatitis. It was used as a biocide and for embalming, but is banned for these in Europe. In the EU, the maximum allowed concentration of formaldehyde in finished products is 0.2%, and any product that exceeds 0.05% has to include a warning that the product contains formaldehyde, though this rarely seems to be the case in construction materials and products.

FSC Forest Stewardship Council www.fsc-uk.org/

GHA Good Homes Alliance www.goodhomes.org.uk/

Glu-lam A method for gluing together strips of timber to create very strong structural beams and columns

Green Deal A much-criticised measure introduced by the Conservative Liberal Coalition Government in the UK (DECC) to encourage retrofitting of existing property, to be funded by various private organisations though some local authorities are attempting to set up alternative green deal measures www.greendealinitiative.co.uk/

Green Guide to Specification A much-criticised system for awarding 'environmental classifications' to most building products and materials www.bre.co.uk/greenguide

HAB OAKUS A private development company established by Kevin McCloud working with the GreenSquare group www.haboakus.co.uk

HAB Shimmy An in-home computer system developed for the Hab Oakus Triangle development in Swindon

HCA UK Homes and Communities Agency www.homesandcommunities.co.uk/

Hempcrete A method of constructing insulating walls with the name Hemcrete registered by Lime Technology; generic names not registered are hempcrete and hemp-lime

Hemp The plant Cannabis sativa, being the drug-free version of cannabis or marijuana; there are other versions and many hundreds of varieties

Hemp fibre The hemp plant produces very tough fibre which can be stripped off the stalk

Hemp shiv or hurd The chopped up straw of the plant once the fibre has been stripped off

Heraklith Trade name for a wood wool slab, which used to be described as made with magnesium silicate but, since being taken over by Knauf, only a mineral binder is referred to www.heraklith.com/

Hygroscopicity The science of how a material deals with moisture

IAQ indoor air quality, a measure of the levels of pollutants inside buildings

IBPSA The International Building Performance Simulation Association

ICE Inventory of Carbon and Energy compiled by Bath University www.bath.ac.uk/mech-eng/research/sert

IES Integrated Environmental Solutions computer performance modelling www.iesve.com/

ISO International Standards Organisation www.iso.org/

Iso-cyanate iso-cynates are mixed with polyols to make polyurethane insulation. Methyl isocyanate was the toxic chemical that killed thousands in the Bhopal disaster. Serious respiratory problems have occurred in firemen exposed to polyurethane and isocyanates spillages and fires

JRHT Joseph Rowntree Housing Trust

Knauf Knauf Insulation Ltd (St Helens, UK) but in 75 countries, a German company, said to be family-owned in Bavaria. Manufacturer of mineral, glass fibre, polyfoam insulations, plasterboard and owner of Heraklith wood wool

LABC Local Authority Building Control www.labc.uk.com/

LCA life cycle analysis, a life cycle assessment (LCA) is the assessment of the environmental impact of a given product throughout its lifespan

LCBP Low Carbon Building Programme, a UK Government acronym for constructing low impact buildings which disappeared as soon as it appeared and is now used for grant funding of renewable energy installations www.bre.co.uk/page.jsp?id=1332

LCIF Low Carbon Innovation Fund: Another UK Government acronym that disappeared as a general fund but a new version now exists: https://www.lowcarbonfund.co.uk/LCIF/

LEED US Green Building Council rating system for slightly greener buildings www.usgbc.org

LHOIST A multinational lime products company that owns the 'Tradical' brand of hemp-lime materials www.lhoist.co.uk/Frame_Home.htm

LID Low Impact Development policy: initially introduced in Pembrokeshire, this is now adopted throughout Wales as the One Planet Development policy (Technical Advice Note 6), best accessed through www.lammas.org.uk/lowimpact/index.htm

LILAC Low Impact Living Affordable Community (Leeds) www.lilac.coop

LMU Leeds Metropolitan University

Magnesite Magnesium carbonate, used as a binder in board and other building materials, similar to calcium carbonate but not as widely occurring

Magnesium silicate Claimed to be a low carbon alterative to cement, it is used in composite boards and has a high resistance to moisture

Manmade Materials used in building construction that are derived from synthetic rather than materials, or where chemical and manufacturing processes remove any natural characteristics

MHOS Mutual Home Ownership Society, one of a number of models of collective or cooperative home ownership where house occupants may have a share in the equity of the property www.cds.coop

MIMA Mineralwool Insulation Manufacturers Association, previously known as EURISOL www.mima.info

MMC Modern Methods of Construction, usually assumed to mean prefabricated or off-site methods, usually using synthetic manmade materials

MMMF Man made mineral fibre as used in insulation

Modcell A proprietary name for a form of prefabricated construction using strawbales compressed into timber frames www.modcell.com

MVHR Mechanical ventilation and heat recovery, an electrical powered system to import fresh air which can be heated by heat extracted from stale air which is being evacuated from a building. This is normally a requirement of meeting the passiv haus standard though it is not a passive system

Nanosil A proprietary additive used in some render systems as a form of waterproofing

Natureplus A certification standard for ecological materials widely used throughout Europe; certificates only awarded to the best specific (not generic) products, which must only have a very low petrochemical usage www.natureplus.org/

NBA National Building Agency, a UK Government agency in the 1960s and 1970s that promoted and certified 'system' building; there is an Irish National Building Agency which still exists

NBT Natural Building Technologies, one of the leading UK distributors of ecological and natural building products www.natural-building.co.uk

NNFCC National Non-food Crops Centre www.nnfcc.co.uk

OSB Oriented strand board, a form of wooden building board in which scraps of timber are glued together, often using phenol or urea formaldehyde, a highly toxic and carcinogenic glue; OSB is widely used in current construction, particularly in MMC and SIPS construction; a small number of companies offer OSB with what they describe as 'safe' resins

Passivhaus/SPHC There are number of passiv haus organisations in the UK and internationally, most of which seem to collaborate, though there is also some competition for certification. www.passivhaus.org.uk/ (BRE) www.passivhaustrust.org.uk www.passivehouse-international.org www.sphc.co.uk

Pavatex/Diffutherm/Pavaflex Wood fibre products made in Switzerland but available from NBT in the UK www.pavatex.com/

PBDEs Poly brominated di-phenol ethers, a family of highly dangerous synthetic chemicals that have been widely used in flame retardants in furnishings, electrical products and construction materials including synthetic insulation materials. They are not chemically bound to the products in which they are used so can leach out into the environment, and are regarded as high risk in the USA where they are replacing PCBs as the most prevalent organohalogen contaminant particularly in the Arctic. Concern in Europe seems lower and a wide range of alternative chemicals are now used in different products www.epa.gov/oppt/existingchemicals/pubs/actionplans/pbde.html

Phenol Also known as carbolic acid, largely derived from oil, one of the basic products from which a wide range of plastics and synthetic materials are based; it is a dangerous neurotoxin

PIR. Polyisocynaurate (rigid) insulation, similar to PUR

Planning Portal UK Government website giving access to planning and building regulations www.planningportal.gov.uk

Polyol A name for a wide range of chemicals including those used to make polyurethane insulation

Probe Post-Occupancy Review of Buildings and their Engineering www.usablebuildings.co.uk/

PUR Rigid polyurethane insulation similar to PIR

PVA Polyvinyl acetates, used in a wide range of relatively safe glues

PVC Polyvinyl chloride also known as uPVC and PVCu, one of the most controversial substances widely used in buildings and building materials, regarded as highly dangerous to the environment and health by some, issues largely discounted by the PVC industry

RAE Royal Academy of Engineering. www.raeng.org.uk

Rainscreen A form of cladding used on buildings, can be made from timber boards, panels and many other materials to shed rain from wall surfaces

REACH Registration, Evaluation, Authorisation and Restriction of Chemical Substances, a set of European Regulations that were introduced in 2007 http://ec.europa.eu/environment/chemicals/reach/reach_intro.htm

Renewable materials 'Renewable and biodegradable materials not only consume less energy in their preparation, but also are less problematic to dispose of at the end of their useful life. Renewable materials are substances derived from a living tree, plant, animal or ecosystem which has the ability to regenerate itself. A renewable material can be produced again and again. For example, when we use plantation wood to make paper we can plant more trees to replace it. Earth's mineral resources are finite, and often energy-intensive, but timber resources can be produced indefinitely, with strong environmental benefits'. www.csiro.au/Outcomes/Materials-and-Manufacturing/Innovation/renewable-biodegradable-materials.aspx

Resistant A range of proprietary building boards that use magnesium silicate and have been used with hemp lime construction. www.resistant.co.uk/

RHP Renewable House Programme, set up by UK Government Department DECC in 2009 but no longer in existence www.homesandcommunities.co.uk/ourwork/renewable-construction

RIBA Royal Institute of British Architects

RICS Royal Institute of Chartered Surveyors

SAP Standard Assessment Procedure, DECC's methodology for assessing and comparing the energy and environmental performance of dwellings, its purpose is to provide accurate and reliable assessments of dwelling energy performances that are needed to underpin energy and environmental policy initiatives www.decc.gov.uk/en/content/cms/emissions/sap/sap.aspx

SBEM Simplified Building Energy Model

Sedum Flowering succulent plants commonly known as stonecrops, they have water storing leaves and can grow with little soil, commonly used in 'green roofs'

SETAC Society of Environmental Toxicology and Chemistry

SGR Scientists for Global Responsibility, scientists architects, engineers, technologists www.sgr.org.uk/

Sheep's wool Fleece sheared from sheep used in clothing, carpets and insulation etc.

Silicate *See magnesium silicate*

SIPS Structural insulated panels, a form of off-site, prefabricated, usually timber (but sometimes metal) panels incorporating insulation, usually synthetic such as polyurethane which bonds to the timber

Synthetic *See manmade*

TEAGASC The Irish Agriculture and Food Development Authority www.teagasc.ie

Thistle A form of gypsum based plaster that is commonly used in buildings.

TPR Thermo poly rock, a material based on plastic waste bonded together with resins

Tradical A proprietary set of products including lime binders and hemp for hemp lime construction, sold by Lime Technology and LHOIST

TSB UK Technology Strategy Board www.innovateuk.org/

Ty Unnos Welsh term meaning 'house of one night', experimental form of construction using locally grown welsh timber

UKCIP UK Climate Impacts programme, hosted at the Environmental Change Institute, University of Oxford www.ukcip.org.uk/

UKGBC UK Green Building Council

UKTI UK Government Department for Trade and Industry www.ukti.gov.uk/home.html

UWHA United Welsh Housing Association

WATCH UK Working group on Action to Control Chemicals, Health and Safety Executive

WHO World Health Organisation

WUFI Building modelling and energy technique which recognises hygro-thermal behaviour of materials, Fraunhofer Institute for Building Physics www.ibp.fraunhofer.de/en/

Zero Carbon Hub UK organisation to facilitate the mainstream delivery of low and zero carbon homes www.zerocarbonhub.org/

Index

Note: page numbers in italics refer to figures; page numbers in bold refer to tables.

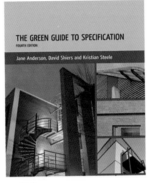
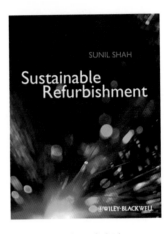
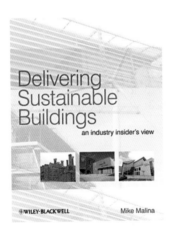
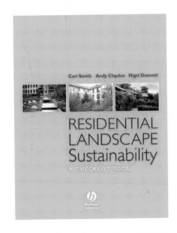
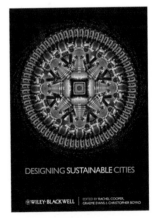